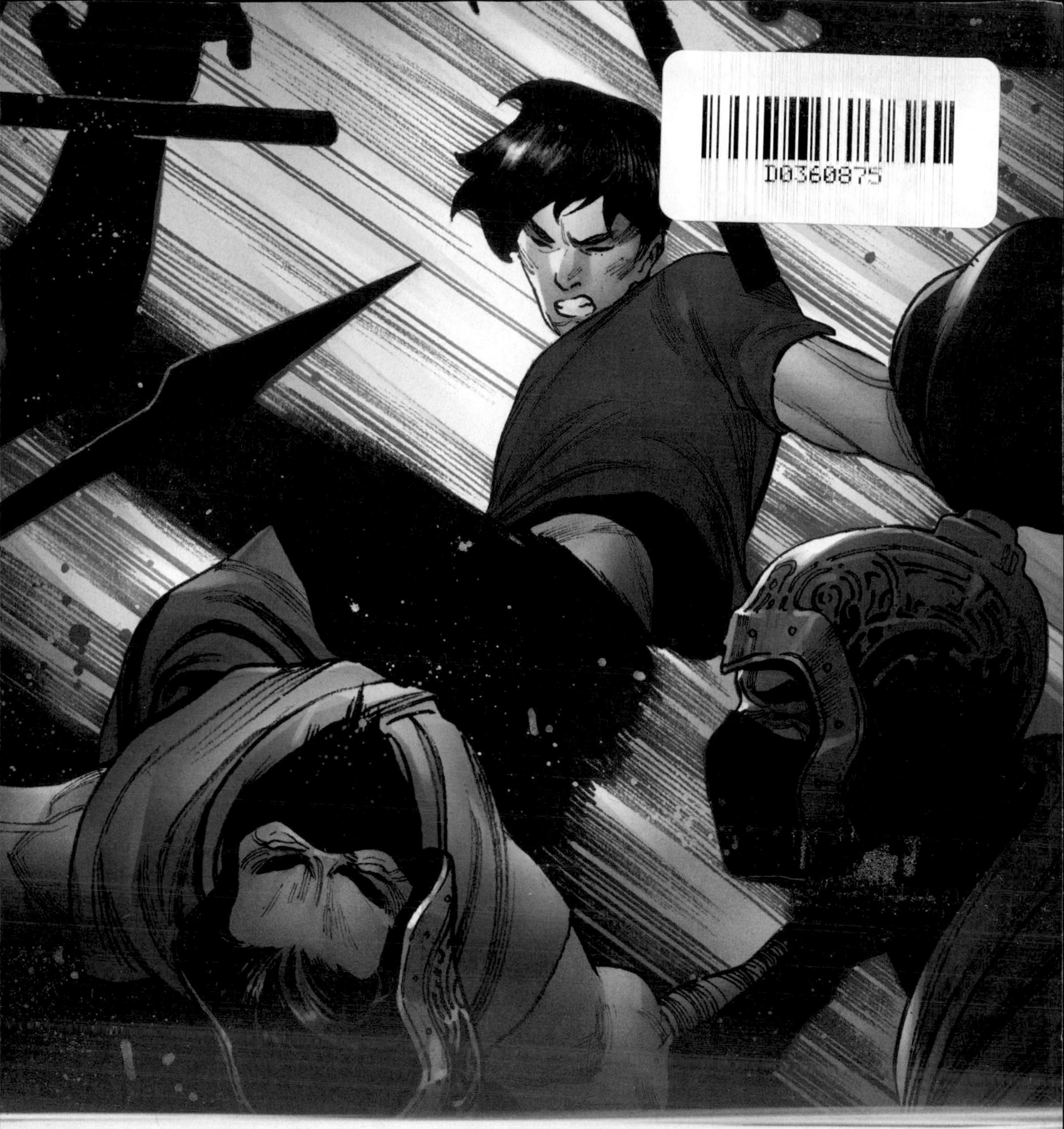

SHANG-CHI

BROTHERS & SISTERS

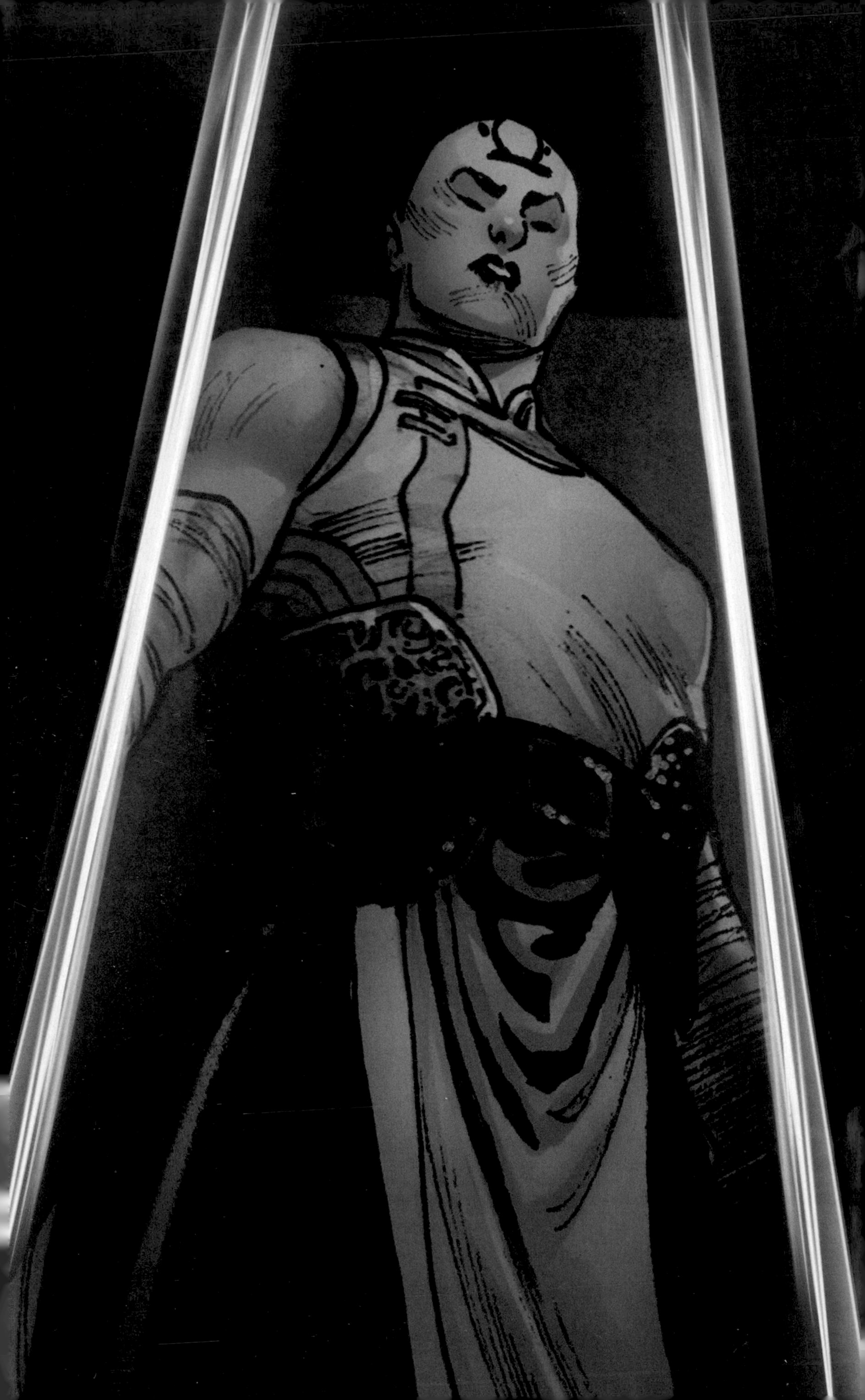

BROTHERS & SISTERS

WRITER **GENE LUEN YANG**

ARTIST **DIKE RUAN**

FLASHBACK ARTIST **PHILIP TAN**

COLOR ARTIST **SEBASTIAN CHENG**

LETTERER **VC'S TRAVIS LANHAM**

COVER ART **JIM CHEUNG** & **LAURA MARTIN** [#1];
PHILIP TAN & **JAY DAVID RAMOS** [#2-3];
BERNARD CHANG [#4];
AND **MARCUS TO** & **SEBASTIAN CHENG** [#5]

ASSISTANT EDITORS **LAUREN AMARO** & **KAT GREGOROWICZ**

EDITOR **DARREN SHAN**

SPECIAL THANKS TO **MARK BASSO**

COLLECTION EDITOR **JENNIFER GRÜNWALD**
ASSISTANT EDITOR **DANIEL KIRCHHOFFER**
ASSISTANT MANAGING EDITOR **MAIA LOY**
ASSISTANT MANAGING EDITOR **LISA MONTALBANO**

VP PRODUCTION & SPECIAL PROJECTS **JEFF YOUNGQUIST**
BOOK DESIGNER **SALENA MAHINA**
SVP PRINT, SALES & MARKETING **DAVID GABRIEL**
EDITOR IN CHIEF **C.B. CEBULSKI**

-CHI BY GENE LUEN YANG VOL. 1: BROTHERS & SISTERS. Contains material originally published in magazine form as SHANG-CHI (2020) #1-5. Second printing 2021. ISBN 978-1-302-92485-0. Published by MARVEL WORLDWIDE, subsidiary of MARVEL ENTERTAINMENT, LLC. OFFICE OF PUBLICATION: 1290 Avenue of the Americas, New York, NY 10104. © 2021 MARVEL. No similarity between any of the names, characters, persons, and/or institutions magazine with those of any living or dead person or institution is intended, and any such similarity which may exist is purely coincidental. **Printed in Canada.** KEVIN FEIGE, Chief Creative Officer; DAN BUCKLEY, President, Entertainment; JOE QUESADA, EVP & Creative Director; DAVID BOGART, Associate Publisher & SVP of Talent Affairs; TOM BREVOORT, VP, Executive Editor; NICK LOWE, Executive Editor, VP of Content, Digital Publishing; DAVID L, VP of Print & Digital Publishing; JEFF YOUNGQUIST, VP of Production & Special Projects; ALEX MORALES, Director of Publishing Operations; DAN EDINGTON, Managing Editor; RICKEY PURDIN, Director of Talent Relations; ER GRÜNWALD, Senior Editor, Special Projects; SUSAN CRESPI, Production Manager; STAN LEE, Chairman Emeritus. For information regarding advertising in Marvel Comics or on Marvel.com, please contact Vit DeBellis, Custom ns & Integrated Advertising Manager, at vdebellis@marvel.com. For Marvel subscription inquiries, please call 888-511-5480. **Manufactured between 6/11/2021 and 7/13/2021 by SOLISCO PRINTERS, SCOTT, QC, CANADA.**

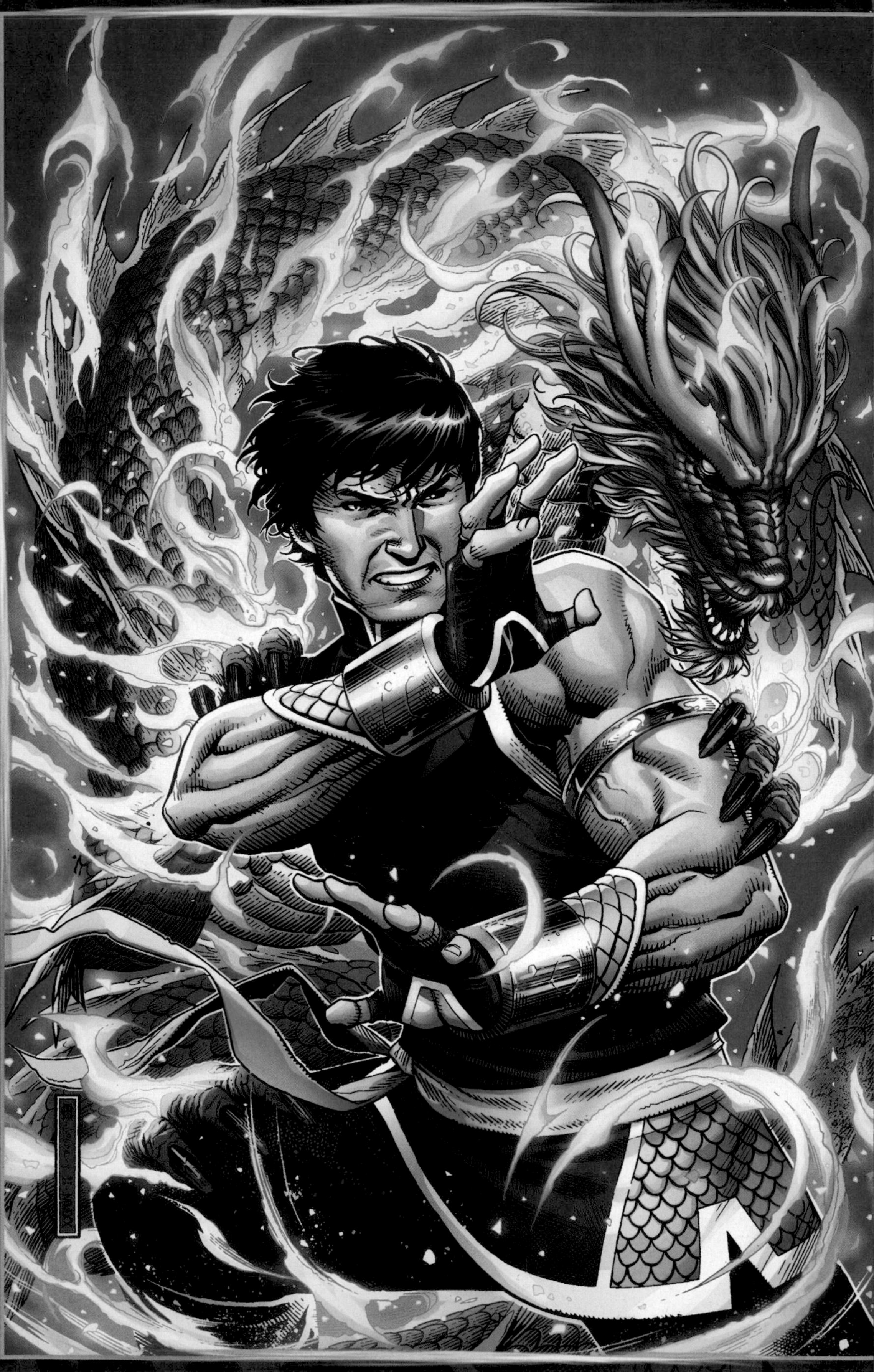

ONE

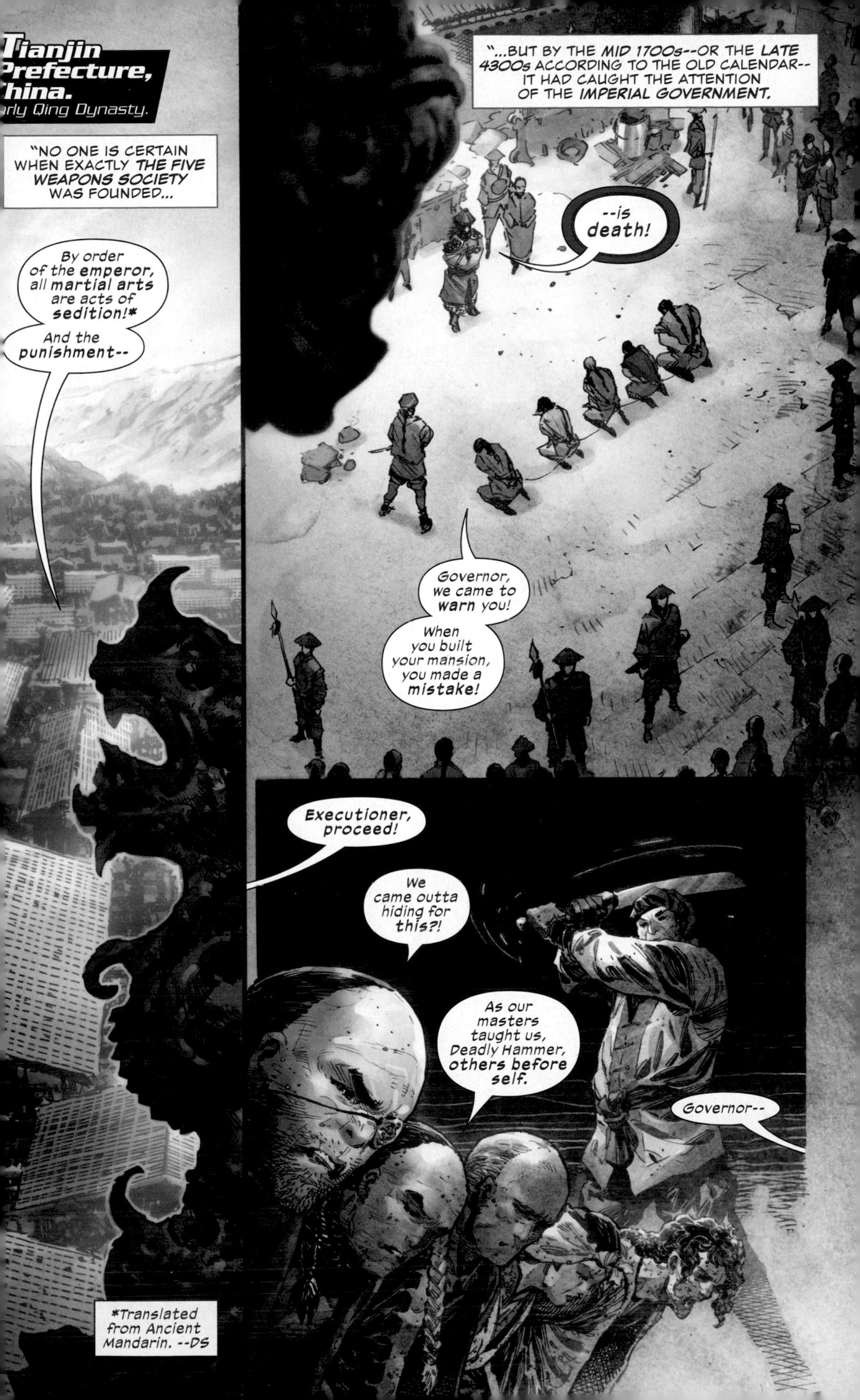
Tianjin Prefecture, China.
arly Qing Dynasty.
"NO ONE IS CERTAIN WHEN EXACTLY THE FIVE WEAPONS SOCIETY WAS FOUNDED...
By order of the emperor, all martial arts are acts of sedition!*
And the punishment--
*Translated from Ancient Mandarin. --DS
"...BUT BY THE MID 1700s--OR THE LATE 4300s ACCORDING TO THE OLD CALENDAR--IT HAD CAUGHT THE ATTENTION OF THE IMPERIAL GOVERNMENT.
--is death!
Governor, we came to warn you!
When you built your mansion, you made a mistake!
Executioner, proceed!
We came outta hiding for this?!
As our masters taught us, Deadly Hammer, others before self.
Governor--

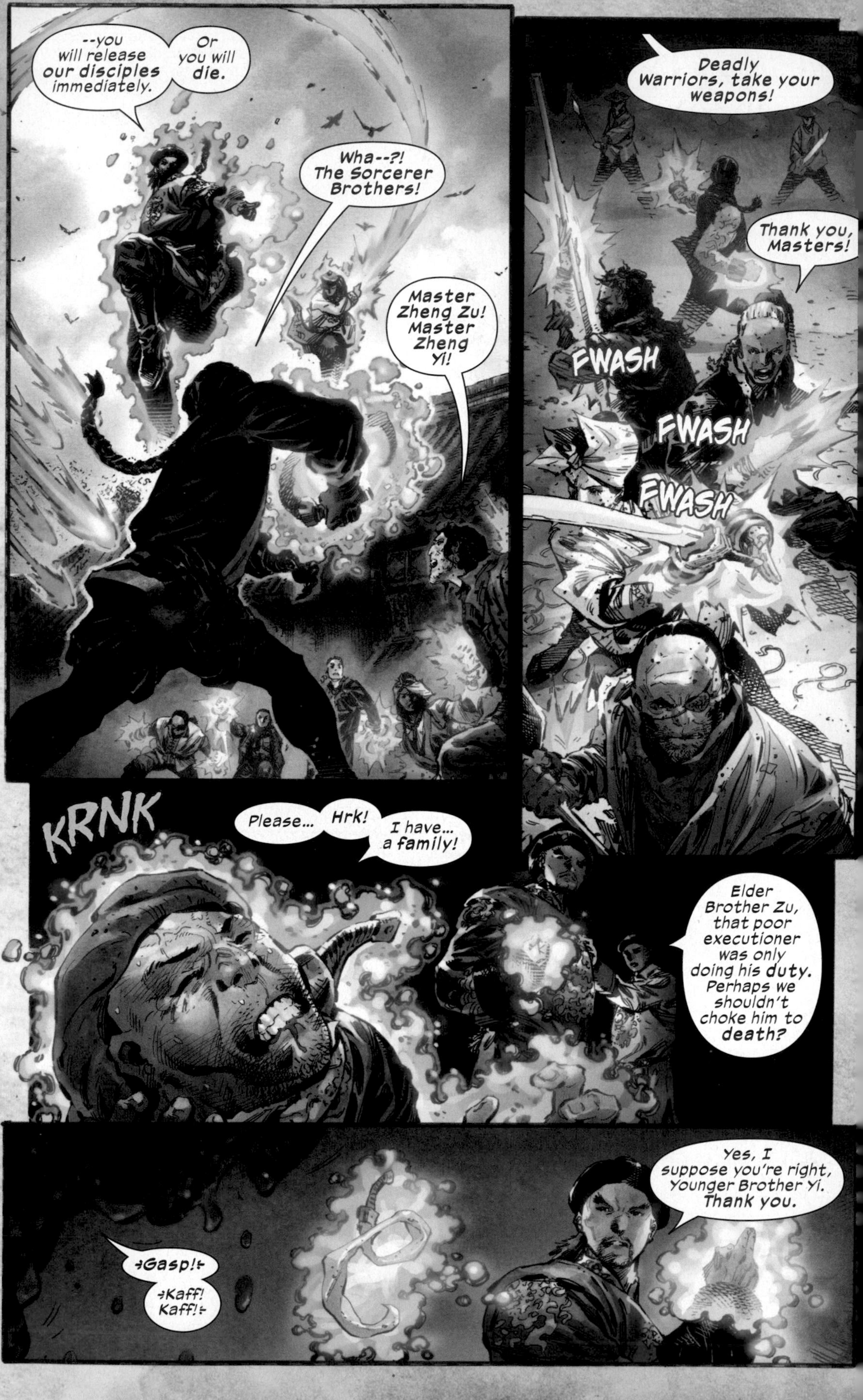
--you will release our disciples immediately.
Or you will die.
Wha--?! The Sorcerer Brothers!
Master Zheng Zu! Master Zheng Yi!
Deadly Warriors, take your weapons!
Thank you, Masters!
FWASH
FWASH
FWASH
KRNK
Please...
Hrk!
I have... a family!
Elder Brother Zu, that poor executioner was only doing his duty. Perhaps we shouldn't choke him to death?
Yes, I suppose you're right, Younger Brother Yi. Thank you.
Gasp!
Kaff! Kaff!

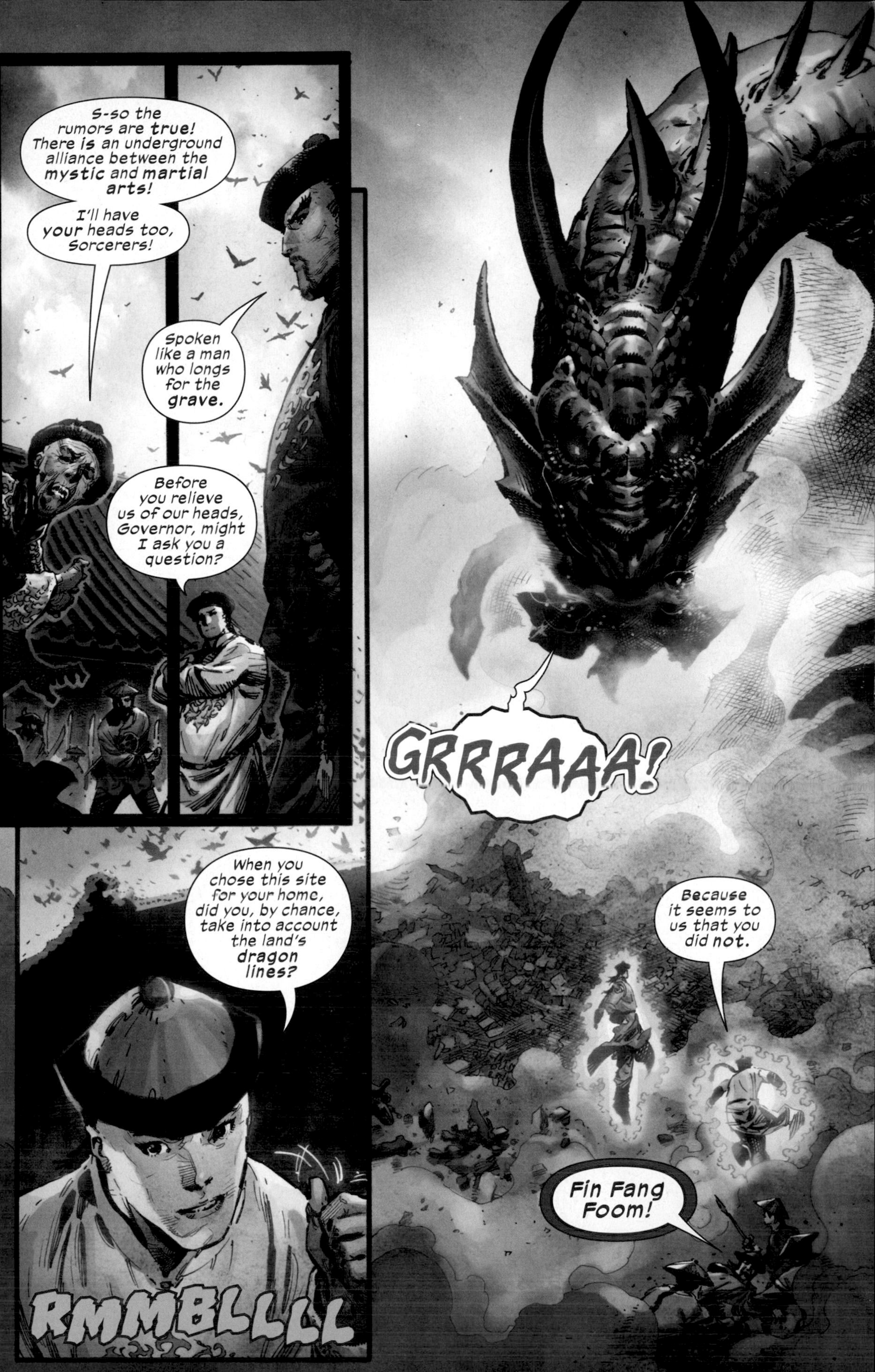
S-so the rumors are true! There is an underground alliance between the mystic and martial arts!
I'll have your heads too, Sorcerers!
Spoken like a man who longs for the grave.
Before you relieve us of our heads, Governor, might I ask you a question?
When you chose this site for your home, did you, by chance, take into account the land's dragon lines?
RMMBLLLL
GRRRAAA!
Because it seems to us that you did not.
Fin Fang Foom!

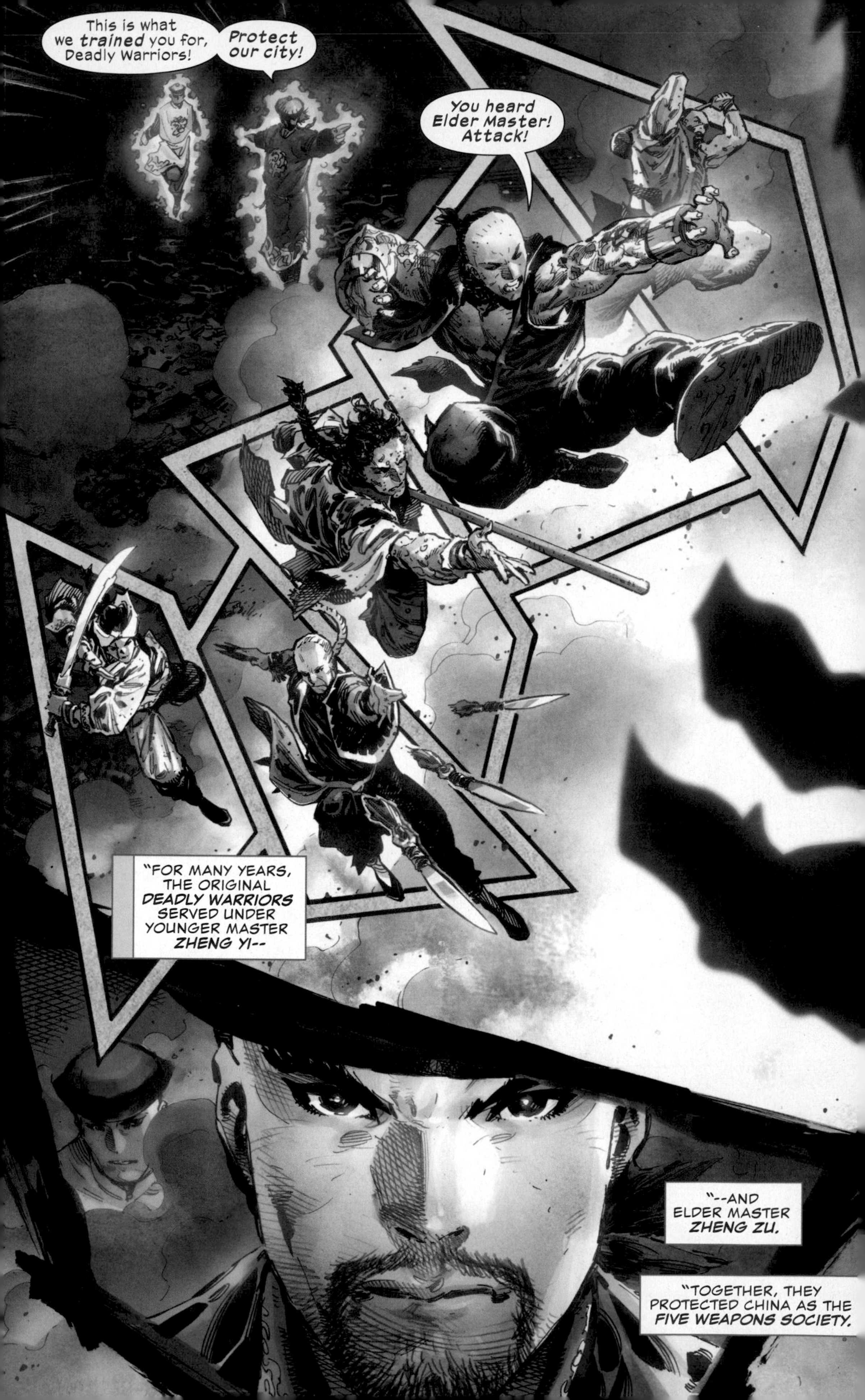
This is what we trained you for, Deadly Warriors!
Protect our city!
You heard Elder Master! Attack!
"FOR MANY YEARS, THE ORIGINAL DEADLY WARRIORS SERVED UNDER YOUNGER MASTER ZHENG YI--
"--AND ELDER MASTER ZHENG ZU.
"TOGETHER, THEY PROTECTED CHINA AS THE FIVE WEAPONS SOCIETY.

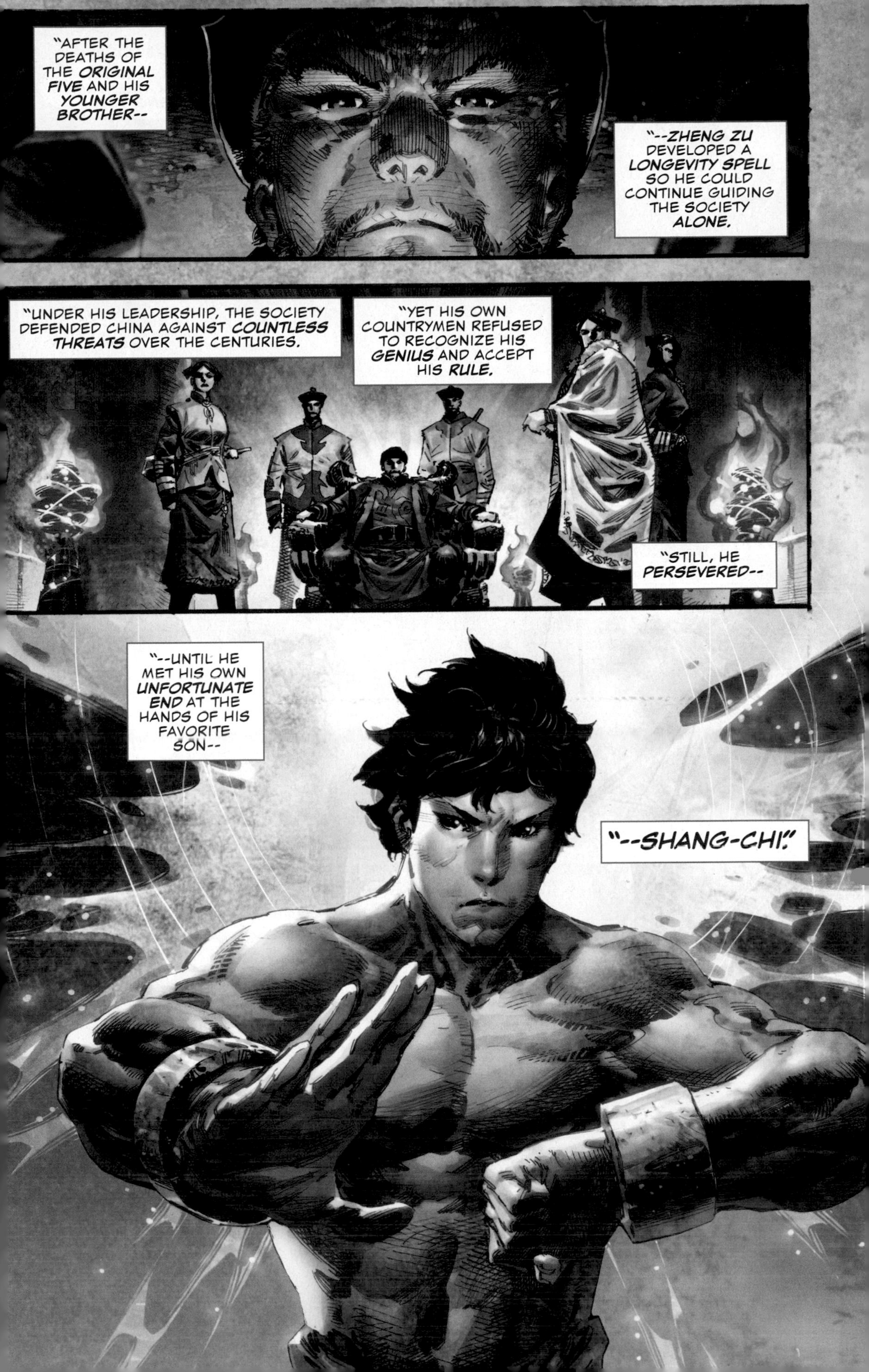
"AFTER THE DEATHS OF THE ORIGINAL FIVE AND HIS YOUNGER BROTHER--
"--ZHENG ZU DEVELOPED A LONGEVITY SPELL SO HE COULD CONTINUE GUIDING THE SOCIETY ALONE.
"UNDER HIS LEADERSHIP, THE SOCIETY DEFENDED CHINA AGAINST COUNTLESS THREATS OVER THE CENTURIES.
"YET HIS OWN COUNTRYMEN REFUSED TO RECOGNIZE HIS GENIUS AND ACCEPT HIS RULE.
"STILL, HE PERSEVERED--
"--UNTIL HE MET HIS OWN UNFORTUNATE END AT THE HANDS OF HIS FAVORITE SON--
"--SHANG-CHI."

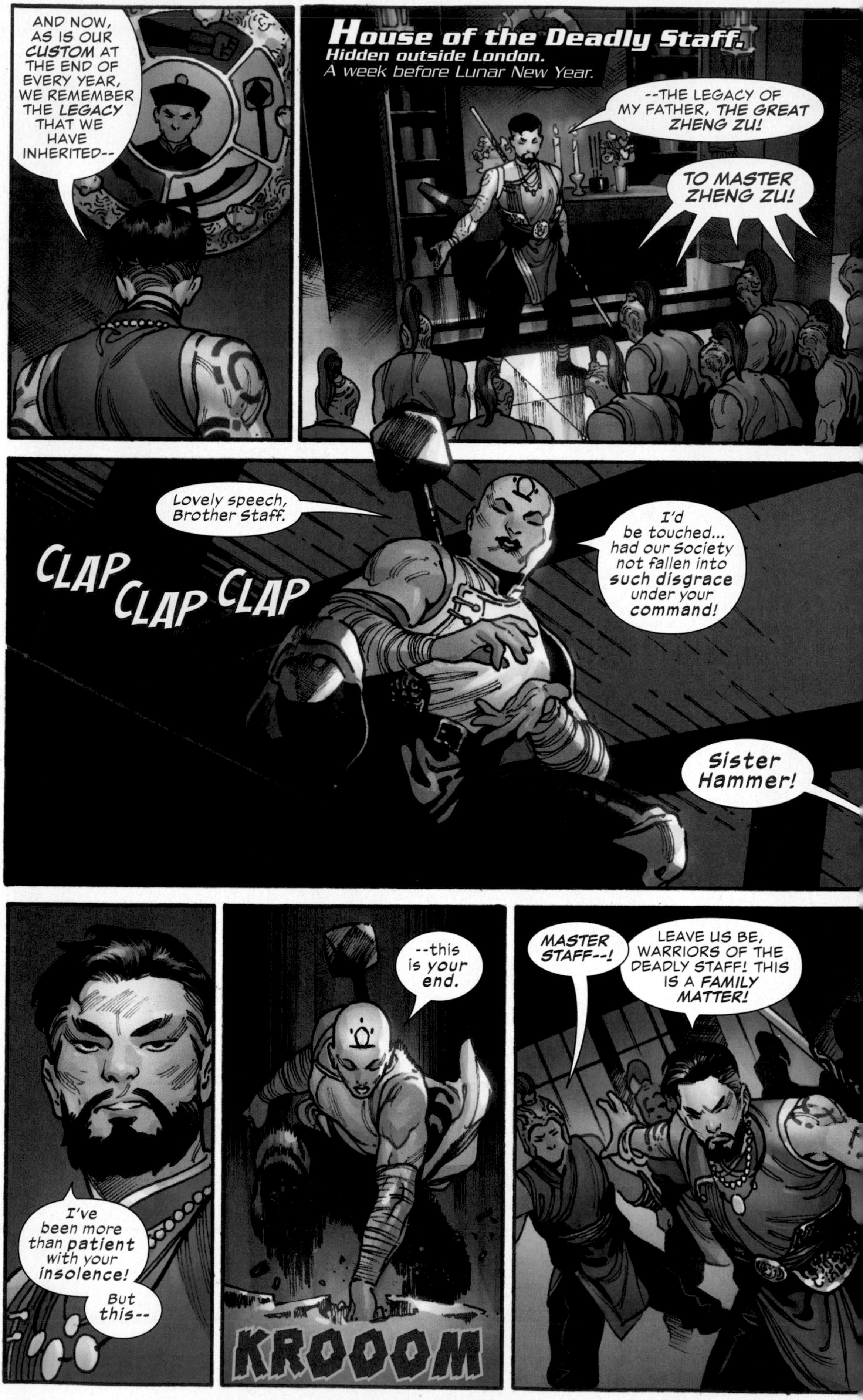
AND NOW, AS IS OUR CUSTOM AT THE END OF EVERY YEAR, WE REMEMBER THE LEGACY THAT WE HAVE INHERITED--
House of the Deadly Staff.
Hidden outside London.
A week before Lunar New Year.
--THE LEGACY OF MY FATHER, THE GREAT ZHENG ZU!
TO MASTER ZHENG ZU!
Lovely speech, Brother Staff.
CLAP CLAP CLAP
I'd be touched... had our Society not fallen into such disgrace under your command!
Sister Hammer!
I've been more than patient with your insolence!
But this--
--this is your end.
KROOOM
MASTER STAFF--!
LEAVE US BE, WARRIORS OF THE DEADLY STAFF! THIS IS A FAMILY MATTER!

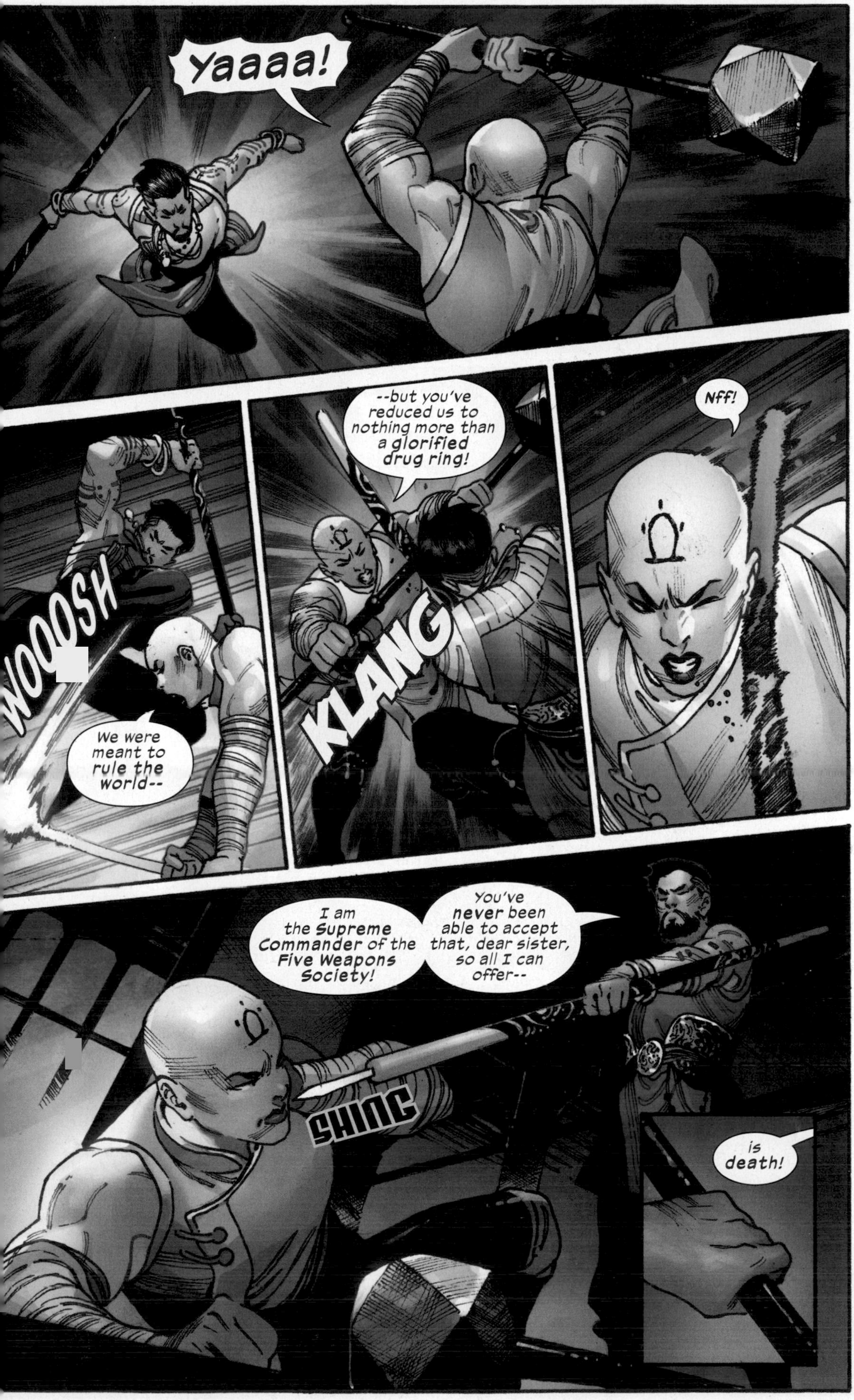
Yaaaa!
WOOOSH
We were meant to rule the world--
--but you've reduced us to nothing more than a glorified drug ring!
KLANG
Nff!
I am the Supreme Commander of the Five Weapons Society!
You've never been able to accept that, dear sister, so all I can offer--
SHING
is death!

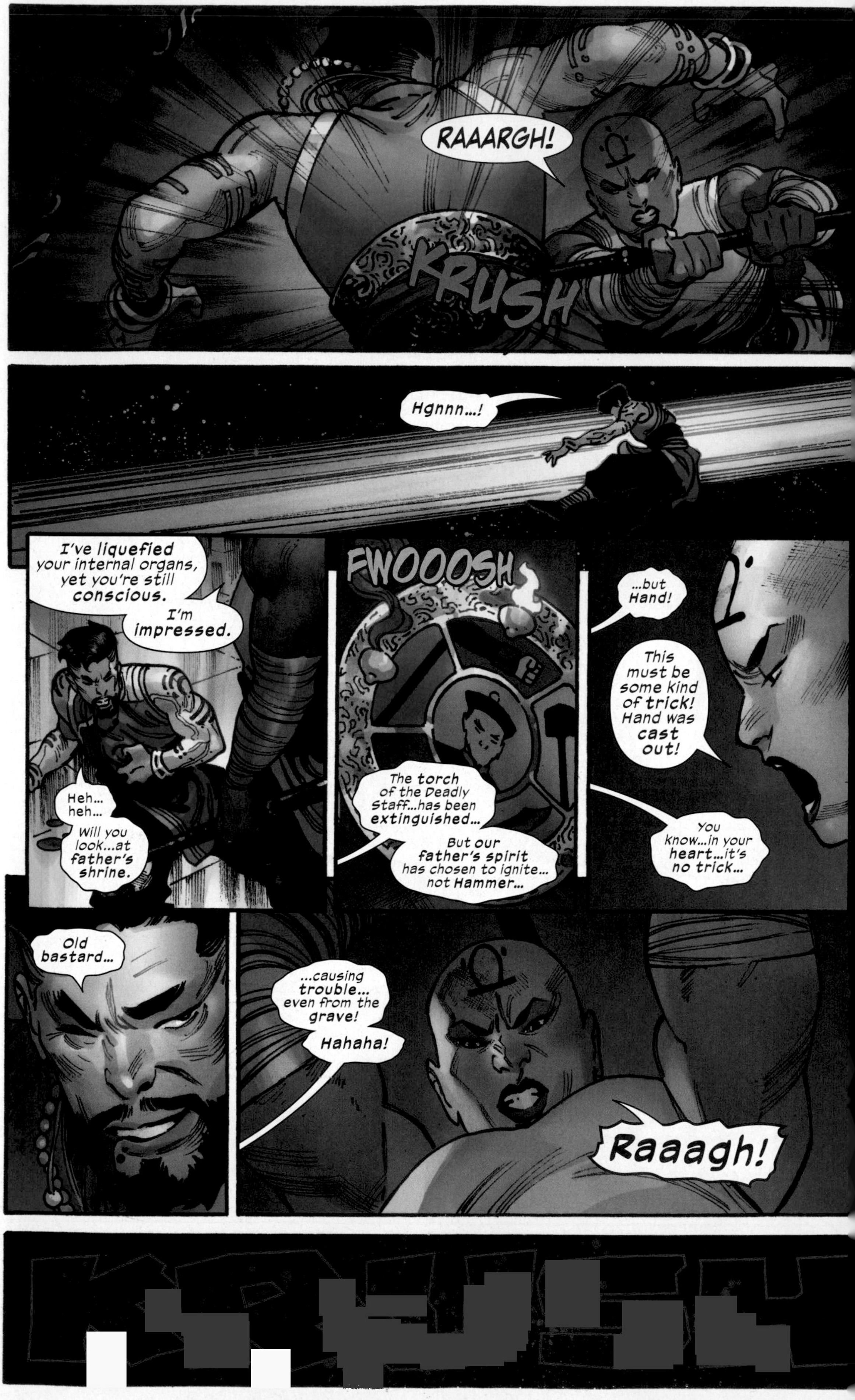
RAAARGH!
KRUSH
Hgnnn...!
I've liquefied your internal organs, yet you're still conscious.
I'm impressed.
Heh... heh...
Will you look...at father's shrine.
FWOOOSH
The torch of the Deadly Staff...has been extinguished...
But our father's spirit has chosen to ignite... not Hammer...
...but Hand!
This must be some kind of trick! Hand was cast out!
You know...in your heart...it's no trick...
Old bastard...
...causing trouble... even from the grave!
Hahaha!
Raaagh!

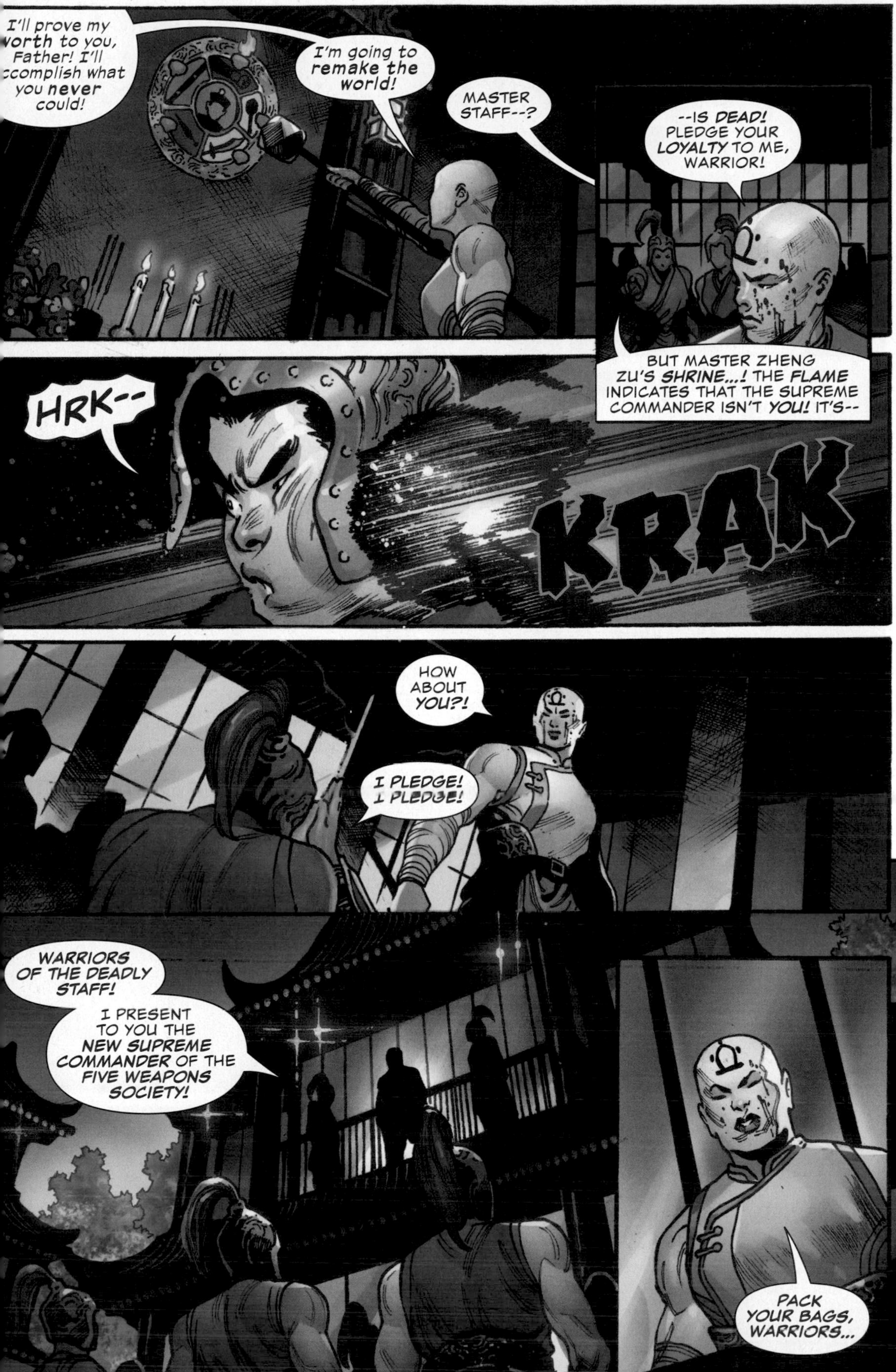

I'll prove my worth to you, Father! I'll accomplish what you never could!
I'm going to remake the world!
MASTER STAFF--?
--IS DEAD! PLEDGE YOUR LOYALTY TO ME, WARRIOR!
BUT MASTER ZHENG ZU'S SHRINE...! THE FLAME INDICATES THAT THE SUPREME COMMANDER ISN'T YOU! IT'S--
HRK--
KRAK
HOW ABOUT YOU?!
I PLEDGE! I PLEDGE!
WARRIORS OF THE DEADLY STAFF!
I PRESENT TO YOU THE NEW SUPREME COMMANDER OF THE FIVE WEAPONS SOCIETY!
ONG LIVE COMMANDER HAMMER!
PACK YOUR BAGS, WARRIORS...

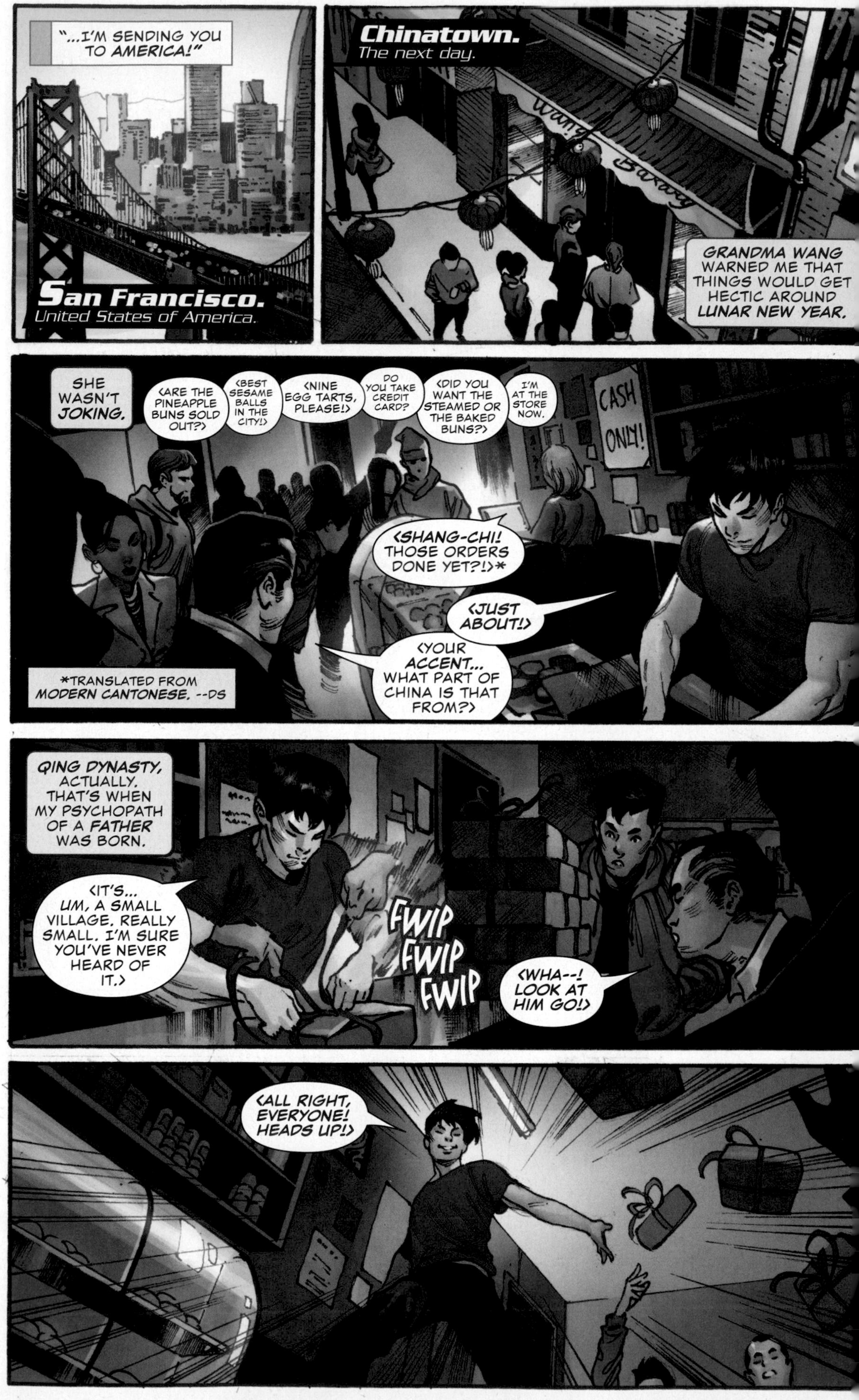
"...I'M SENDING YOU TO AMERICA!"
San Francisco.
United States of America.
Chinatown.
The next day.
GRANDMA WANG WARNED ME THAT THINGS WOULD GET HECTIC AROUND LUNAR NEW YEAR.
SHE WASN'T JOKING.
<ARE THE PINEAPPLE BUNS SOLD OUT?>
<BEST SESAME BALLS IN THE CITY!>
<NINE EGG TARTS, PLEASE!>
DO YOU TAKE CREDIT CARD?
<DID YOU WANT THE STEAMED OR THE BAKED BUNS?>
I'M AT THE STORE NOW.
CASH ONLY!
<SHANG-CHI! THOSE ORDERS DONE YET?!>*
<JUST ABOUT!>
<YOUR ACCENT... WHAT PART OF CHINA IS THAT FROM?>
*TRANSLATED FROM MODERN CANTONESE. --DS
QING DYNASTY, ACTUALLY. THAT'S WHEN MY PSYCHOPATH OF A FATHER WAS BORN.
<IT'S... UM, A SMALL VILLAGE. REALLY SMALL. I'M SURE YOU'VE NEVER HEARD OF IT.>
FWIP FWIP FWIP
<WHA--! LOOK AT HIM GO!>
<ALL RIGHT, EVERYONE! HEADS UP!>

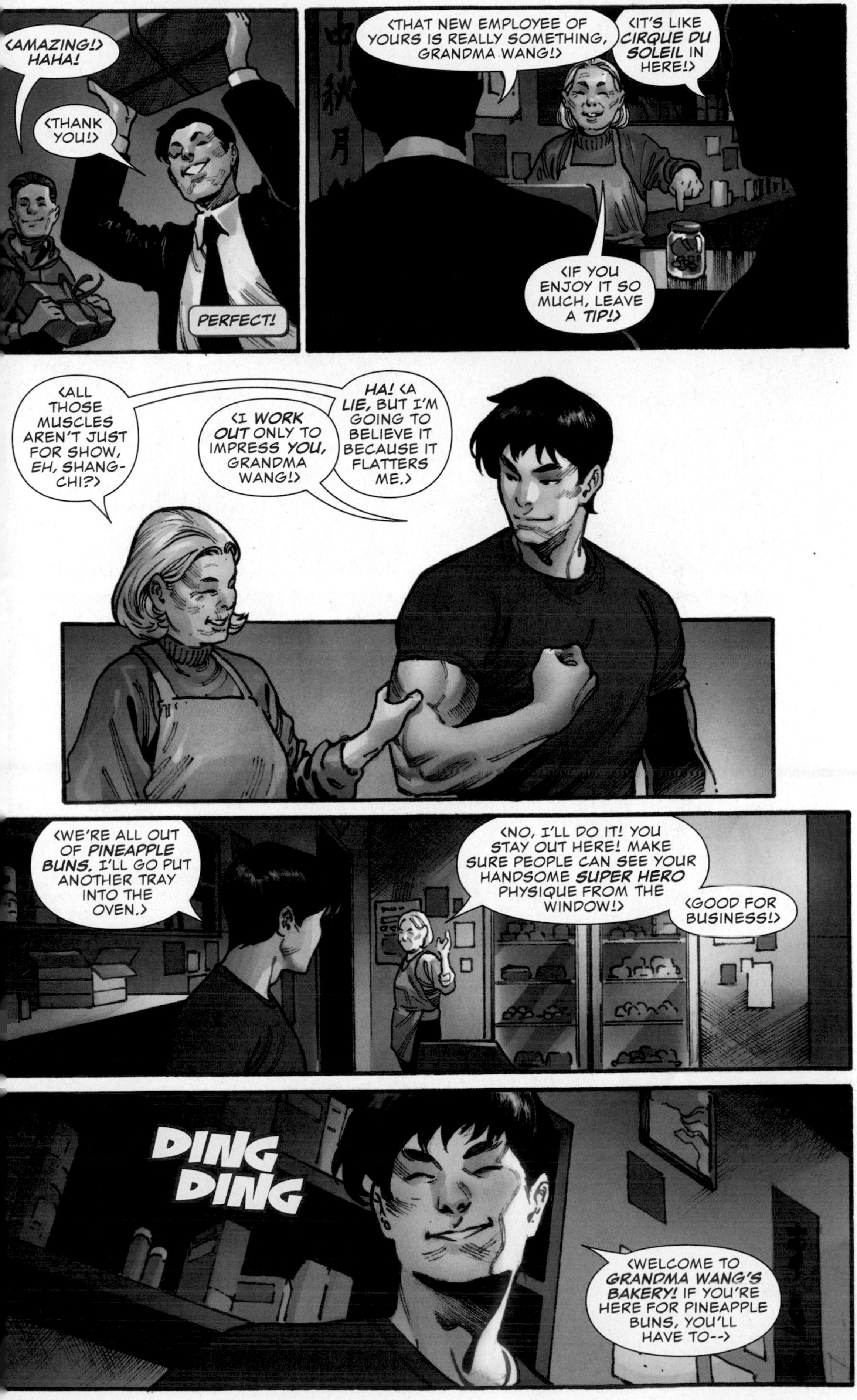

<AMAZING!> HAHA!
<THANK YOU!>
PERFECT!
<THAT NEW EMPLOYEE OF YOURS IS REALLY SOMETHING, GRANDMA WANG!>
<IT'S LIKE CIRQUE DU SOLEIL IN HERE!>
<IF YOU ENJOY IT SO MUCH, LEAVE A TIP!>
<ALL THOSE MUSCLES AREN'T JUST FOR SHOW, EH, SHANG-CHI?>
<I WORK OUT ONLY TO IMPRESS YOU, GRANDMA WANG!>
HA! <A LIE, BUT I'M GOING TO BELIEVE IT BECAUSE IT FLATTERS ME.>
<WE'RE ALL OUT OF PINEAPPLE BUNS. I'LL GO PUT ANOTHER TRAY INTO THE OVEN.>
<NO, I'LL DO IT! YOU STAY OUT HERE! MAKE SURE PEOPLE CAN SEE YOUR HANDSOME SUPER HERO PHYSIQUE FROM THE WINDOW!>
<GOOD FOR BUSINESS!>
DING DING
<WELCOME TO GRANDMA WANG'S BAKERY! IF YOU'RE HERE FOR PINEAPPLE BUNS, YOU'LL HAVE TO-->

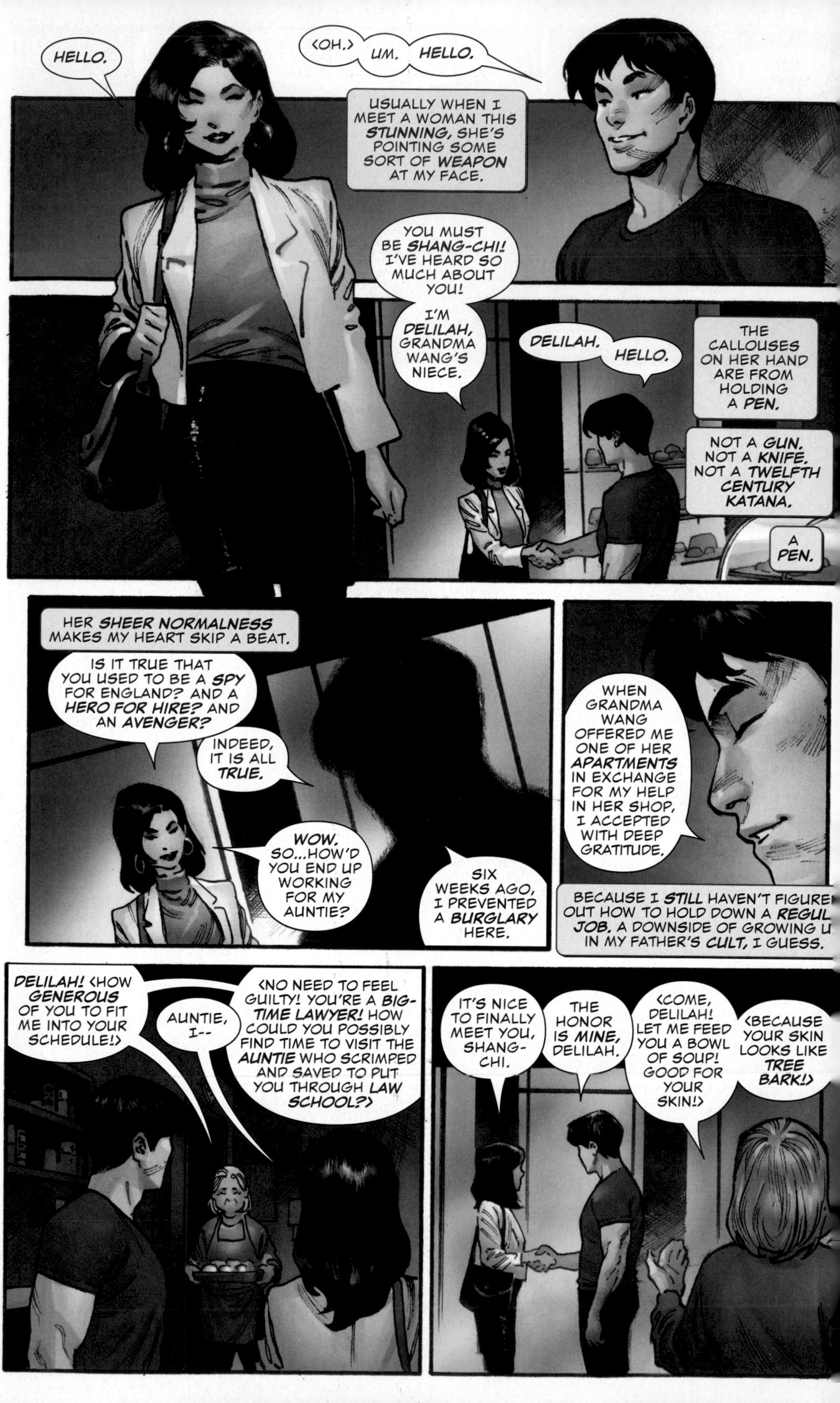
HELLO.
<OH.> UM. HELLO.
USUALLY WHEN I MEET A WOMAN THIS STUNNING, SHE'S POINTING SOME SORT OF WEAPON AT MY FACE.
YOU MUST BE SHANG-CHI! I'VE HEARD SO MUCH ABOUT YOU!
I'M DELILAH, GRANDMA WANG'S NIECE.
DELILAH. HELLO.
THE CALLOUSES ON HER HAND ARE FROM HOLDING A PEN.
NOT A GUN. NOT A KNIFE. NOT A TWELFTH CENTURY KATANA.
A PEN.
HER SHEER NORMALNESS MAKES MY HEART SKIP A BEAT.
IS IT TRUE THAT YOU USED TO BE A SPY FOR ENGLAND? AND A HERO FOR HIRE? AND AN AVENGER?
INDEED, IT IS ALL TRUE.
WOW. SO...HOW'D YOU END UP WORKING FOR MY AUNTIE?
SIX WEEKS AGO, I PREVENTED A BURGLARY HERE.
WHEN GRANDMA WANG OFFERED ME ONE OF HER APARTMENTS IN EXCHANGE FOR MY HELP IN HER SHOP, I ACCEPTED WITH DEEP GRATITUDE.
BECAUSE I STILL HAVEN'T FIGURE OUT HOW TO HOLD DOWN A REGUL JOB. A DOWNSIDE OF GROWING U IN MY FATHER'S CULT, I GUESS.
DELILAH! <HOW GENEROUS OF YOU TO FIT ME INTO YOUR SCHEDULE!>
AUNTIE, I--
<NO NEED TO FEEL GUILTY! YOU'RE A BIG-TIME LAWYER! HOW COULD YOU POSSIBLY FIND TIME TO VISIT THE AUNTIE WHO SCRIMPED AND SAVED TO PUT YOU THROUGH LAW SCHOOL?>
IT'S NICE TO FINALLY MEET YOU, SHANG-CHI.
THE HONOR IS MINE, DELILAH.
<COME, DELILAH! LET ME FEED YOU A BOWL OF SOUP! GOOD FOR YOUR SKIN!>
<BECAUSE YOUR SKIN LOOKS LIKE TREE BARK!>

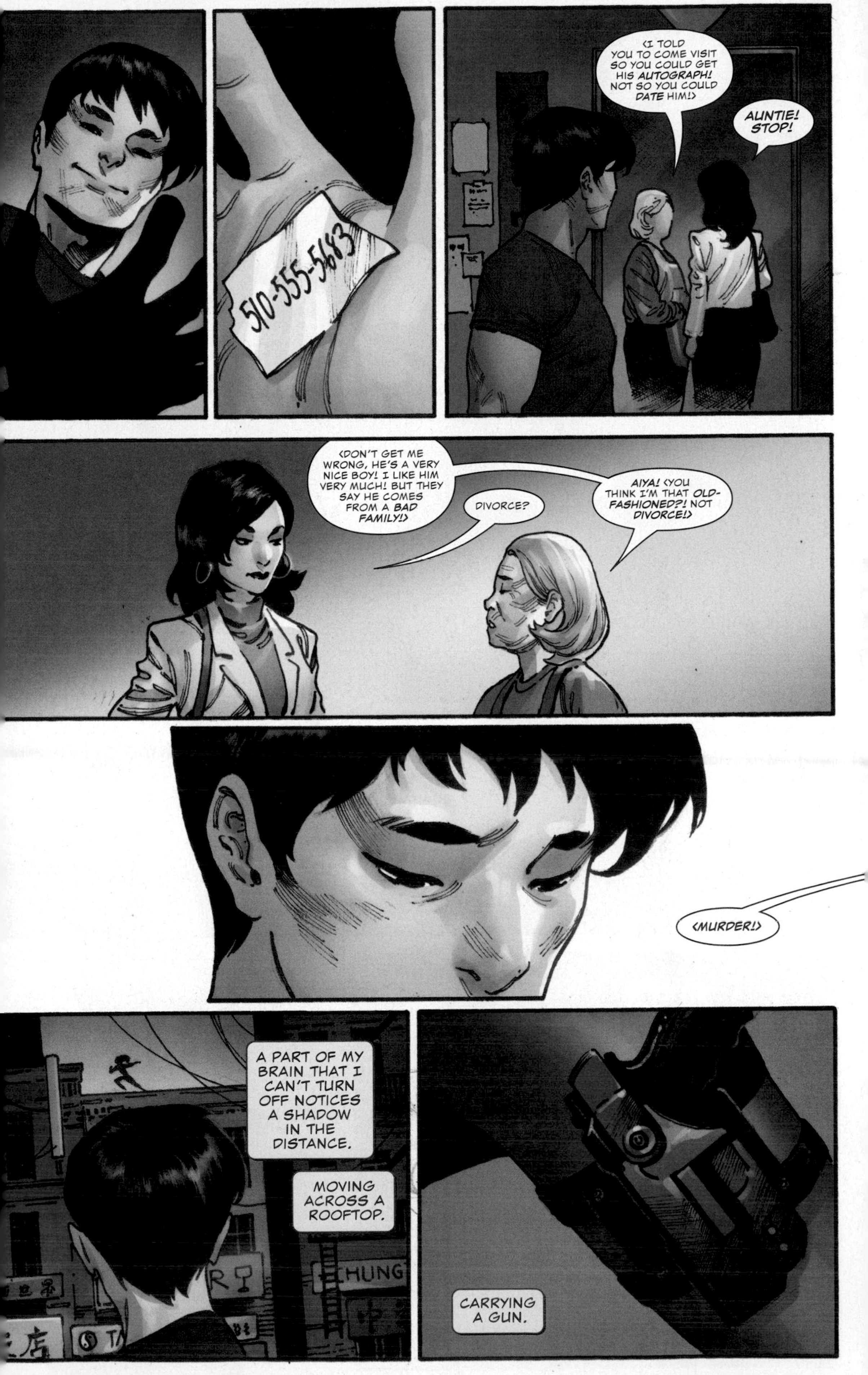
510-555-5683
<I TOLD YOU TO COME VISIT SO YOU COULD GET HIS *AUTOGRAPH!* NOT SO YOU COULD *DATE* HIM!>
AUNTIE! STOP!
<DON'T GET ME WRONG, HE'S A VERY NICE BOY! I LIKE HIM VERY MUCH! BUT THEY SAY HE COMES FROM A *BAD FAMILY!*>
DIVORCE?
AIYA! <YOU THINK I'M THAT *OLD-FASHIONED?!* NOT *DIVORCE!*>
<MURDER!>
A PART OF MY BRAIN THAT I CAN'T TURN OFF NOTICES A SHADOW IN THE DISTANCE.
MOVING ACROSS A ROOFTOP.
CHUNG
CARRYING A GUN.

I PRAY TO THE *HEAVENS* THAT MY PRESENCE DOESN'T ENDANGER GRANDMA WANG OR ANY OF HER CUSTOMERS.

OR DELILAH.

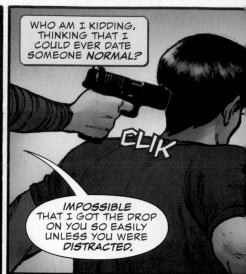

WHO AM I KIDDING, THINKING THAT I COULD EVER DATE SOMEONE *NORMAL*?

CLIK

IMPOSSIBLE THAT I GOT THE DROP ON YOU SO EASILY UNLESS YOU WERE *DISTRACTED.*

WHAT'S ON YOUR MIND, LOVE?

LEIKO WU.

BEAUTIFUL BRITISH SECRET AGENT.

GUN IN MY FACE.

THIS IS MY LIFE.

WHAP

AH! THERE HE IS!

FOR WHAT REASON HAVE YOU COME, LEIKO WU?

TO KEEP YOU *ALIVE*, LOVE.

WE NEED TO TALK, PRIVATEL

KNOW PLACE?

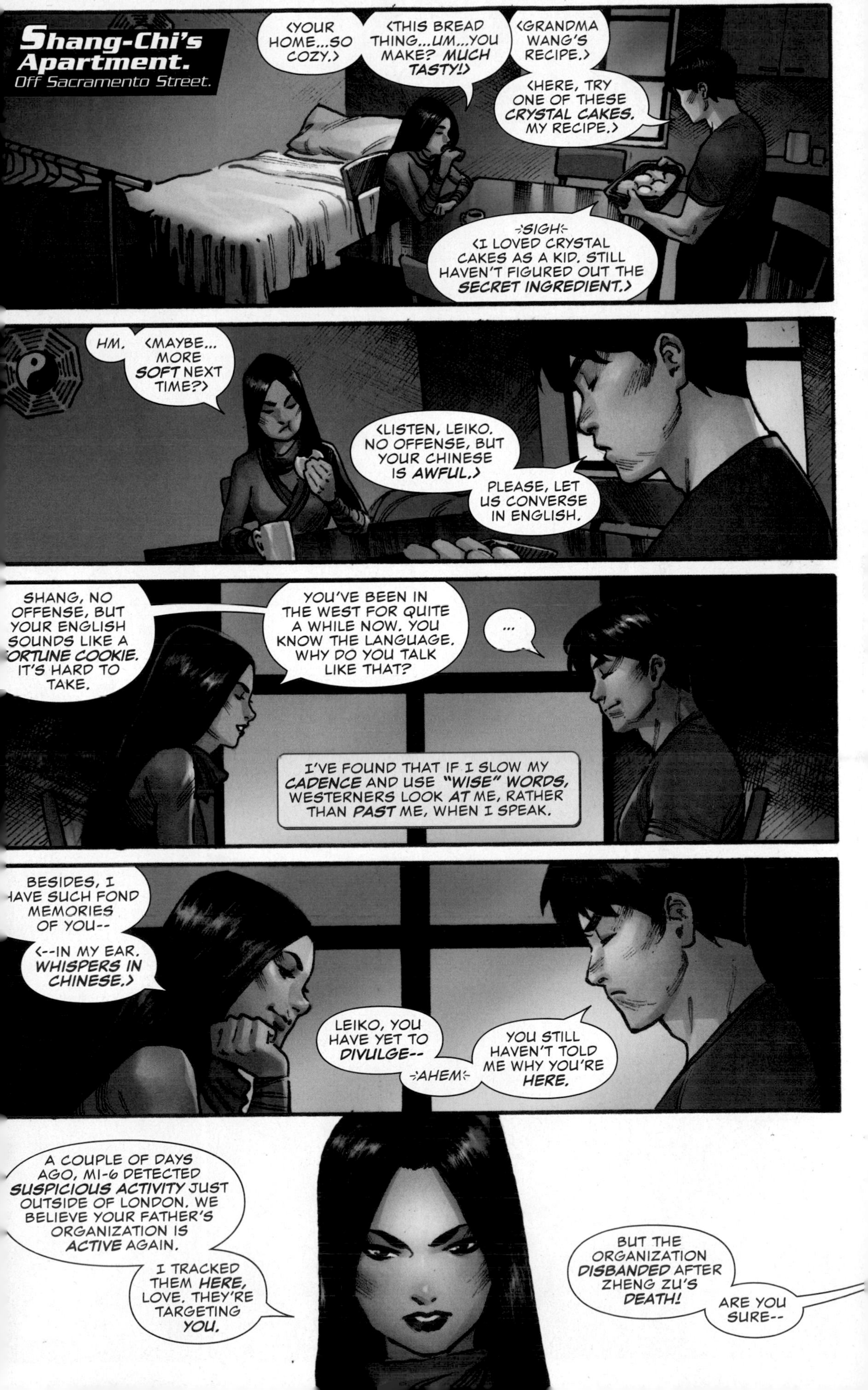
Shang-Chi's Apartment.
Off Sacramento Street.
<YOUR HOME...SO COZY.>
<THIS BREAD THING...UM...YOU MAKE? MUCH TASTY!>
<GRANDMA WANG'S RECIPE.>
<HERE, TRY ONE OF THESE CRYSTAL CAKES. MY RECIPE.>
-SIGH-
<I LOVED CRYSTAL CAKES AS A KID. STILL HAVEN'T FIGURED OUT THE SECRET INGREDIENT.>
HM.
<MAYBE... MORE SOFT NEXT TIME?>
<LISTEN, LEIKO. NO OFFENSE, BUT YOUR CHINESE IS AWFUL.>
PLEASE, LET US CONVERSE IN ENGLISH.
SHANG, NO OFFENSE, BUT YOUR ENGLISH SOUNDS LIKE A FORTUNE COOKIE. IT'S HARD TO TAKE.
YOU'VE BEEN IN THE WEST FOR QUITE A WHILE NOW. YOU KNOW THE LANGUAGE. WHY DO YOU TALK LIKE THAT?
...
I'VE FOUND THAT IF I SLOW MY CADENCE AND USE "WISE" WORDS, WESTERNERS LOOK AT ME, RATHER THAN PAST ME, WHEN I SPEAK.
BESIDES, I HAVE SUCH FOND MEMORIES OF YOU--
<--IN MY EAR. WHISPERS IN CHINESE.>
LEIKO, YOU HAVE YET TO DIVULGE--
-AHEM-
YOU STILL HAVEN'T TOLD ME WHY YOU'RE HERE.
A COUPLE OF DAYS AGO, MI-6 DETECTED SUSPICIOUS ACTIVITY JUST OUTSIDE OF LONDON. WE BELIEVE YOUR FATHER'S ORGANIZATION IS ACTIVE AGAIN.
I TRACKED THEM HERE, LOVE. THEY'RE TARGETING YOU.
BUT THE ORGANIZATION DISBANDED AFTER ZHENG ZU'S DEATH!
ARE YOU SURE--

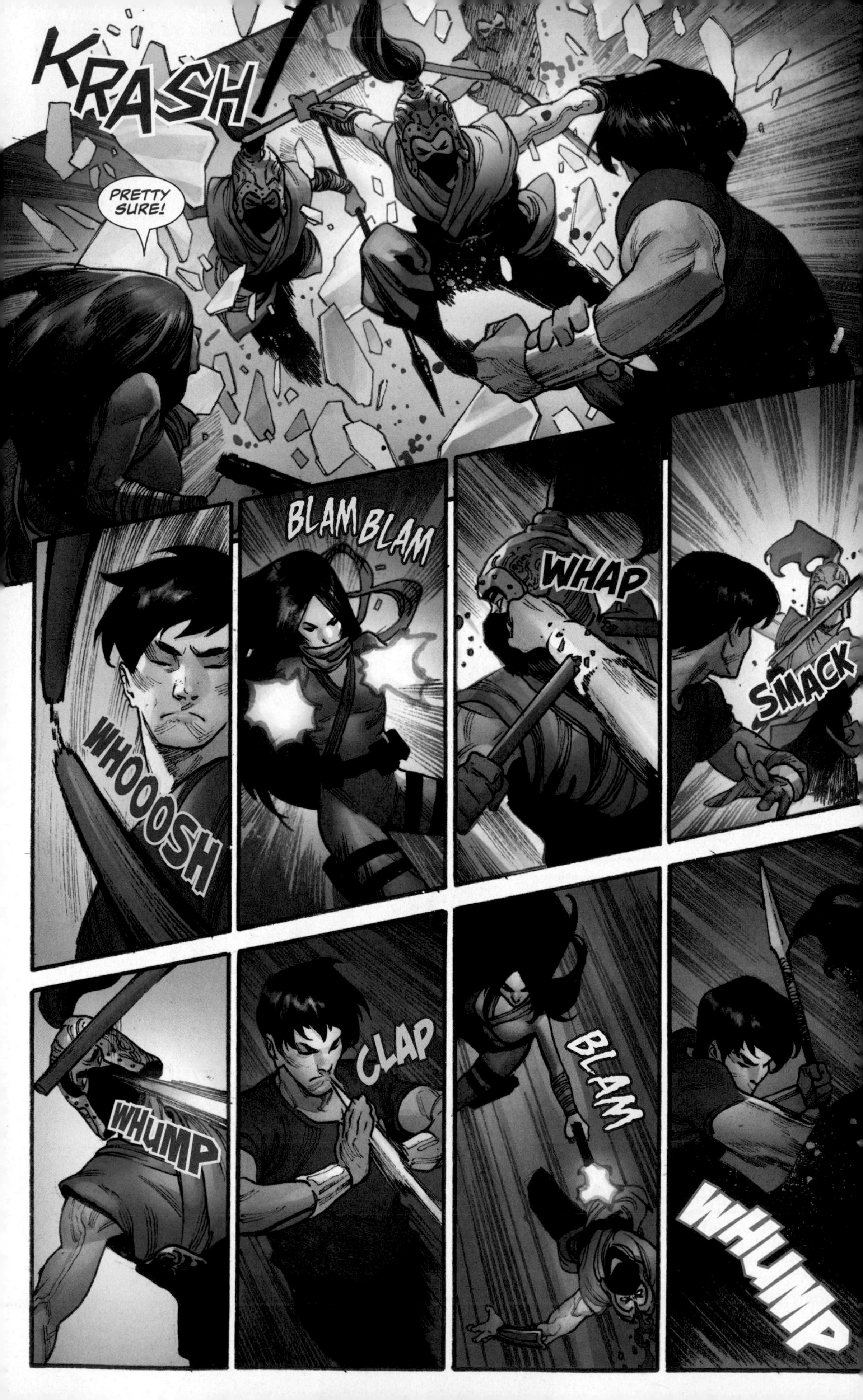
KRASH
PRETTY SURE!
WHOOOSH
BLAM BLAM
WHAP
SMACK
WHUMP
CLAP
BLAM
WHUMP

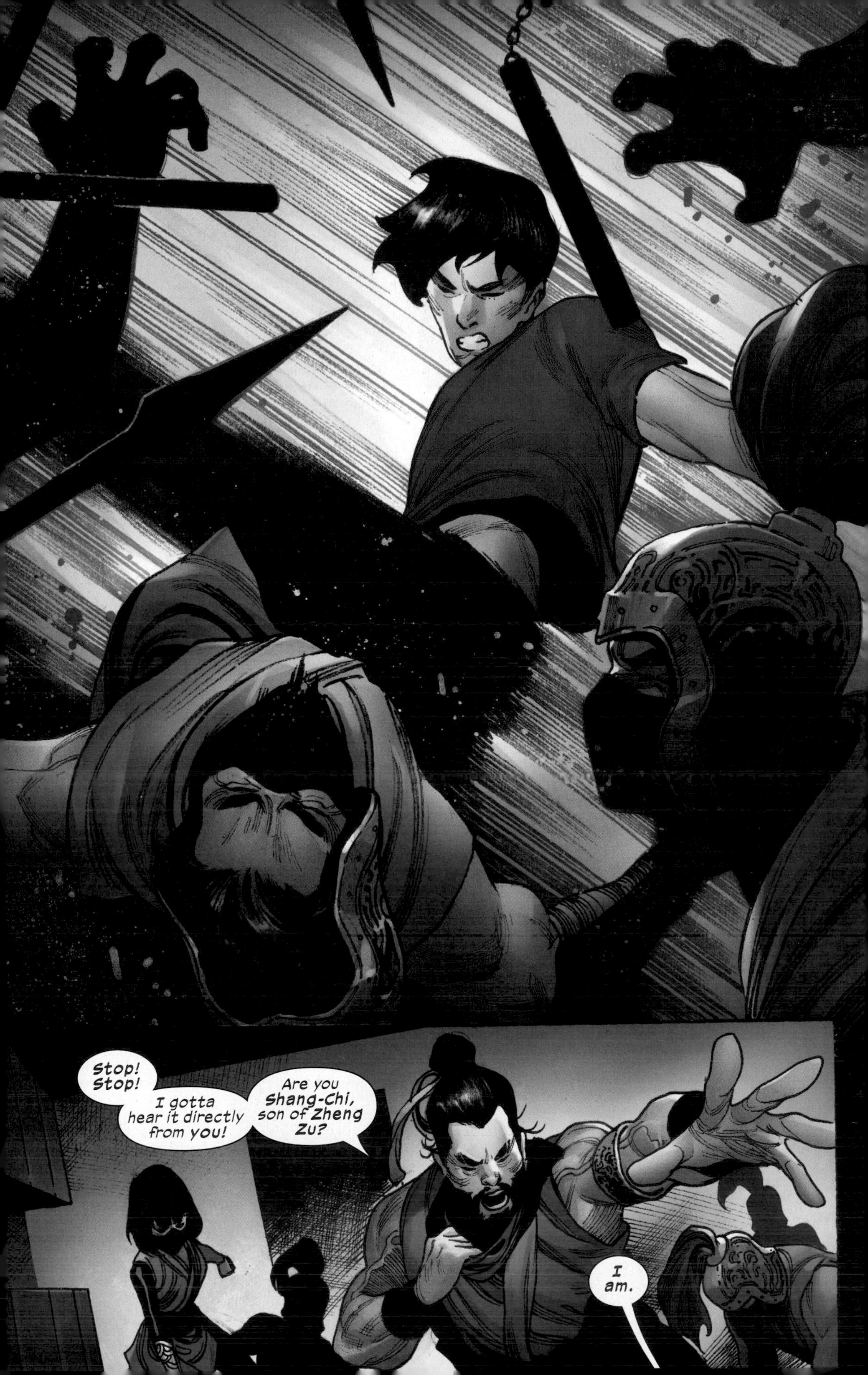
Stop! Stop!
I gotta hear it directly from you!
Are you Shang-Chi, son of Zheng Zu?
I am.

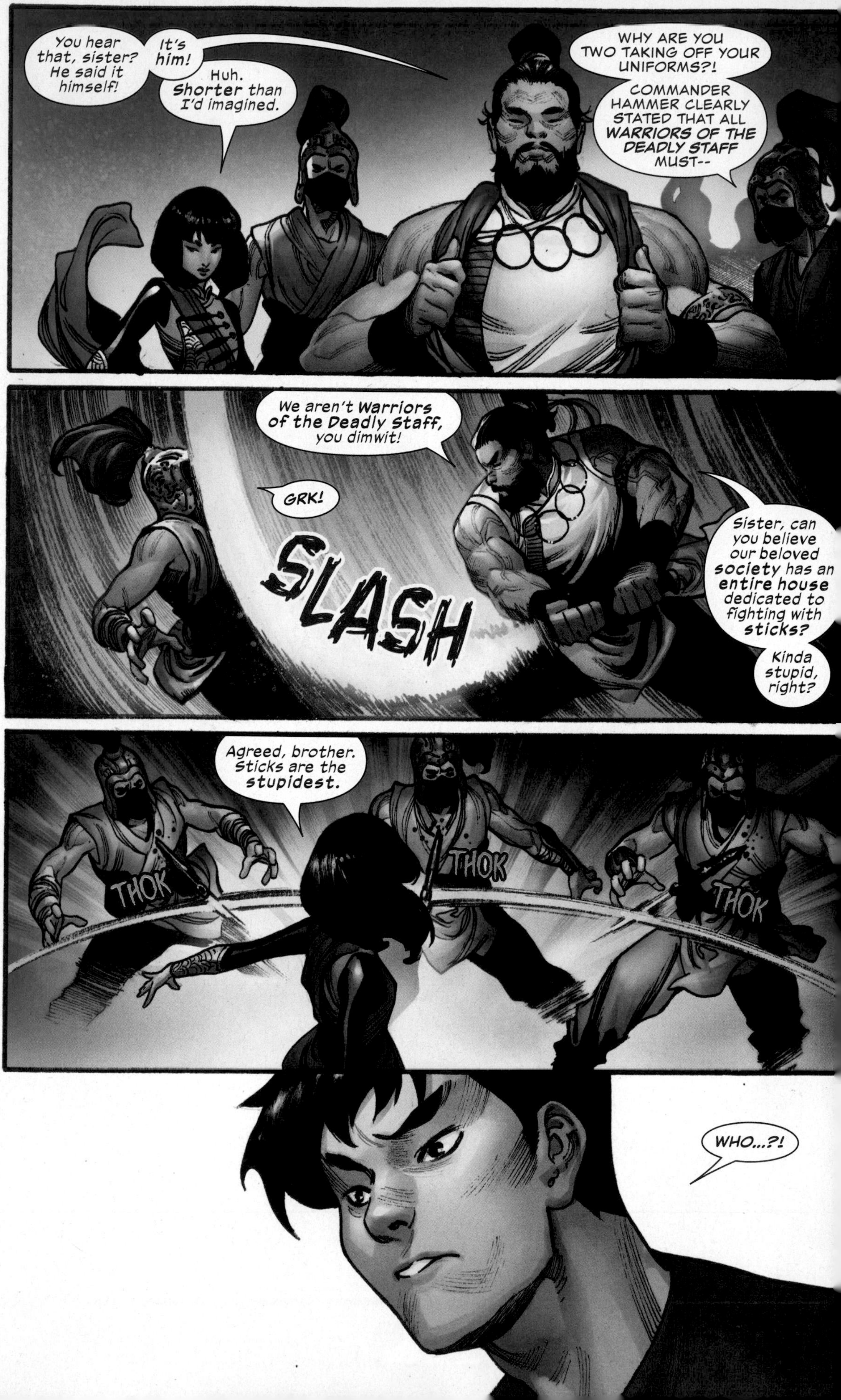
You hear that, sister? He said it himself!
It's him!
Huh. Shorter than I'd imagined.
WHY ARE YOU TWO TAKING OFF YOUR UNIFORMS?!
COMMANDER HAMMER CLEARLY STATED THAT ALL WARRIORS OF THE DEADLY STAFF MUST--
We aren't Warriors of the Deadly Staff, you dimwit!
GRK!
SLASH
Sister, can you believe our beloved society has an entire house dedicated to fighting with sticks?
Kinda stupid, right?
Agreed, brother. Sticks are the stupidest.
THOK
THOK
THOK
WHO...?!

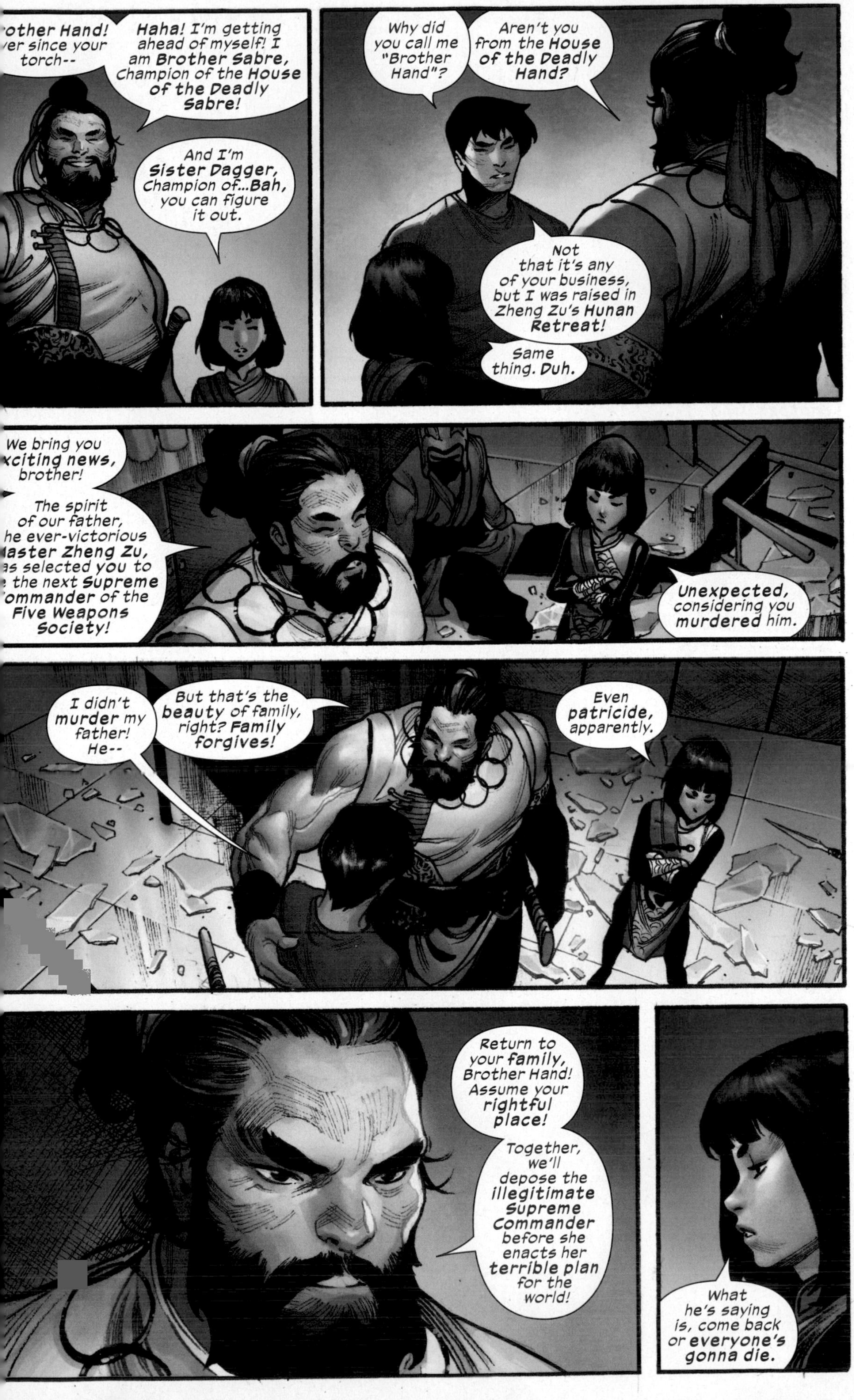
rother Hand! ver since your torch--
Haha! I'm getting ahead of myself! I am Brother Sabre, Champion of the House of the Deadly Sabre!
And I'm Sister Dagger, Champion of...Bah, you can figure it out.
Why did you call me "Brother Hand"?
Aren't you from the House of the Deadly Hand?
Not that it's any of your business, but I was raised in Zheng Zu's Hunan Retreat!
Same thing. Duh.
We bring you xciting news, brother!
The spirit of our father, he ever-victorious laster Zheng Zu, as selected you to the next Supreme ommander of the Five Weapons Society!
Unexpected, considering you murdered him.
I didn't murder my father! He--
But that's the beauty of family, right? Family forgives!
Even patricide, apparently.
Return to your family, Brother Hand! Assume your rightful place!
Together, we'll depose the illegitimate Supreme Commander before she enacts her terrible plan for the world!
What he's saying is, come back or everyone's gonna die.

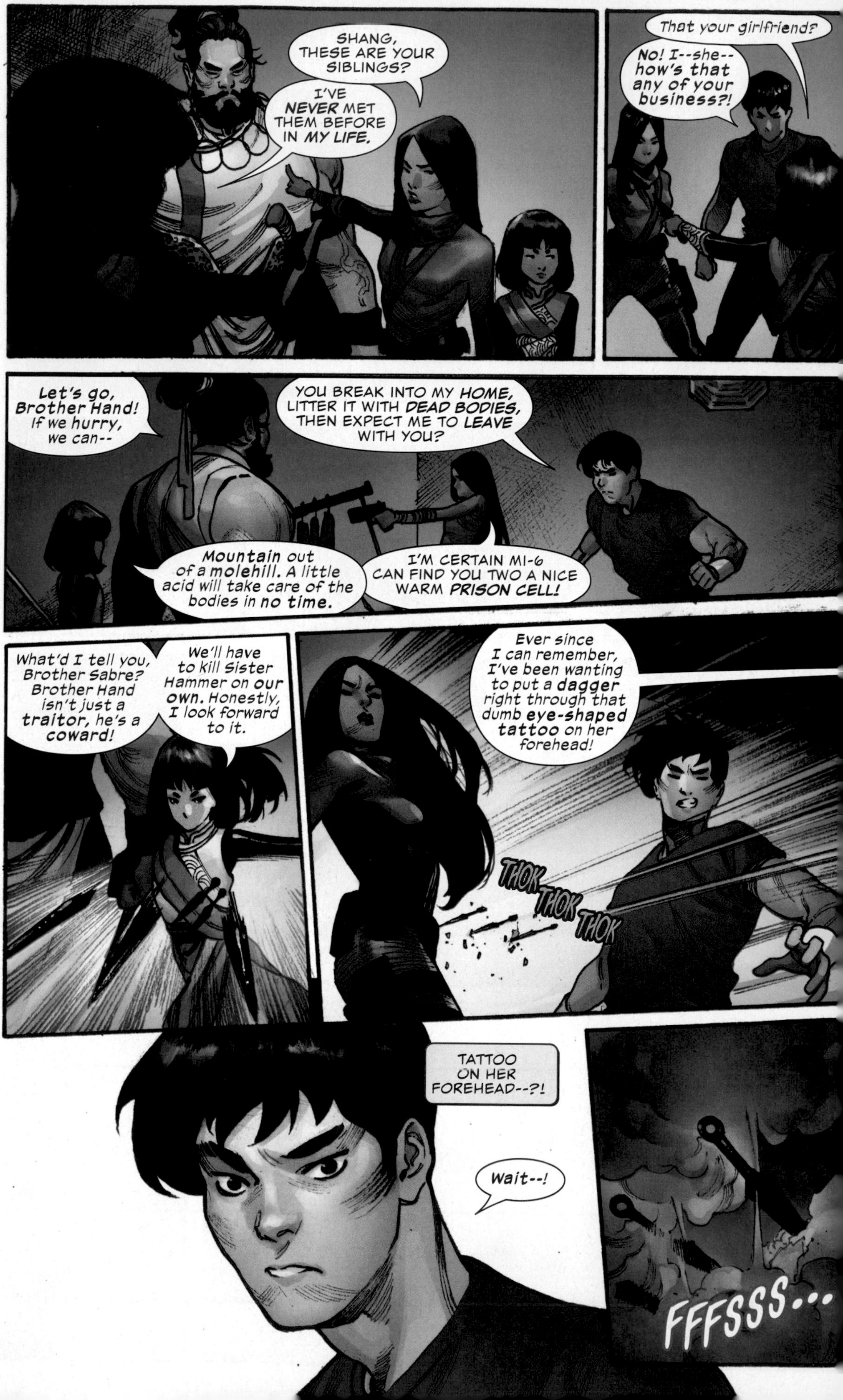

SHANG, THESE ARE YOUR SIBLINGS?
I'VE NEVER MET THEM BEFORE IN MY LIFE.
That your girlfriend?
No! I--she--how's that any of your business?!
Let's go, Brother Hand! If we hurry, we can--
YOU BREAK INTO MY HOME, LITTER IT WITH DEAD BODIES, THEN EXPECT ME TO LEAVE WITH YOU?
Mountain out of a molehill. A little acid will take care of the bodies in no time.
I'M CERTAIN MI-6 CAN FIND YOU TWO A NICE WARM PRISON CELL!
What'd I tell you, Brother Sabre? Brother Hand isn't just a traitor, he's a coward!
We'll have to kill Sister Hammer on our own. Honestly, I look forward to it.
Ever since I can remember, I've been wanting to put a dagger right through that dumb eye-shaped tattoo on her forehead!
THOK THOK THOK
TATTOO ON HER FOREHEAD--?!
Wait--!
FFFSSS...

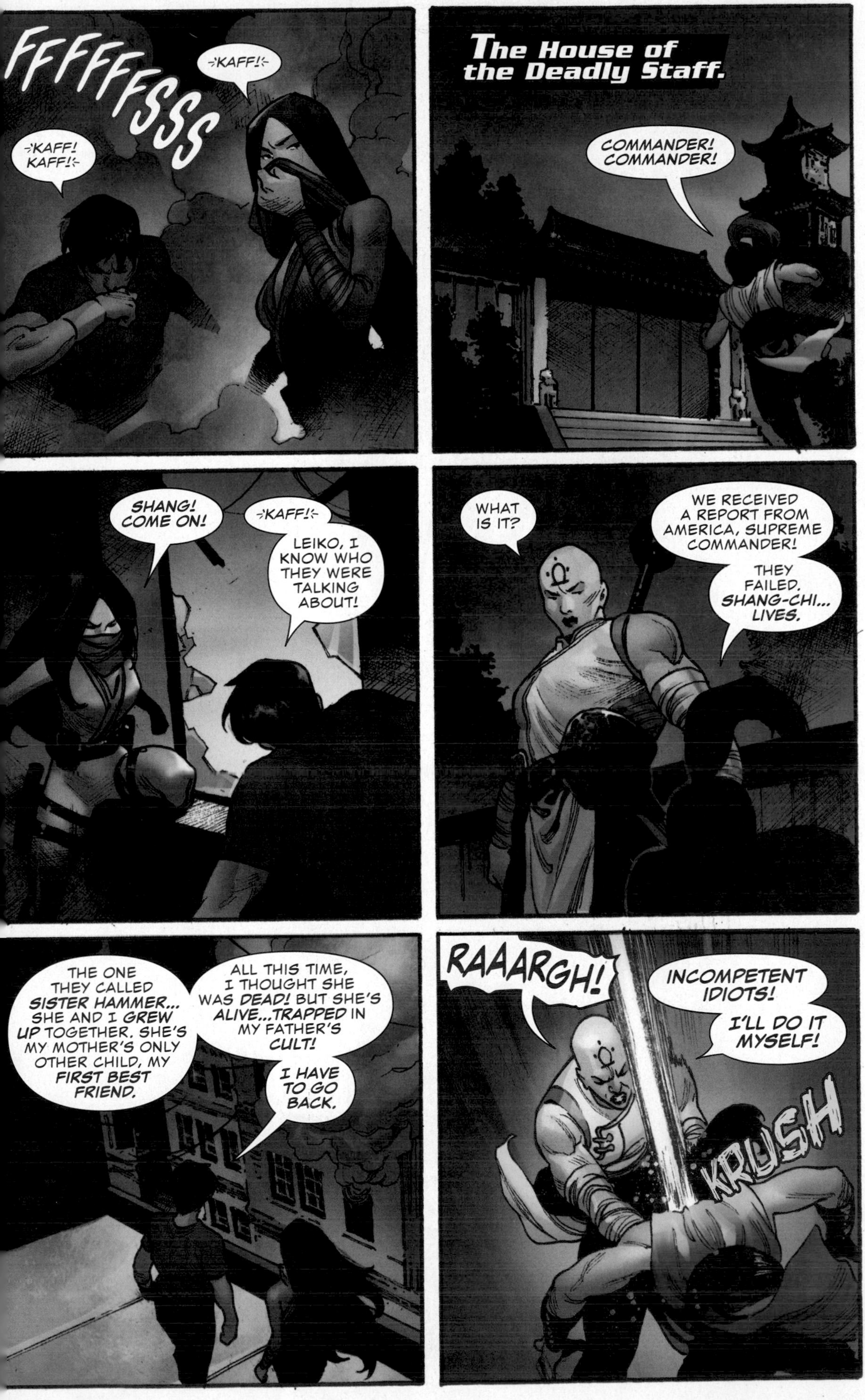
FFFFFFSSS
KAFF!
KAFF! KAFF!
The House of the Deadly Staff.
COMMANDER! COMMANDER!
SHANG! COME ON!
KAFF!
LEIKO, I KNOW WHO THEY WERE TALKING ABOUT!
WHAT IS IT?
WE RECEIVED A REPORT FROM AMERICA, SUPREME COMMANDER!
THEY FAILED. SHANG-CHI... LIVES.
THE ONE THEY CALLED SISTER HAMMER... SHE AND I GREW UP TOGETHER. SHE'S MY MOTHER'S ONLY OTHER CHILD, MY FIRST BEST FRIEND.
ALL THIS TIME, I THOUGHT SHE WAS DEAD! BUT SHE'S ALIVE...TRAPPED IN MY FATHER'S CULT!
I HAVE TO GO BACK.
RAAARGH!
INCOMPETENT IDIOTS!
I'LL DO IT MYSELF!
KRUSH

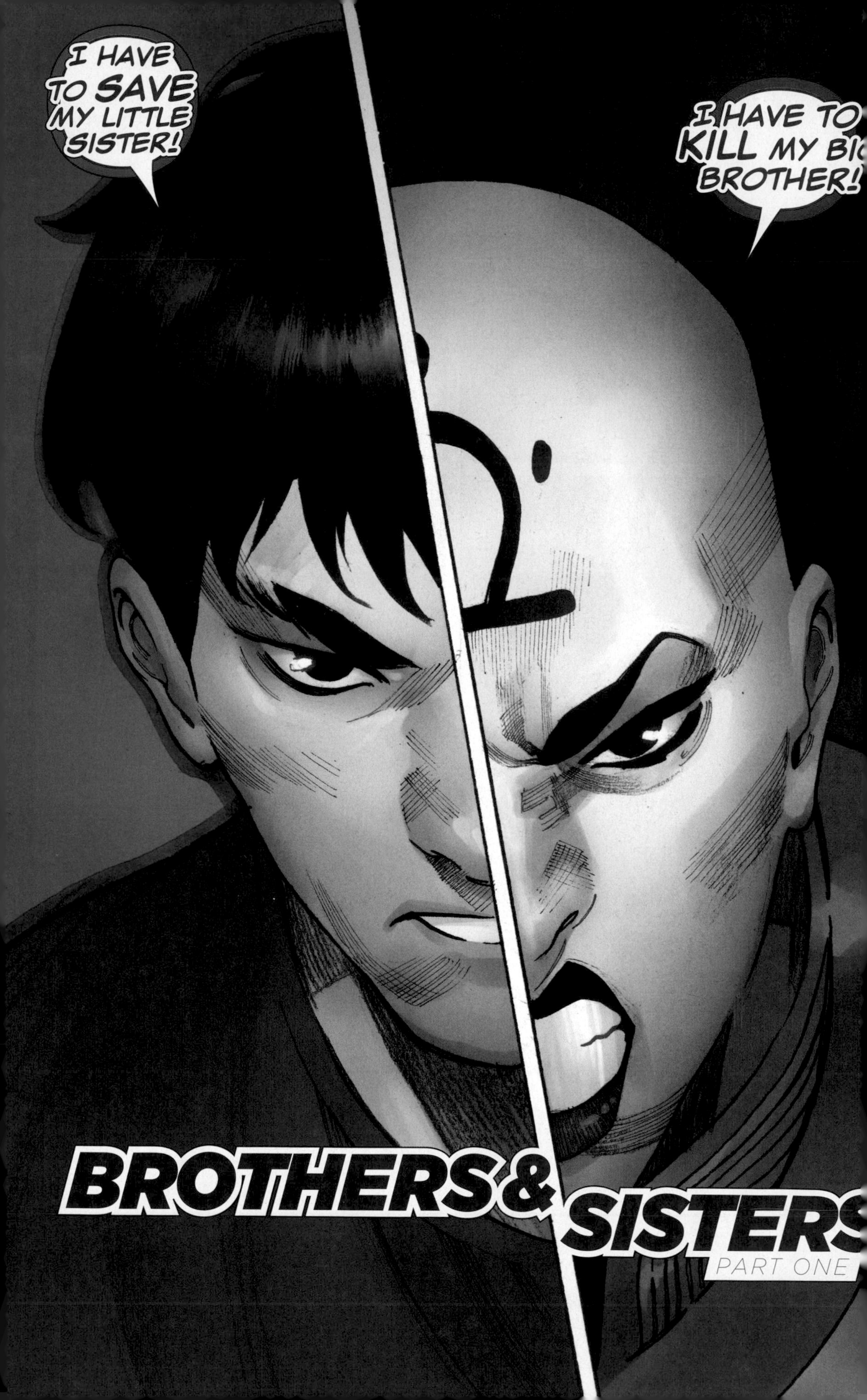
I HAVE TO SAVE MY LITTLE SISTER!
I HAVE TO KILL MY BIG BROTHER!
BROTHERS & SISTERS
PART ONE

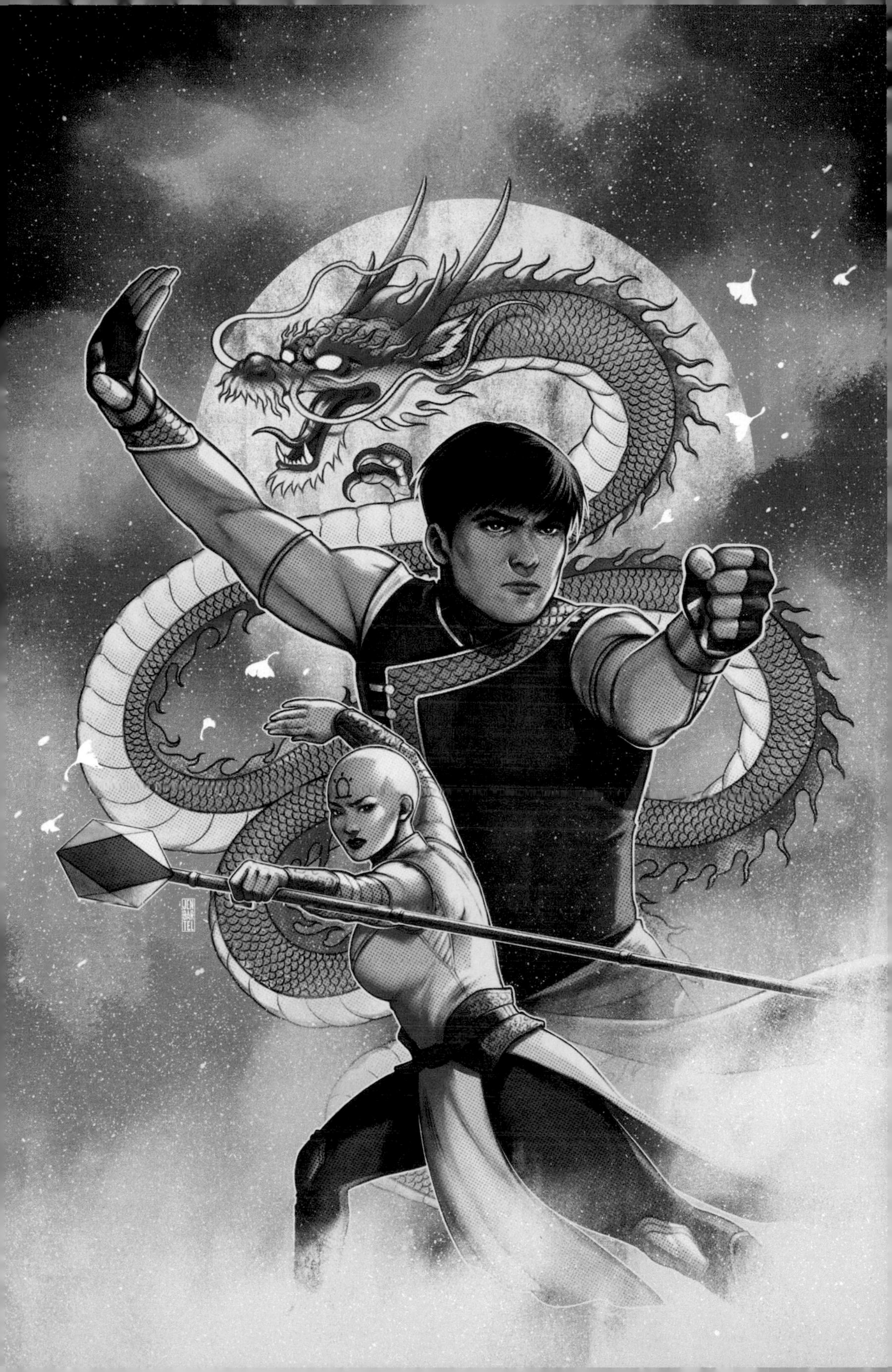
JEN
BAR
TEL

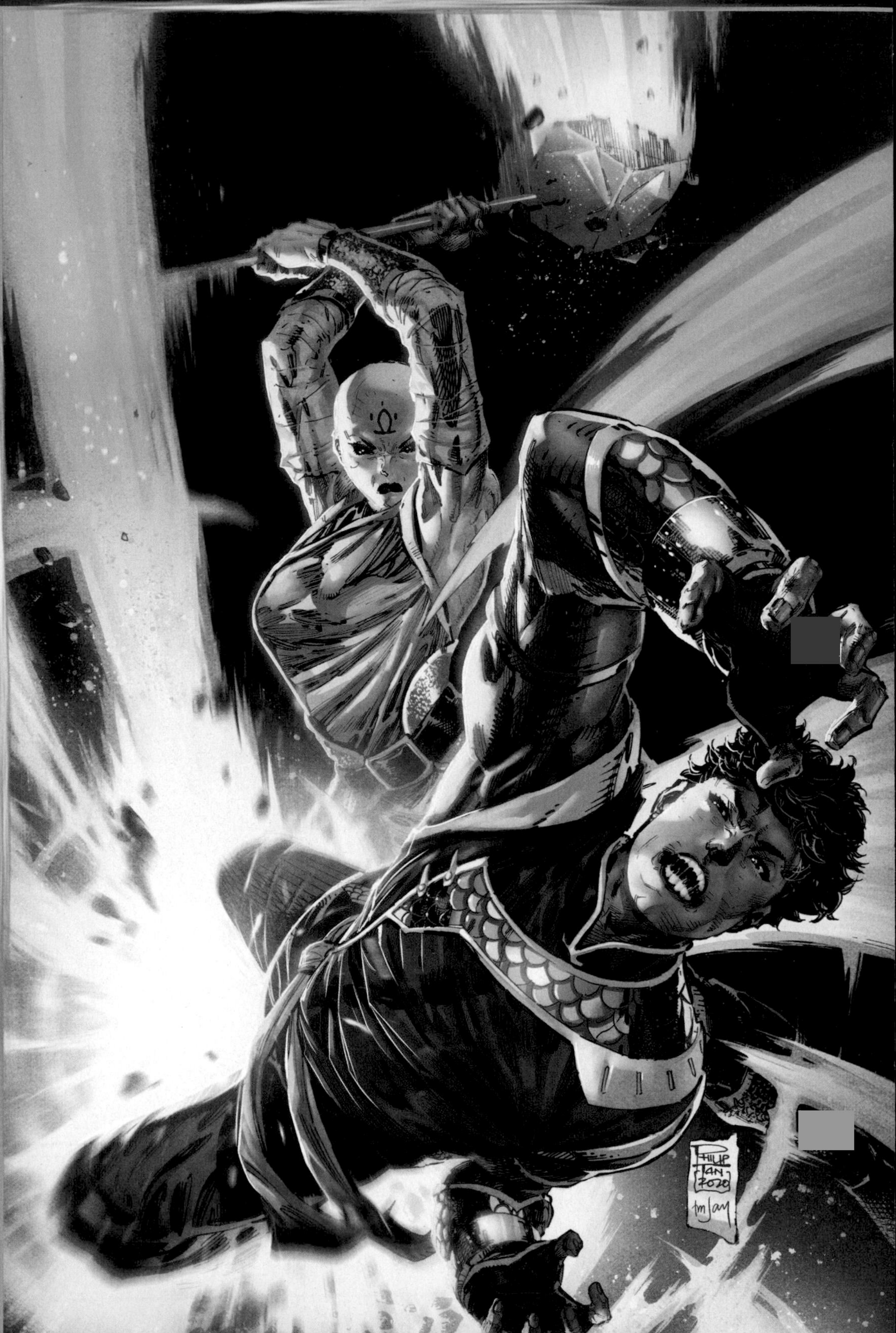
PHILIP TAN 2020
tmJay

TWO

Zheng Zu's Hunan Retreat.
Fifteen years ago.

"MY SISTER AND I WERE THE ONLY ONES WHO REALLY *UNDERSTOOD* EACH OTHER.

"WE BOTH KNEW WHAT IT WAS LIKE TO GROW UP IN A *CULT* THAT PRETENDED THE *QING DYNASTY* HAD NEVER FALLEN.

"THAT THE *REAL WORLD* DID NOT EXIST.

Can you believe the gall of those dumb cooks, Shi-Hua?*

*Translated from ancient Mandarin. --DS

Telling us there are no crystal cakes loft! Don't they know who our dad is?!

I don't know... maybe they're telling the truth, Shang-Chi.

Psh. Those pigs are probably hoarding it all for themselves!

KRUSH

Haha! Are my hands deadly or what?!

Big brother, w-w-we're not supposed to be in here!

Yeah, 'cause it's where they're hiding all the crystal cakes, I bet!

Come on, Shi-Hua! There's nothing to be afr--

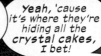

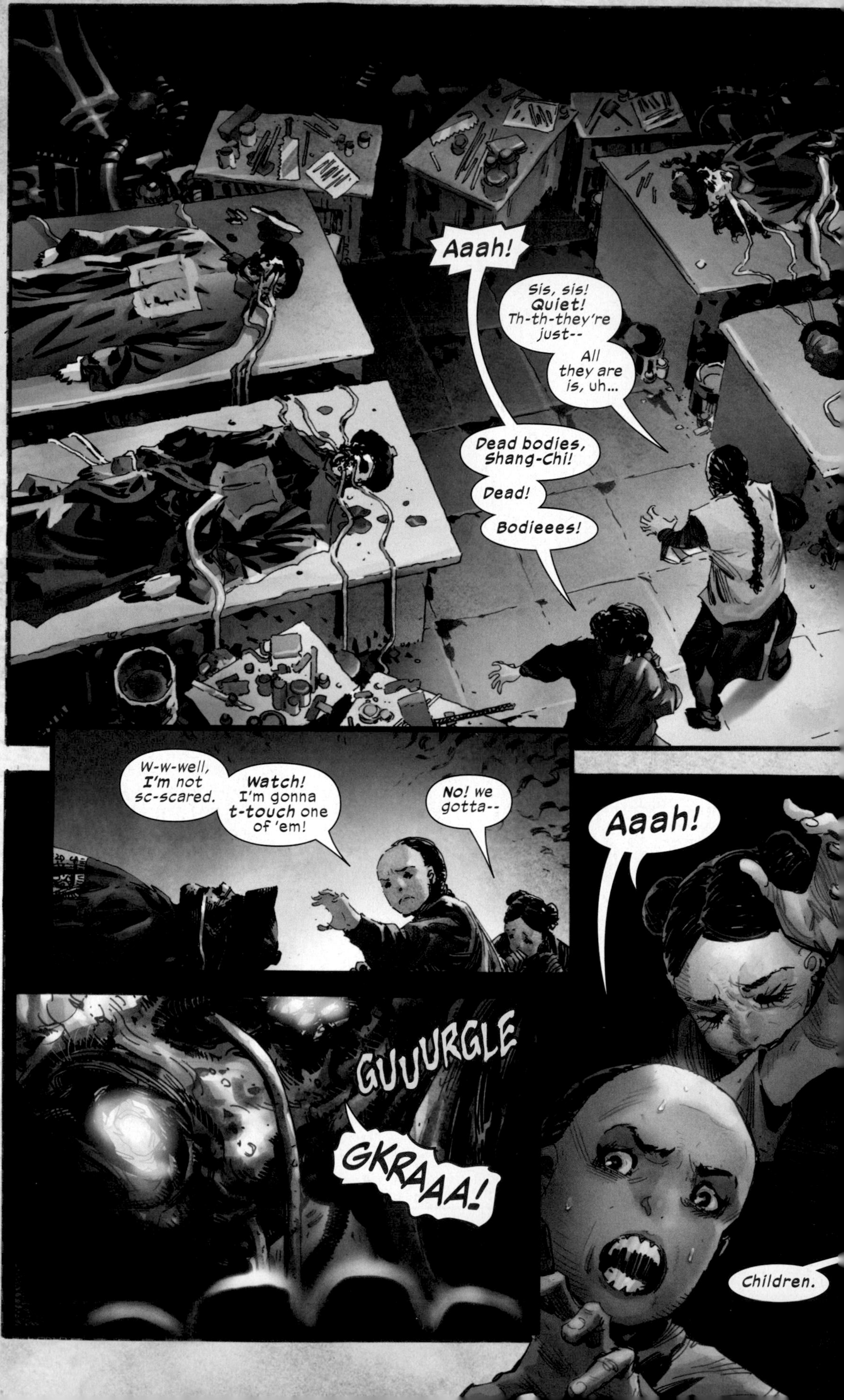
Aaah!
Sis, sis! Quiet! Th-th-they're just--
All they are is, uh...
Dead bodies, Shang-Chi!
Dead!
Bodieees!
W-w-well, I'm not sc-scared.
Watch! I'm gonna t-touch one of 'em!
No! we gotta--
Aaah!
GUUURGLE
GKRAAA!
Children.

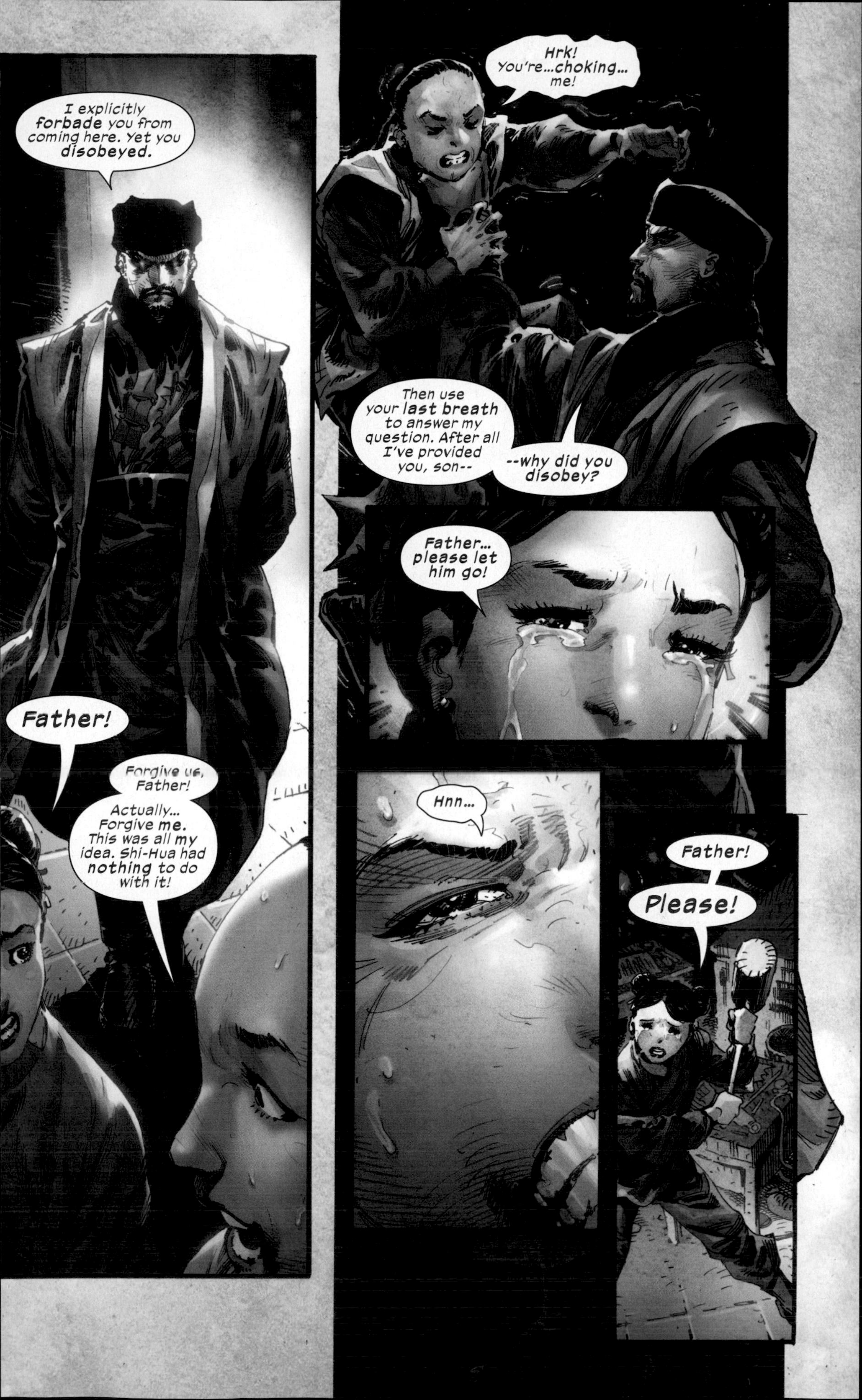
I explicitly forbade you from coming here. Yet you disobeyed.
Father!
Forgive us, Father!
Actually... Forgive me. This was all my idea. Shi-Hua had nothing to do with it!
Hrk! You're...choking... me!
Then use your last breath to answer my question. After all I've provided you, son--
--why did you disobey?
Father... please let him go!
Hnn...
Father!
Please!

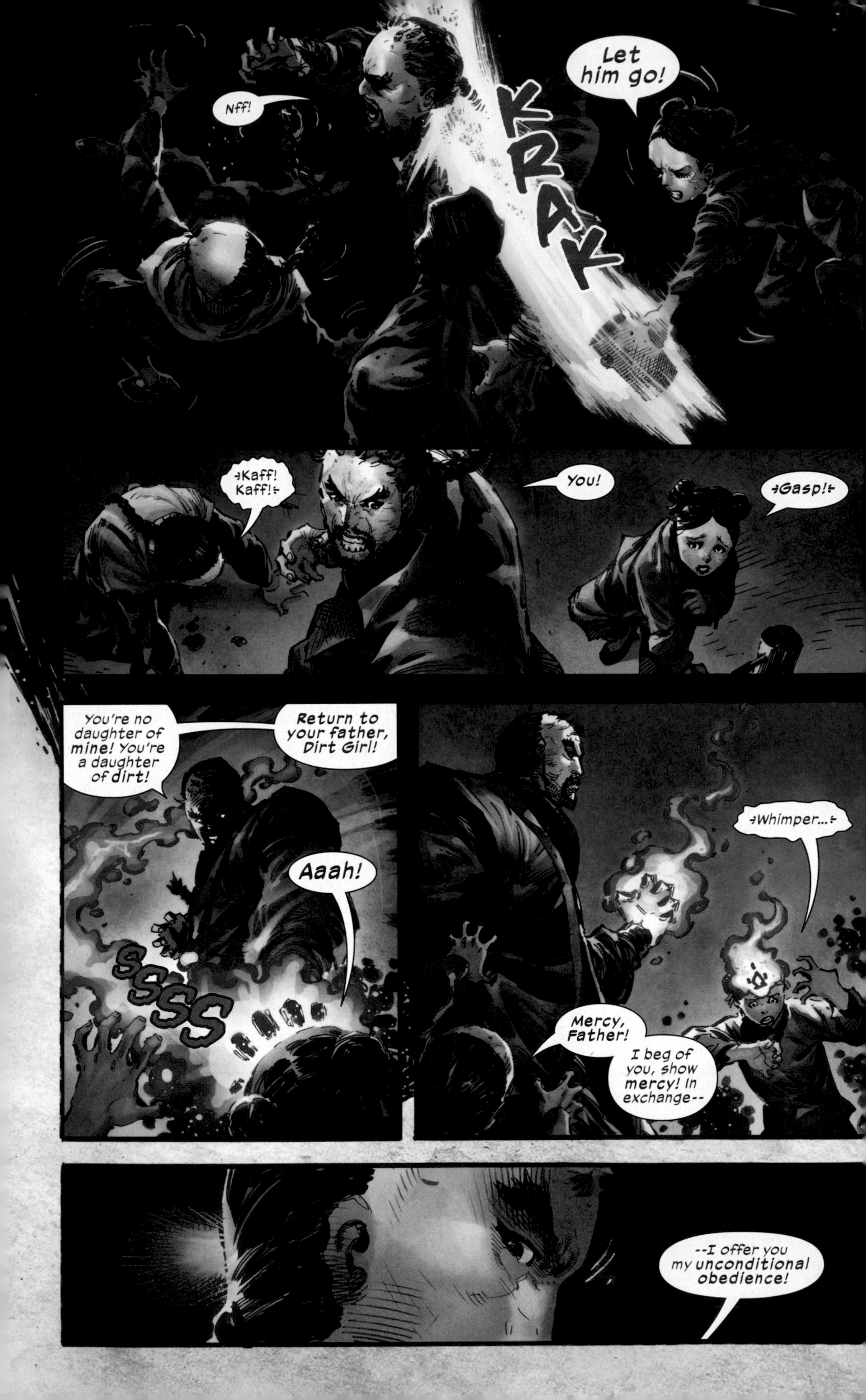
Nff!
KRAK
Let him go!
⊰Kaff! Kaff!⊱
You!
⊰Gasp!⊱
You're no daughter of mine! You're a daughter of dirt!
Return to your father, Dirt Girl!
Aaah!
SSSS
⊰Whimper...⊱
Mercy, Father!
I beg of you, show mercy! In exchange--
--I offer you my unconditional obedience!

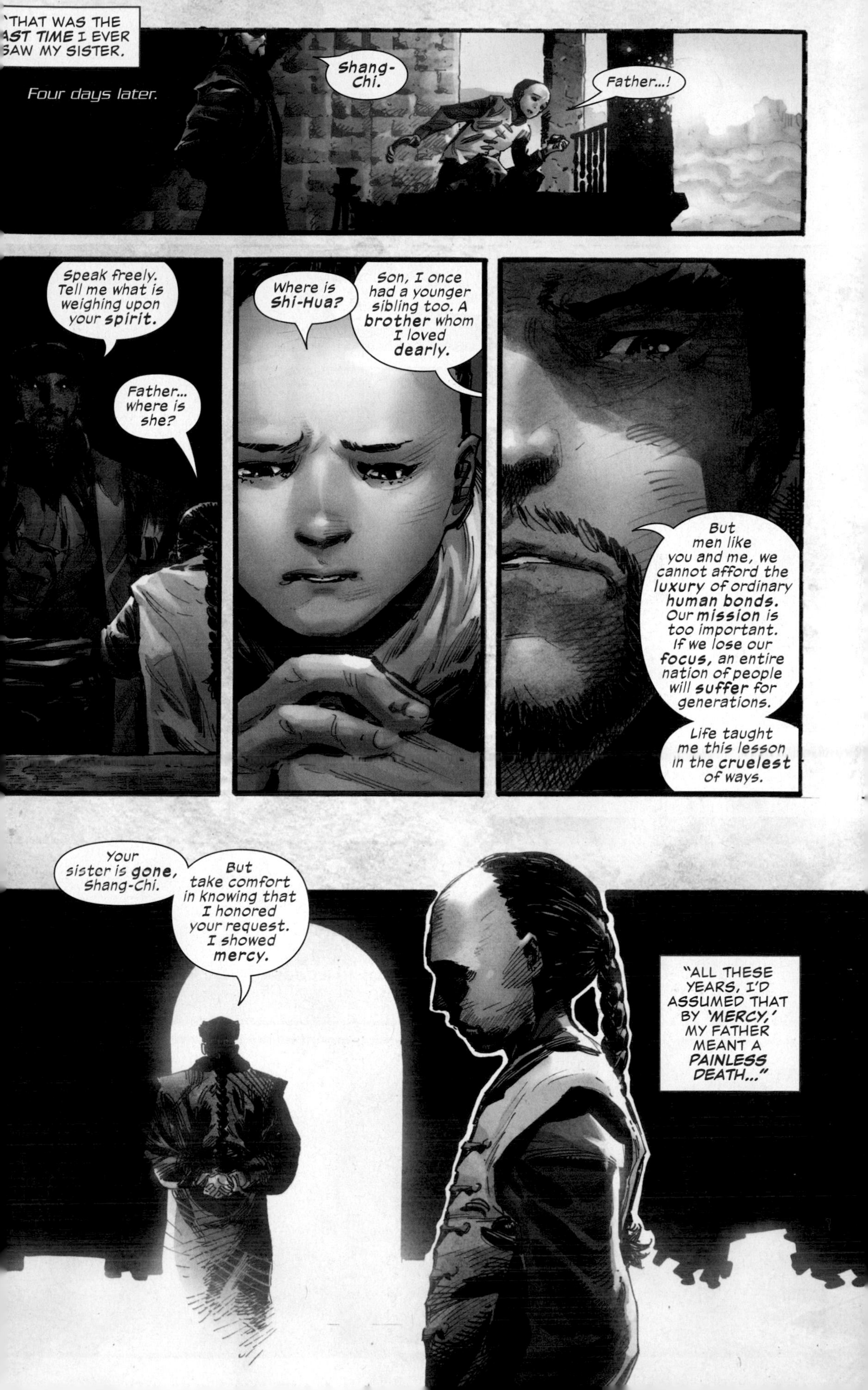

"THAT WAS THE LAST TIME I EVER SAW MY SISTER.
Four days later.
Shang-Chi.
Father...!
Speak freely. Tell me what is weighing upon your spirit.
Father... where is she?
Where is Shi-Hua?
Son, I once had a younger sibling too. A brother whom I loved dearly.
But men like you and me, we cannot afford the luxury of ordinary human bonds. Our mission is too important. If we lose our focus, an entire nation of people will suffer for generations.
Life taught me this lesson in the cruelest of ways.
Your sister is gone, Shang-Chi.
But take comfort in knowing that I honored your request. I showed mercy.
"ALL THESE YEARS, I'D ASSUMED THAT BY 'MERCY,' MY FATHER MEANT A PAINLESS DEATH..."

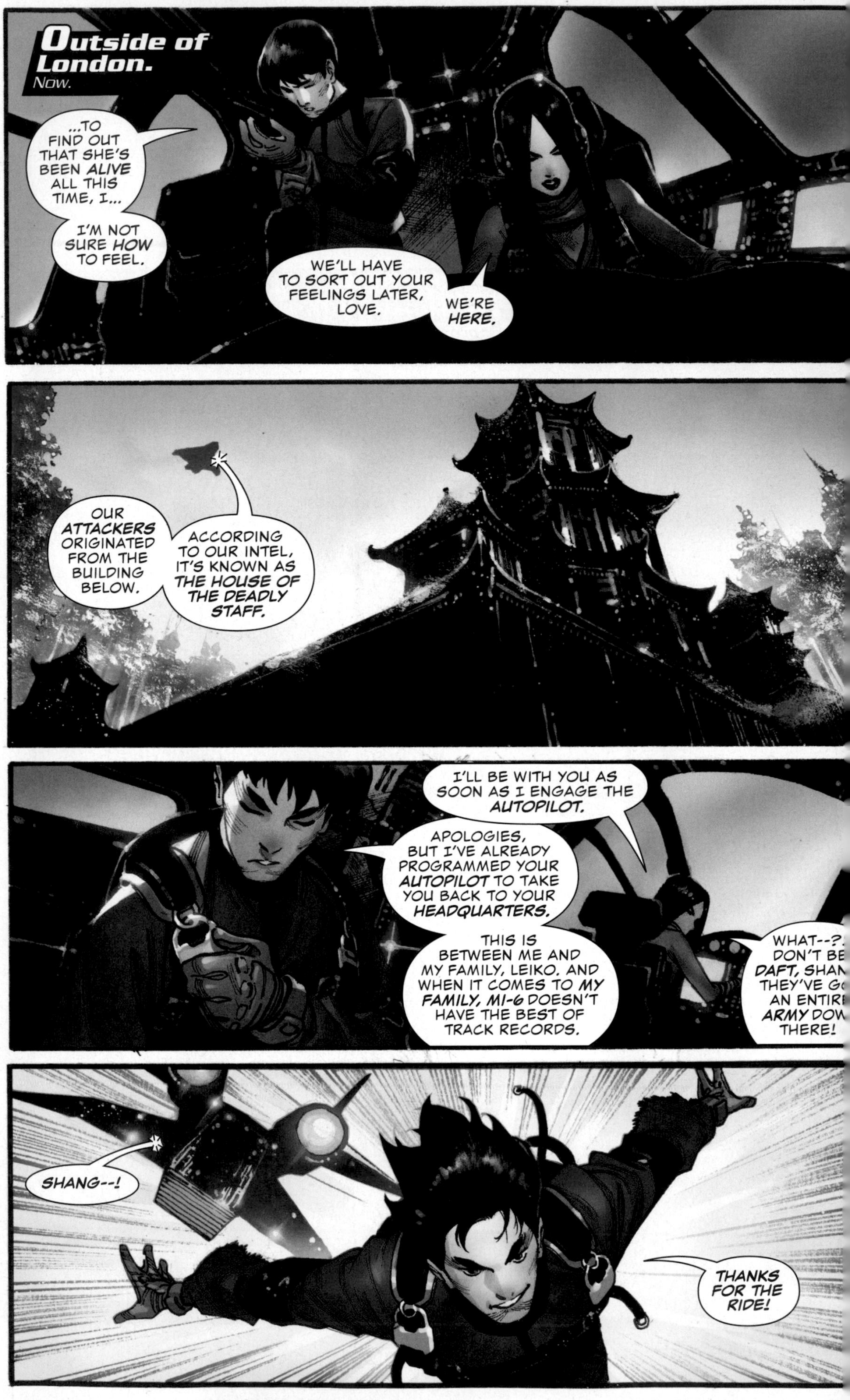
Outside of London.
Now.
...TO FIND OUT THAT SHE'S BEEN ALIVE ALL THIS TIME, I...
I'M NOT SURE HOW TO FEEL.
WE'LL HAVE TO SORT OUT YOUR FEELINGS LATER, LOVE.
WE'RE HERE.
OUR ATTACKERS ORIGINATED FROM THE BUILDING BELOW.
ACCORDING TO OUR INTEL, IT'S KNOWN AS THE HOUSE OF THE DEADLY STAFF.
I'LL BE WITH YOU AS SOON AS I ENGAGE THE AUTOPILOT.
APOLOGIES, BUT I'VE ALREADY PROGRAMMED YOUR AUTOPILOT TO TAKE YOU BACK TO YOUR HEADQUARTERS.
THIS IS BETWEEN ME AND MY FAMILY, LEIKO. AND WHEN IT COMES TO MY FAMILY, MI-6 DOESN'T HAVE THE BEST OF TRACK RECORDS.
WHAT--?! DON'T BE DAFT, SHAN THEY'VE G AN ENTIR ARMY DOW THERE!
SHANG--!
THANKS FOR THE RIDE!

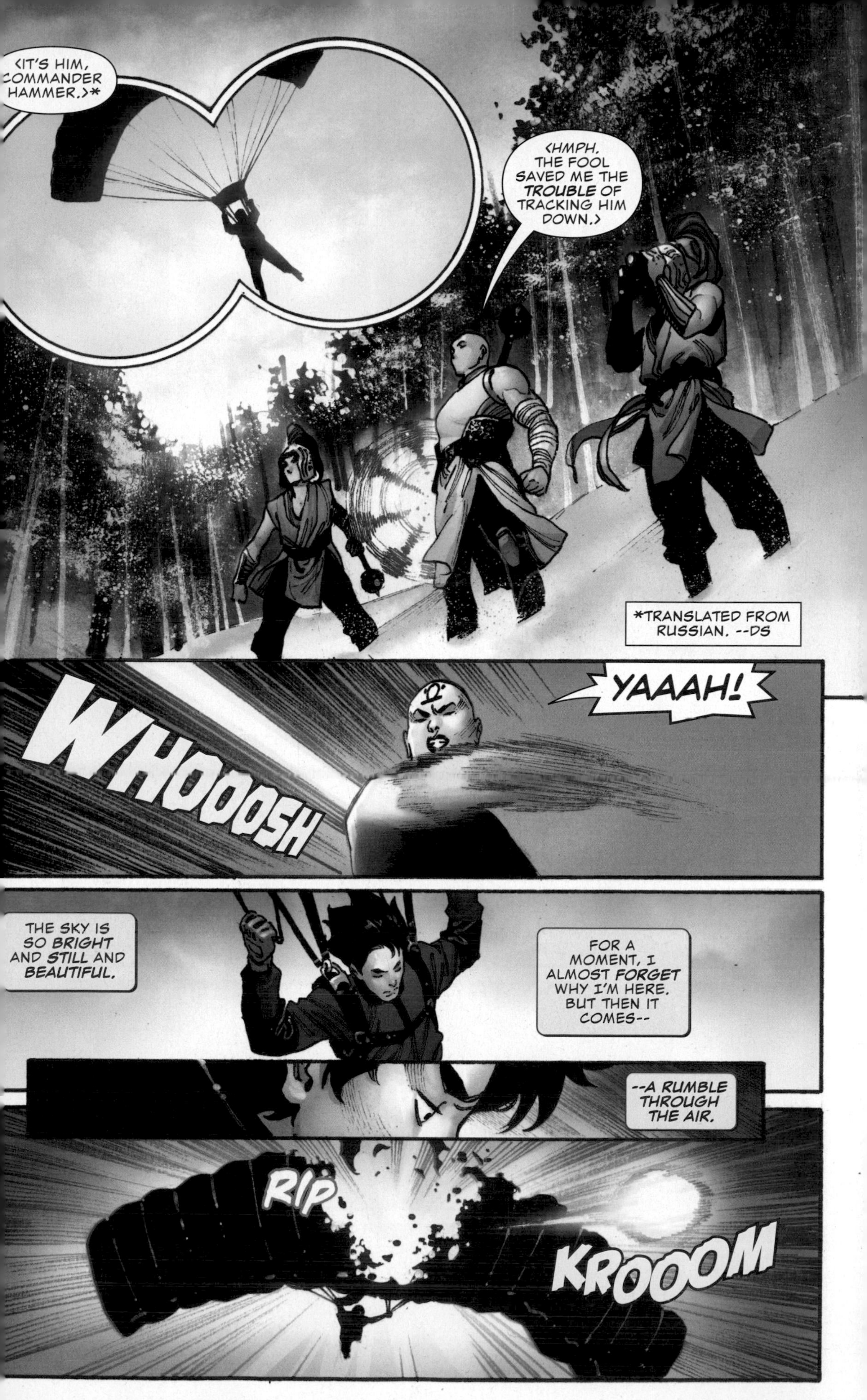
<IT'S HIM, COMMANDER HAMMER.>*
<HMPH. THE FOOL SAVED ME THE TROUBLE OF TRACKING HIM DOWN.>
*TRANSLATED FROM RUSSIAN. --DS
WHOOOSH
YAAAH!
THE SKY IS SO BRIGHT AND STILL AND BEAUTIFUL.
FOR A MOMENT, I ALMOST FORGET WHY I'M HERE. BUT THEN IT COMES--
--A RUMBLE THROUGH THE AIR.
RIP
KROOOM

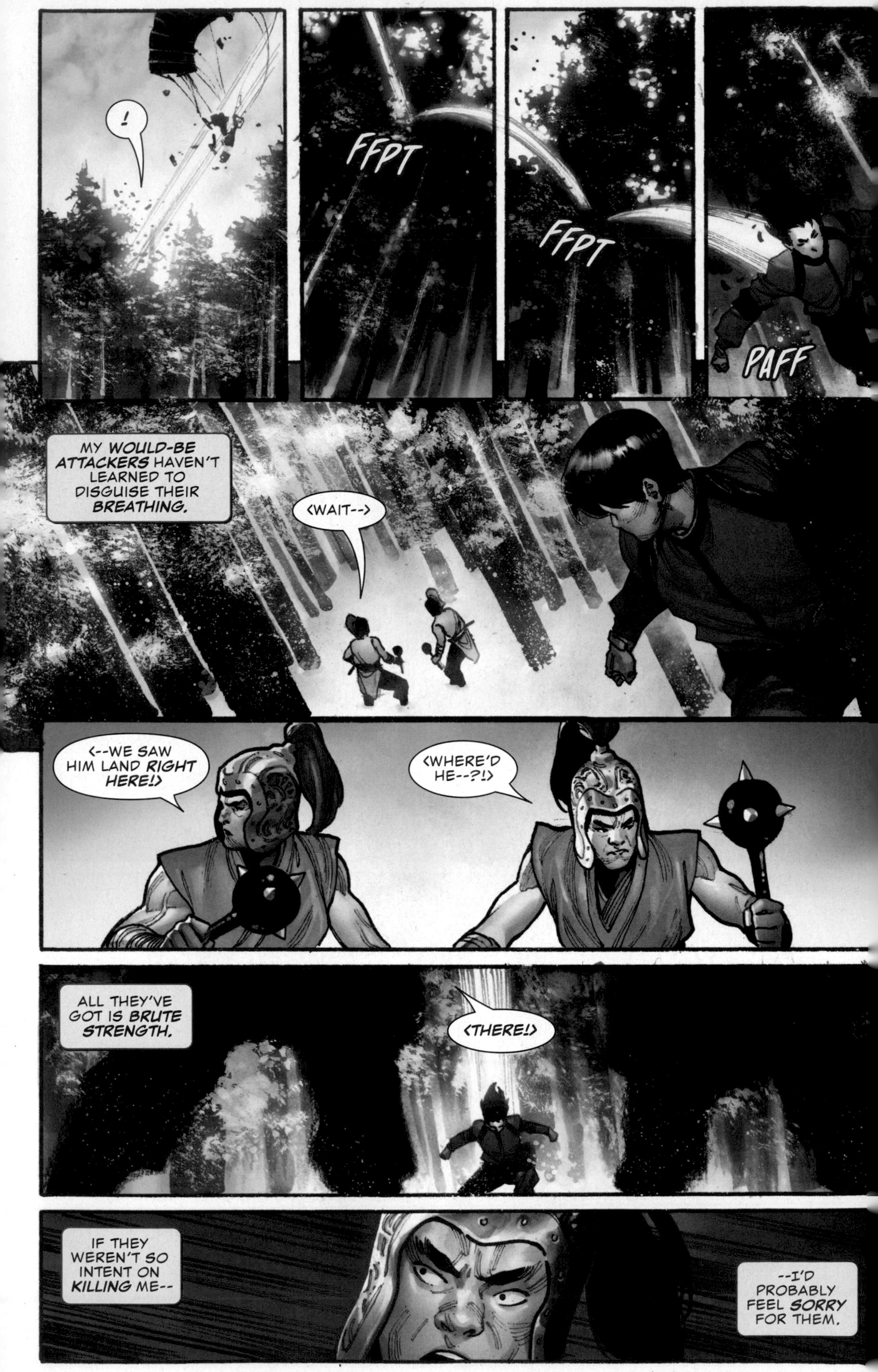
!
FFPT
FFPT
PAFF
MY WOULD-BE ATTACKERS HAVEN'T LEARNED TO DISGUISE THEIR BREATHING.
‹WAIT--›
‹--WE SAW HIM LAND RIGHT HERE!›
‹WHERE'D HE--?!›
ALL THEY'VE GOT IS BRUTE STRENGTH.
‹THERE!›
IF THEY WEREN'T SO INTENT ON KILLING ME--
--I'D PROBABLY FEEL SORRY FOR THEM.

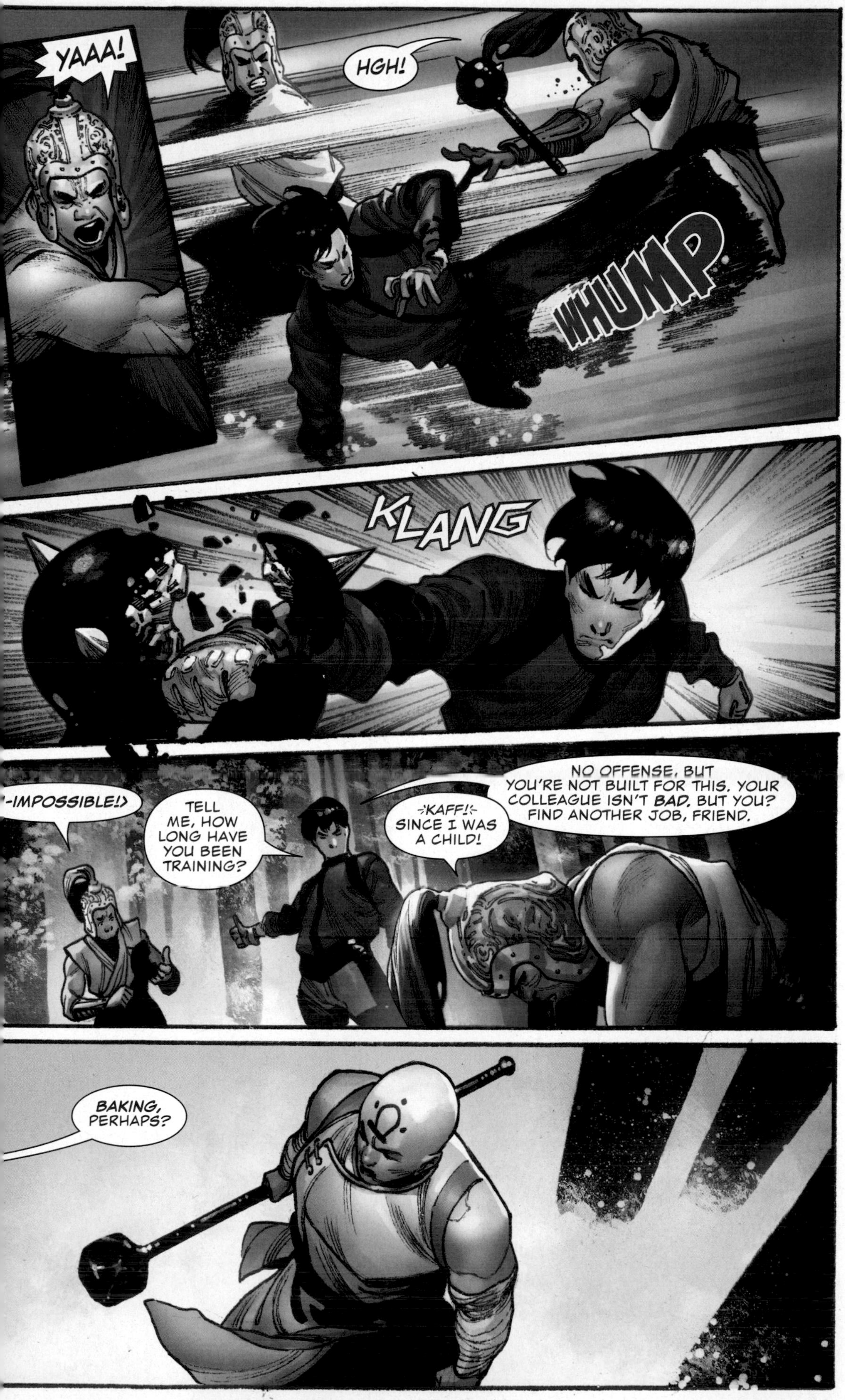
YAAA!
HGH!
WHUMP
KLANG
-IMPOSSIBLE!>
TELL ME, HOW LONG HAVE YOU BEEN TRAINING?
-KAFF!- SINCE I WAS A CHILD!
NO OFFENSE, BUT YOU'RE NOT BUILT FOR THIS. YOUR COLLEAGUE ISN'T BAD, BUT YOU? FIND ANOTHER JOB, FRIEND.
BAKING, PERHAPS?

TAKE IT FROM ME, IT'S NOT A BAD LIFE.

His face... ...he's the same as I remember.

Shang-Chi.

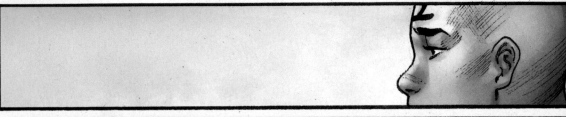

Big brother.

Little sister.

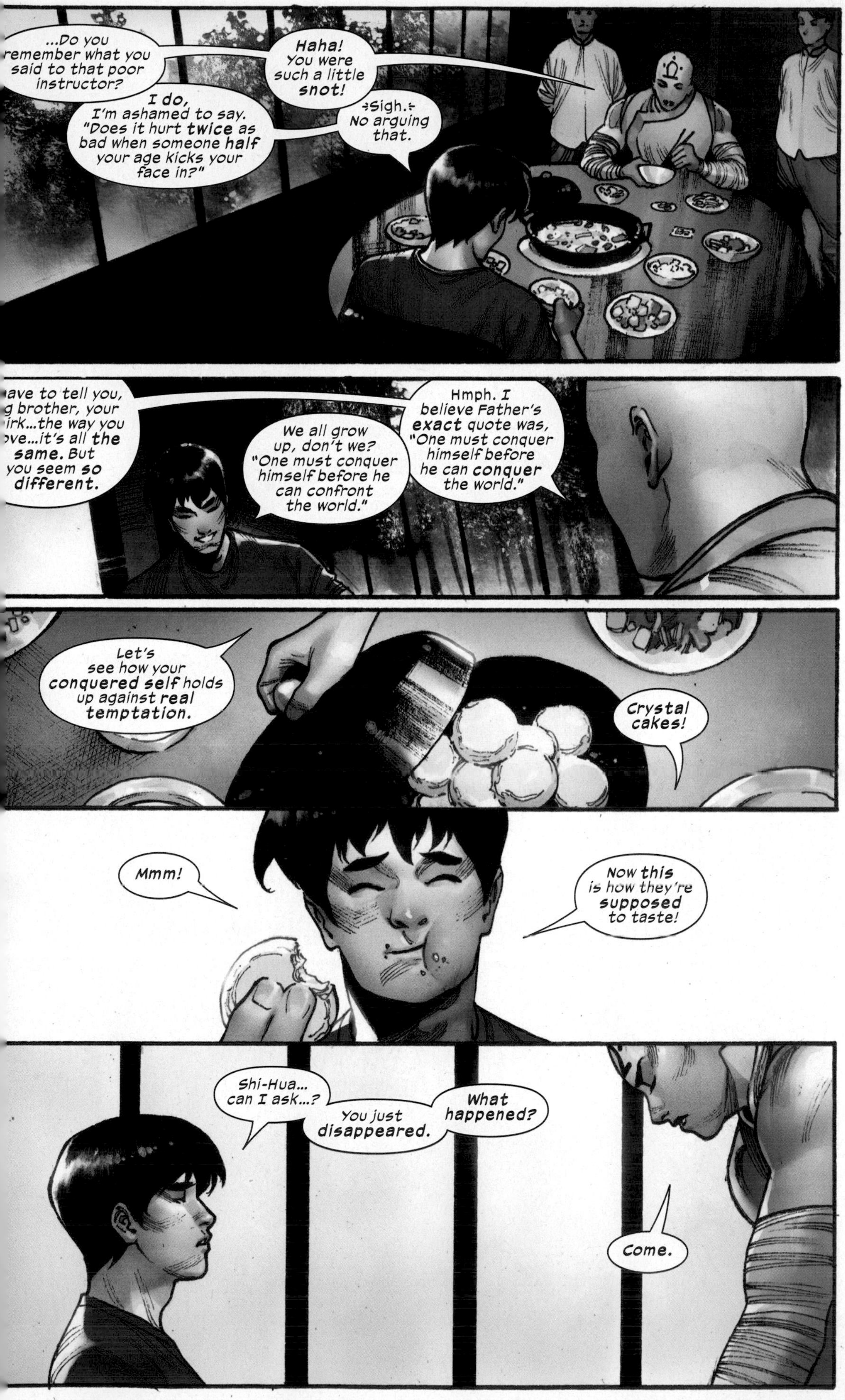
...Do you remember what you said to that poor instructor?
Haha! You were such a little snot!
I do, I'm ashamed to say. "Does it hurt twice as bad when someone half your age kicks your face in?"
⊰Sigh.⊱ No arguing that.
ave to tell you, g brother, your irk...the way you ove...it's all the same. But you seem so different.
We all grow up, don't we? "One must conquer himself before he can confront the world."
Hmph. I believe Father's exact quote was, "One must conquer himself before he can conquer the world."
Let's see how your conquered self holds up against real temptation.
Crystal cakes!
Mmm!
Now this is how they're supposed to taste!
Shi-Hua... can I ask...?
You just disappeared.
What happened?
Come.

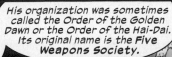

Our father Zheng Zu went by many names. So did everything that was associated with him.

His organization was sometimes called the Order of the Golden Dawn or the Order of the Hai-Dai. Its original name is the *Five Weapons Society*.

Our childhood home, the Hunan Retreat, is also known as the *House of the Deadly Hand*. It's one of the Society's *five* houses, as is the house we're in now.

After that night... the last time we were together...I was sent to the *House of the Deadly Hammer* in Russia.

Russia...!

There, I spent years training to become Champion!

The same way I became Champion of the Hunan Retreat-- of the *House of the Deadly Hand*.

Exactly.

Shi-Hua, all this talk about *Champions* and *Houses*...it's all part of a *make-believe world* created by our *psychopath* of a father!

But there is an actual *real world* out there! And it's better than we ever could have *imagined* when we were kids!

That's why I came *back*, Shi-Hua. To help you *escape*.

Take a look at our Father's shrine. Do you see the flame? It's lit over the symbol of the Deadly Hand.

Not Hammer.

Hand.

I don't understand what that has to do with anything.

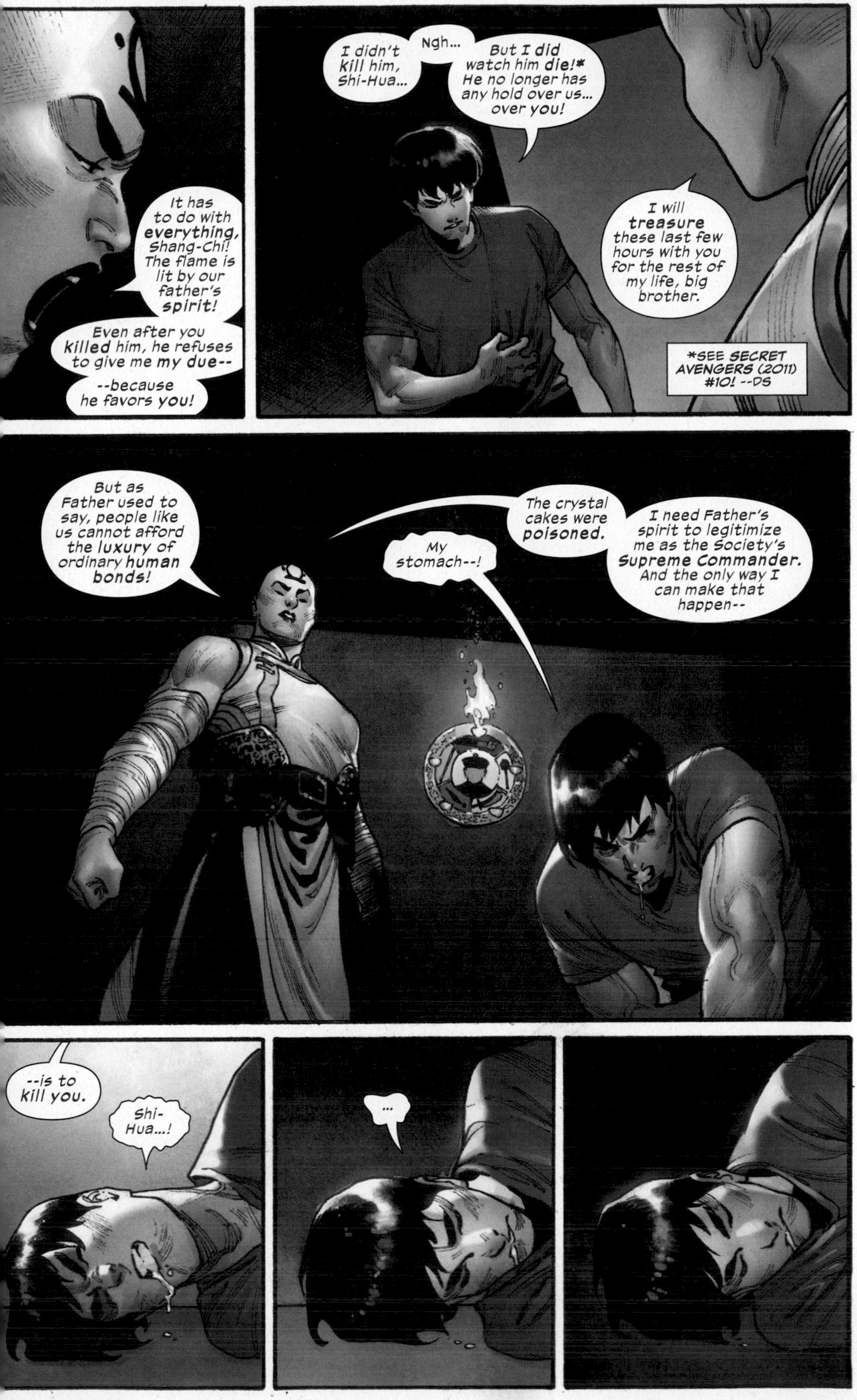
It has to do with everything, Shang-Chi! The flame is lit by our father's spirit!
Even after you killed him, he refuses to give me my due--
--because he favors you!
I didn't kill him, Shi-Hua...
Ngh...
But I did watch him die!* He no longer has any hold over us... over you!
I will treasure these last few hours with you for the rest of my life, big brother.
*SEE SECRET AVENGERS (2011) #10! --DS
But as Father used to say, people like us cannot afford the luxury of ordinary human bonds!
My stomach--!
The crystal cakes were poisoned.
I need Father's spirit to legitimize me as the Society's Supreme Commander. And the only way I can make that happen--
--is to kill you.
Shi-Hua...!
...

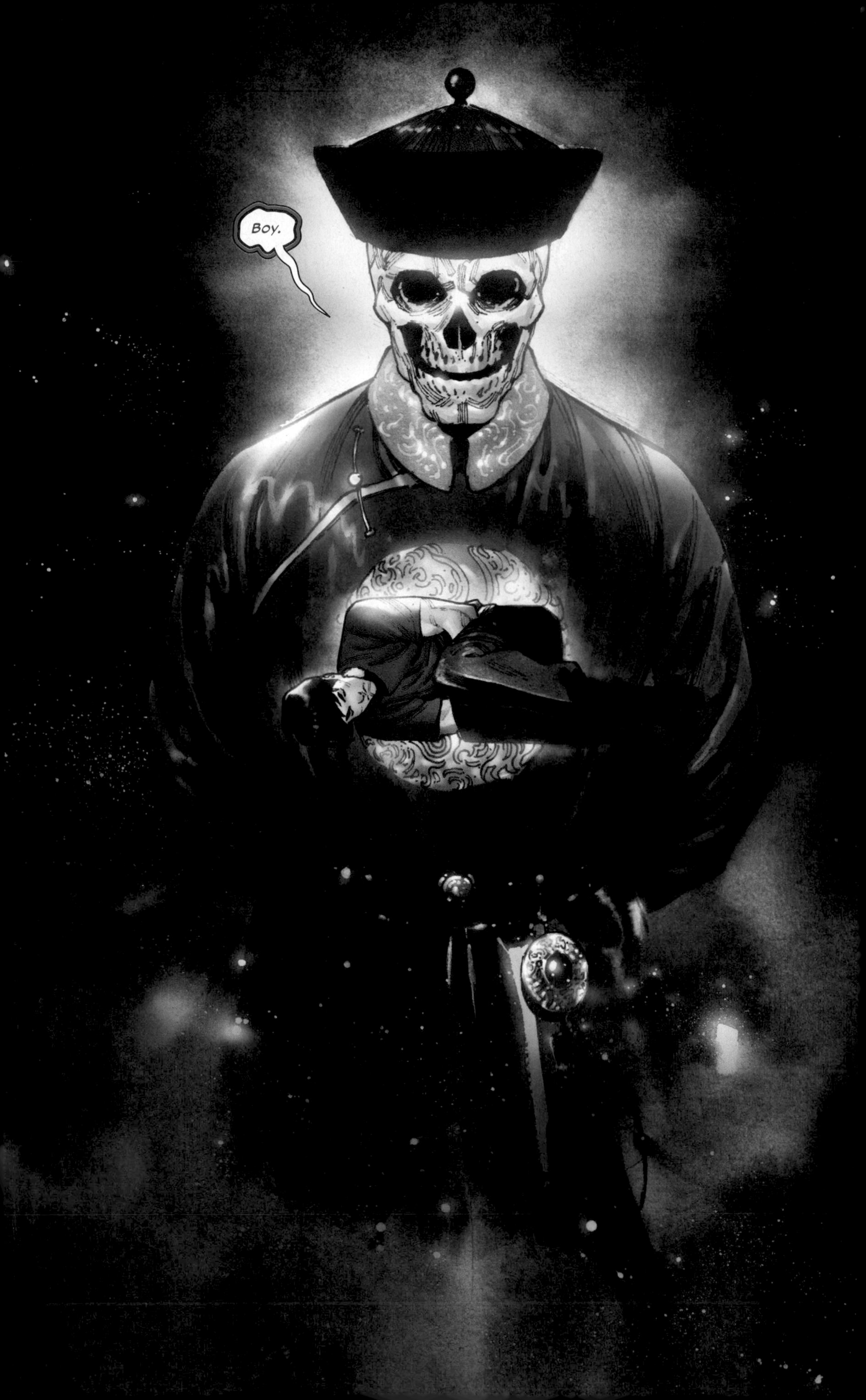
Boy.

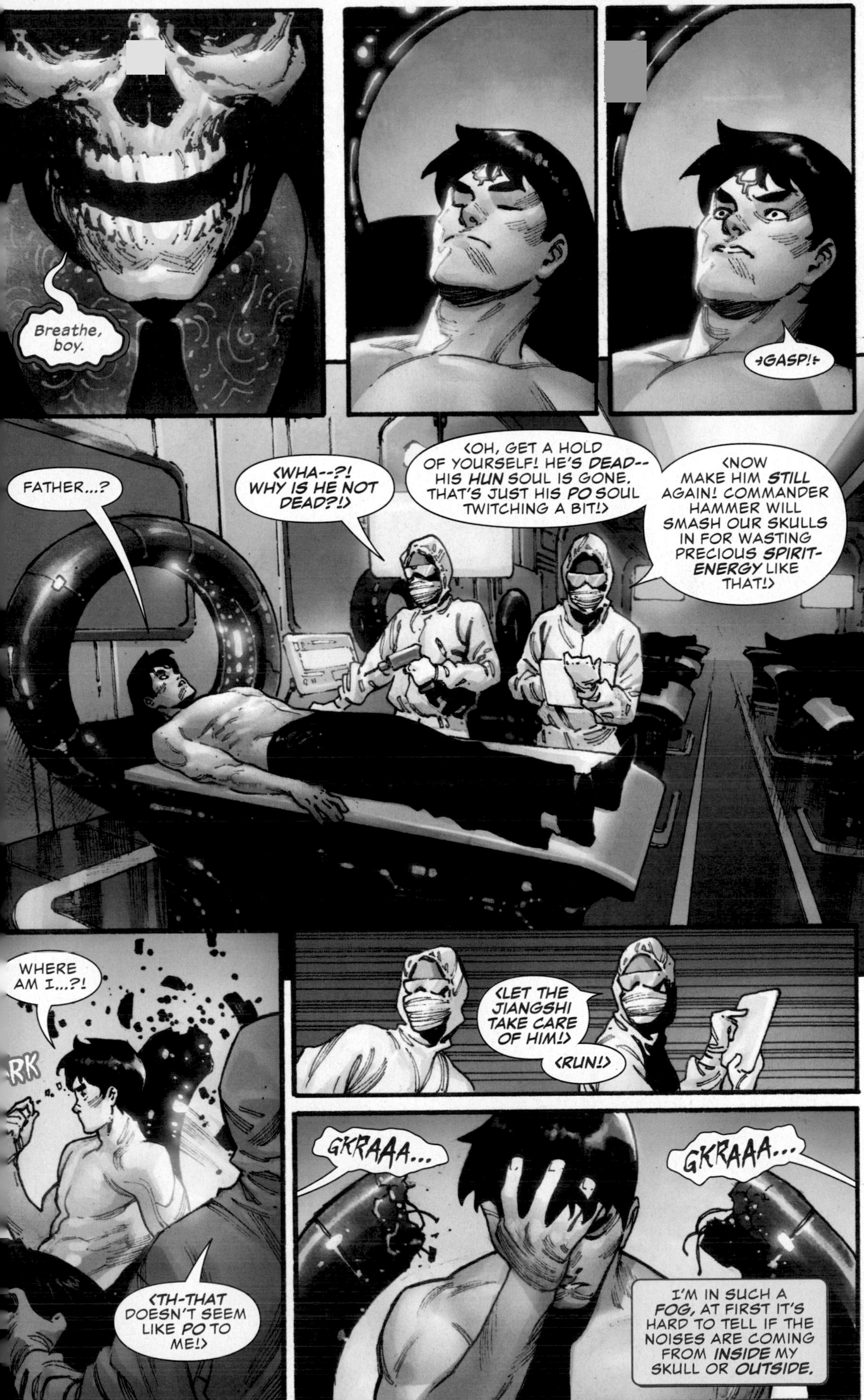
Breathe, boy.
-GASP!-
FATHER...?
<WHA--?! WHY IS HE NOT DEAD?!>
<OH, GET A HOLD OF YOURSELF! HE'S DEAD-- HIS HUN SOUL IS GONE. THAT'S JUST HIS PO SOUL TWITCHING A BIT!>
<NOW MAKE HIM STILL AGAIN! COMMANDER HAMMER WILL SMASH OUR SKULLS IN FOR WASTING PRECIOUS SPIRIT-ENERGY LIKE THAT!>
WHERE AM I...?!
RK
<TH-THAT DOESN'T SEEM LIKE PO TO ME!>
<LET THE JIANGSHI TAKE CARE OF HIM!>
<RUN!>
GKRAAA...
GKRAAA...
I'M IN SUCH A FOG, AT FIRST IT'S HARD TO TELL IF THE NOISES ARE COMING FROM INSIDE MY SKULL OR OUTSIDE.

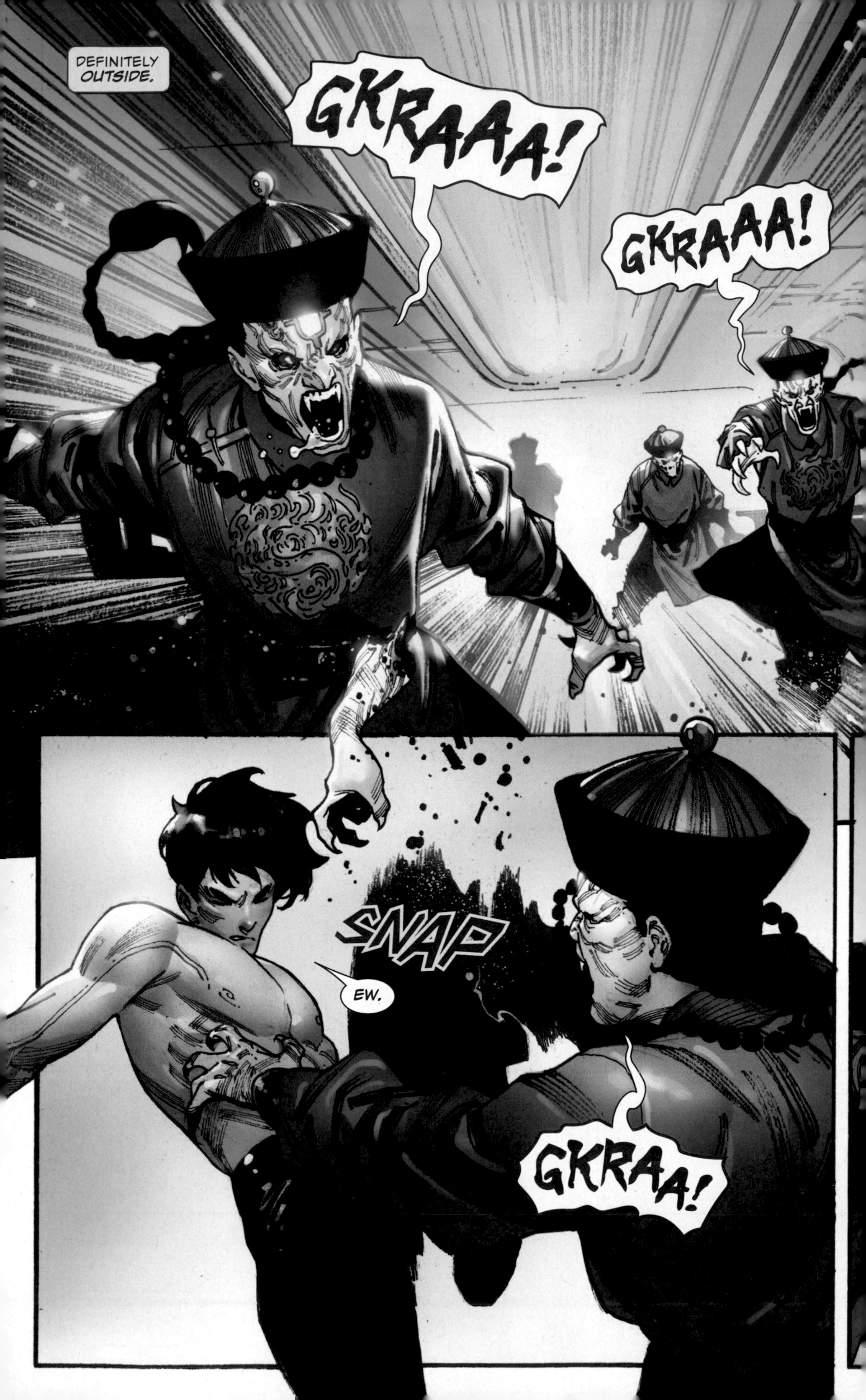
DEFINITELY OUTSIDE.
GKRAAA!
GKRAAA!
SNAP
EW.
GKRAA!

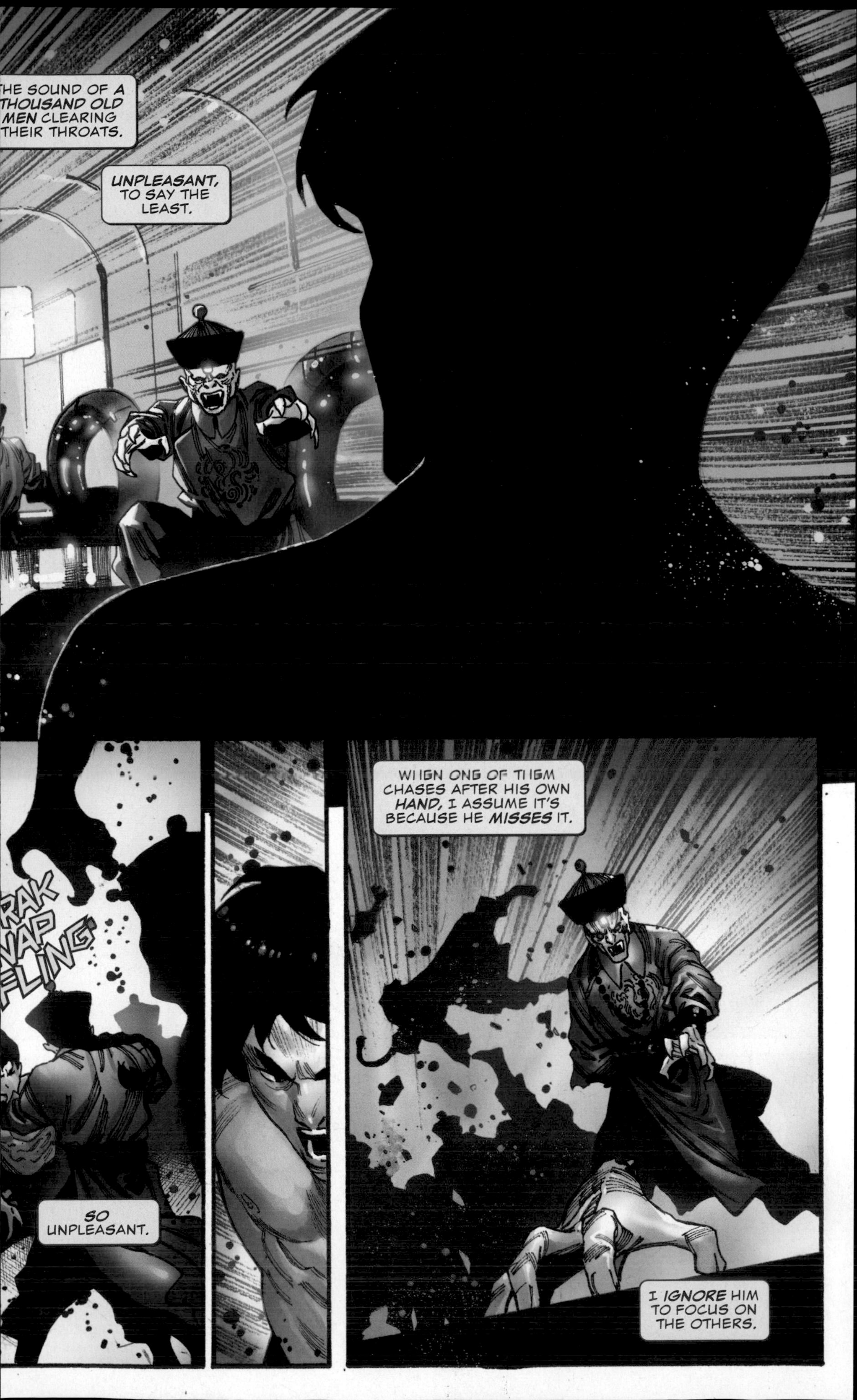
THE SOUND OF A *THOUSAND OLD MEN* CLEARING THEIR THROATS.
UNPLEASANT, TO SAY THE LEAST.
RAK
NAP
FLING
SO UNPLEASANT.
WHEN ONE OF THEM CHASES AFTER HIS OWN *HAND,* I ASSUME IT'S BECAUSE HE *MISSES* IT.
I *IGNORE* HIM TO FOCUS ON THE OTHERS.

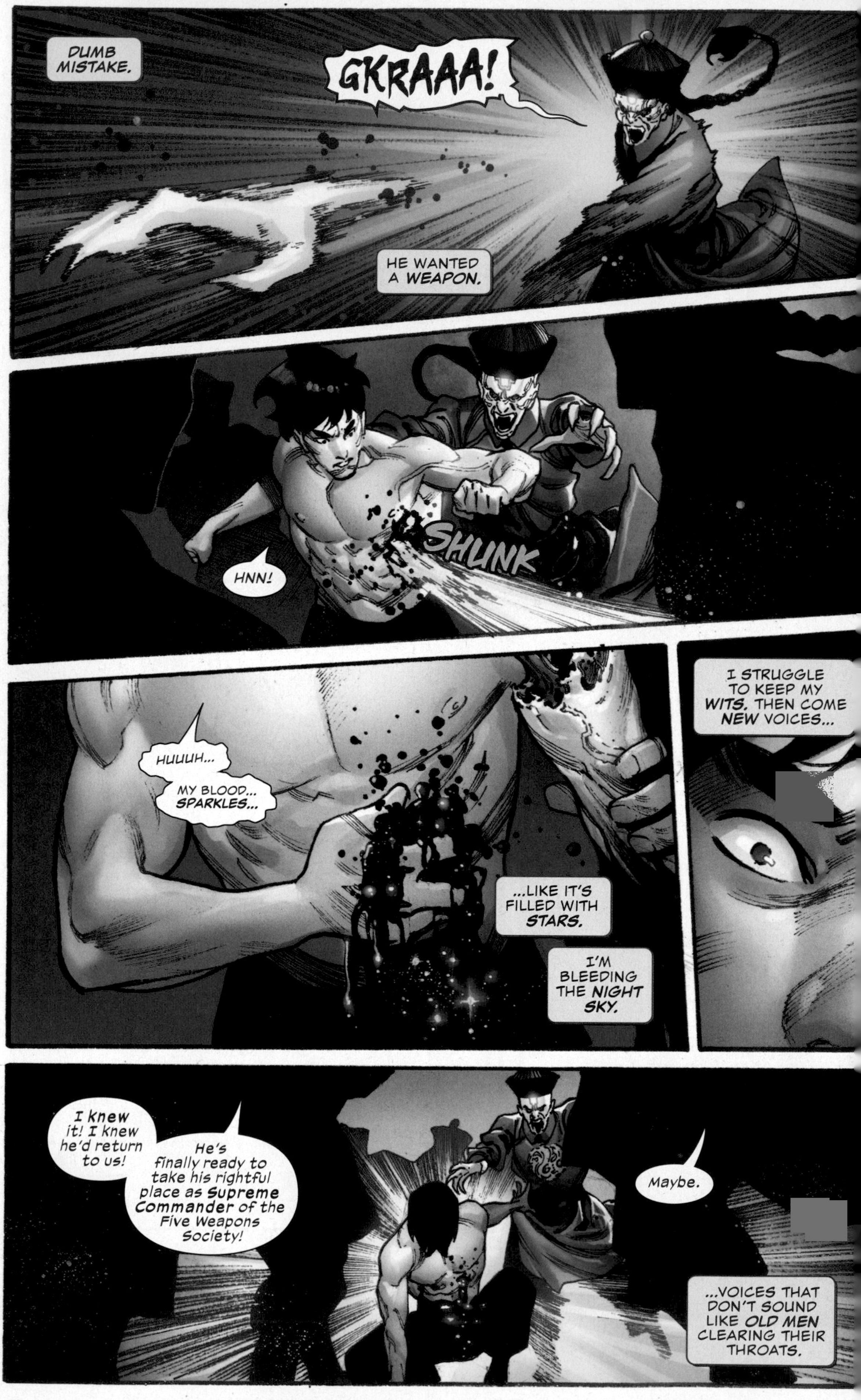
DUMB MISTAKE.
GKRAAA!
HE WANTED A WEAPON.
SHUNK
HNN!
HUUUH...
MY BLOOD... SPARKLES...
...LIKE IT'S FILLED WITH STARS.
I'M BLEEDING THE NIGHT SKY.
I STRUGGLE TO KEEP MY WITS. THEN COME NEW VOICES...
I knew it! I knew he'd return to us!
He's finally ready to take his rightful place as Supreme Commander of the Five Weapons Society!
Maybe.
...VOICES THAT DON'T SOUND LIKE OLD MEN CLEARING THEIR THROATS.

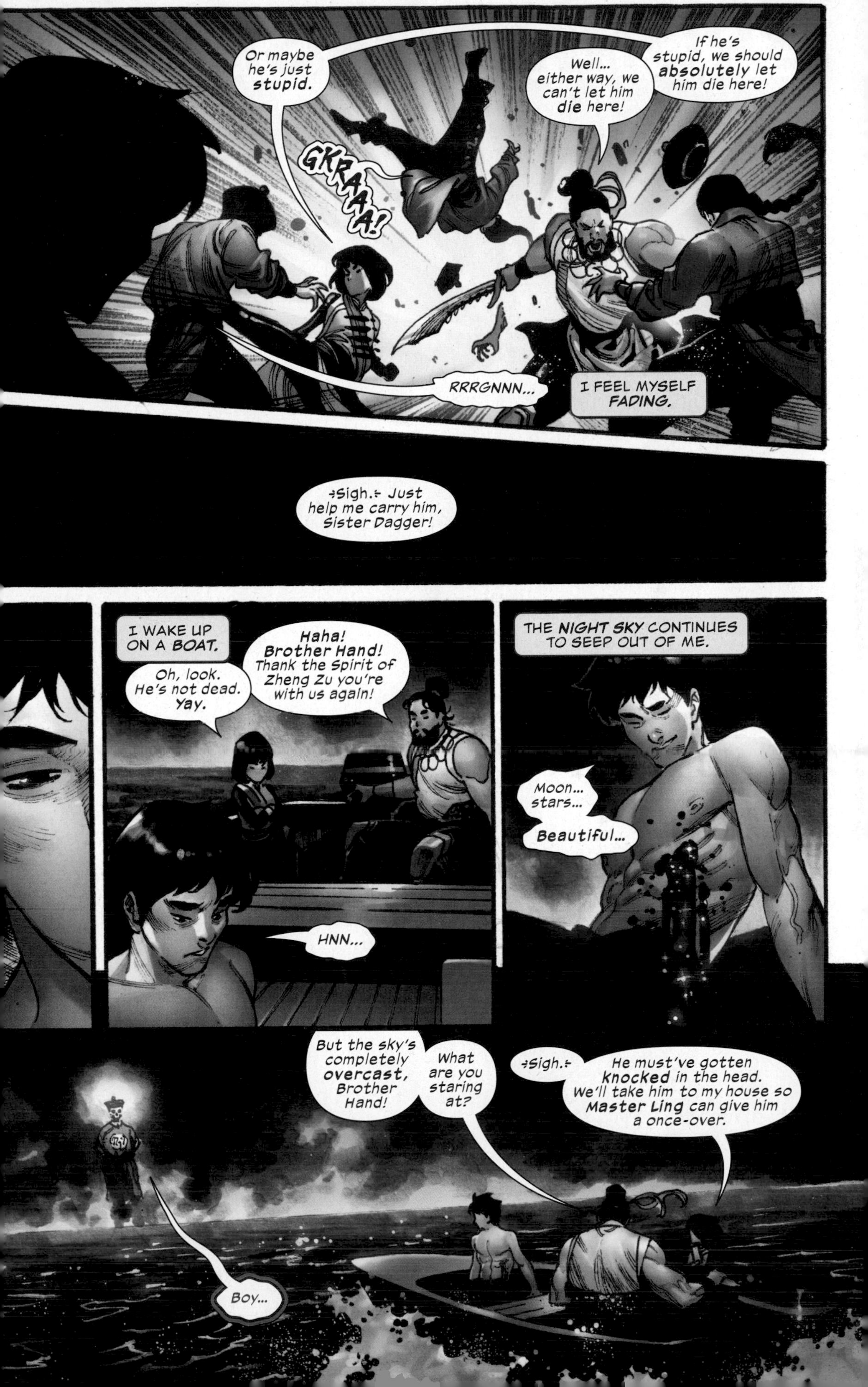
Or maybe he's just stupid.
Well... either way, we can't let him die here!
If he's stupid, we should absolutely let him die here!
GKRAAAA!
RRRGNNN...
I FEEL MYSELF FADING.
Sigh. Just help me carry him, Sister Dagger!
I WAKE UP ON A BOAT.
Oh, look. He's not dead. Yay.
Haha! Brother Hand! Thank the Spirit of Zheng Zu you're with us again!
HNN...
THE NIGHT SKY CONTINUES TO SEEP OUT OF ME.
Moon... stars...
Beautiful...
But the sky's completely overcast, Brother Hand!
What are you staring at?
Sigh. He must've gotten knocked in the head. We'll take him to my house so Master Ling can give him a once-over.
Boy...

BROTHERS & SISTERS
PART TWO

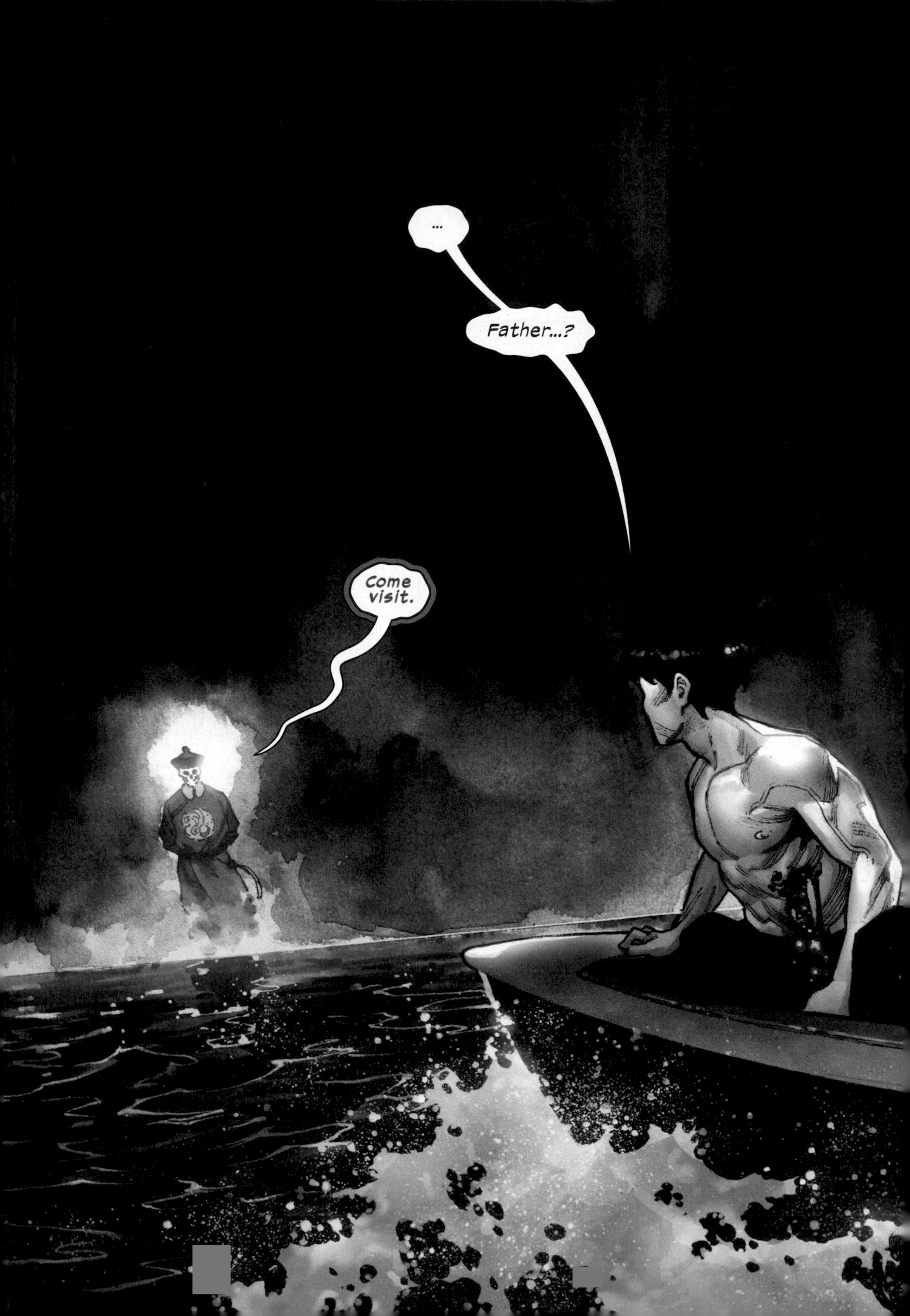
...
Father...?
Come visit.

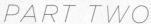

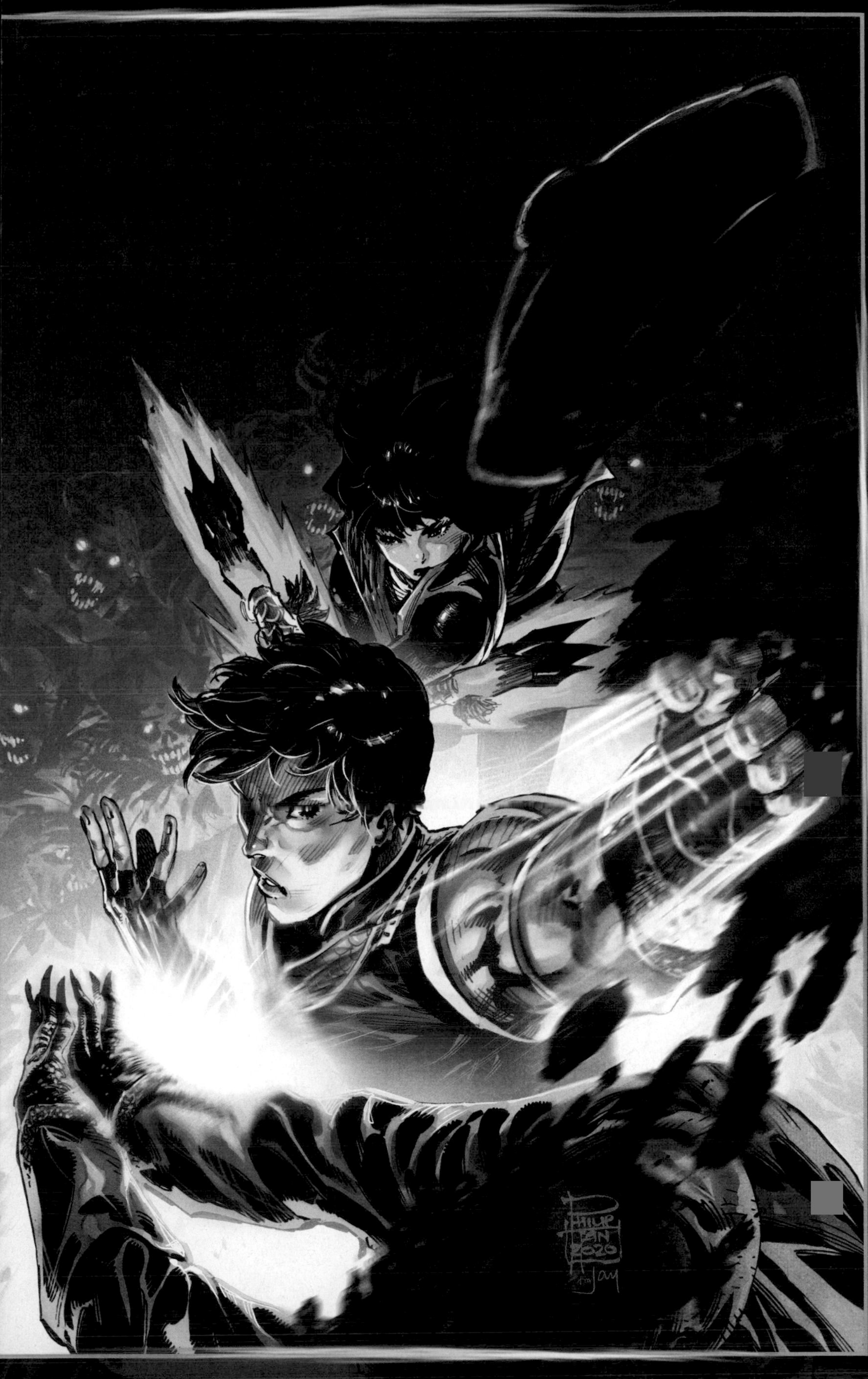

THREE

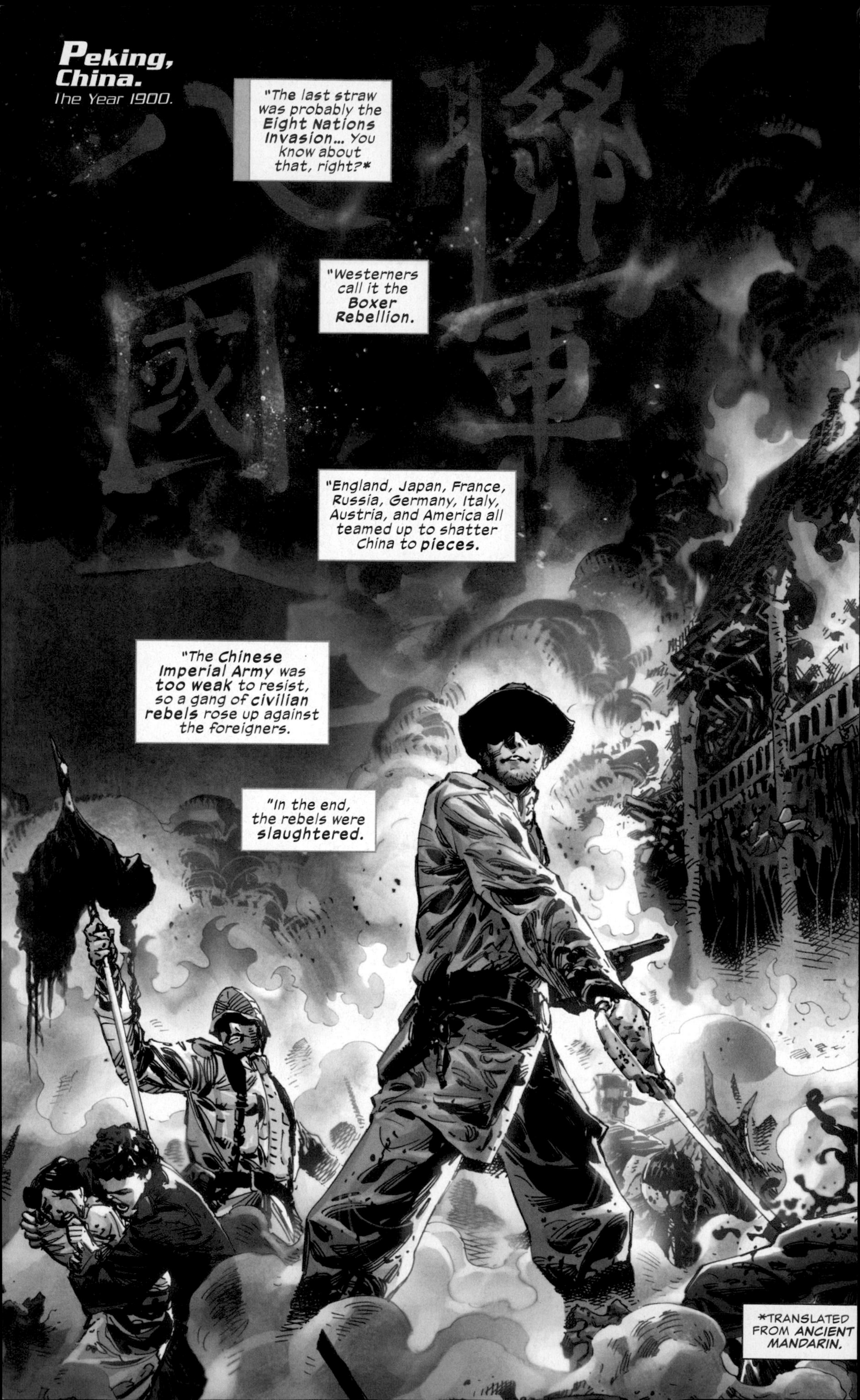
Peking, China.
The Year 1900.
八國聯軍
"The last straw was probably the Eight Nations Invasion... You know about that, right?*
"Westerners call it the Boxer Rebellion.
"England, Japan, France, Russia, Germany, Italy, Austria, and America all teamed up to shatter China to pieces.
"The Chinese Imperial Army was too weak to resist, so a gang of civilian rebels rose up against the foreigners.
"In the end, the rebels were slaughtered.
*TRANSLATED FROM ANCIENT MANDARIN.

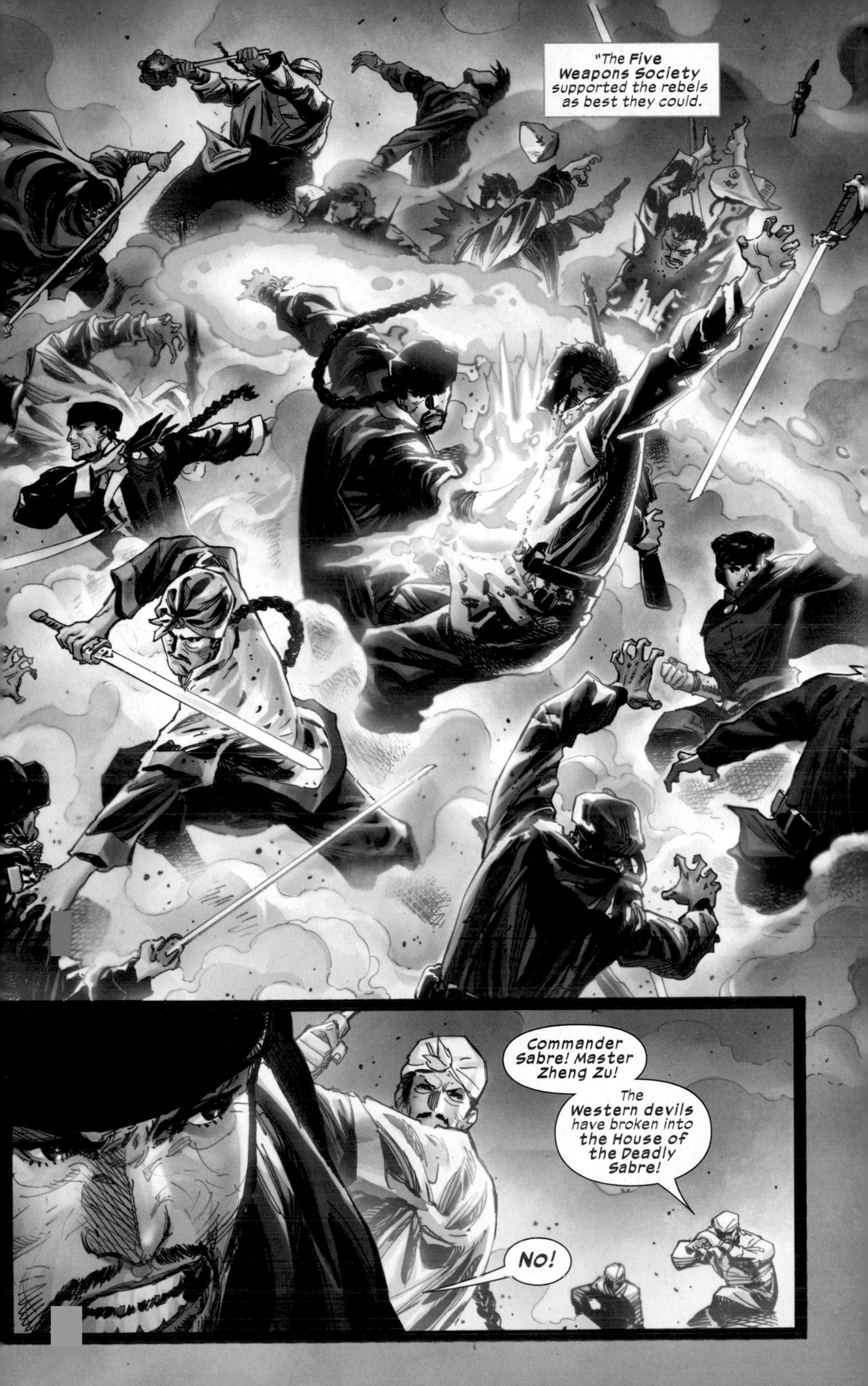
"The Five Weapons Society supported the rebels as best they could.
Commander Sabre! Master Zheng Zu!
The Western devils have broken into the House of the Deadly Sabre!
No!

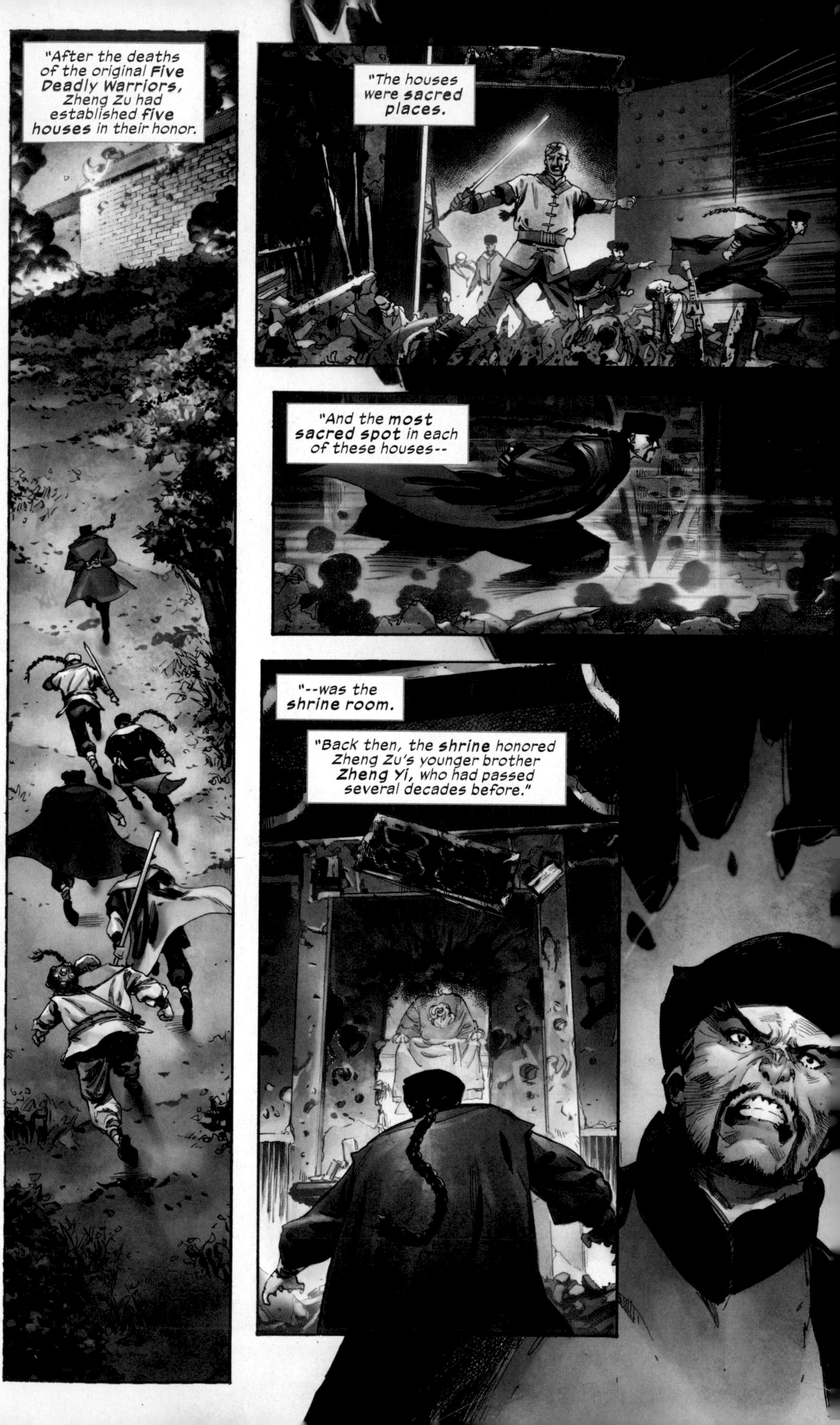
"After the deaths of the original Five Deadly Warriors, Zheng Zu had established five houses in their honor.
"The houses were sacred places.
"And the most sacred spot in each of these houses--
"--was the shrine room.
"Back then, the shrine honored Zheng Zu's younger brother Zheng Yi, who had passed several decades before."

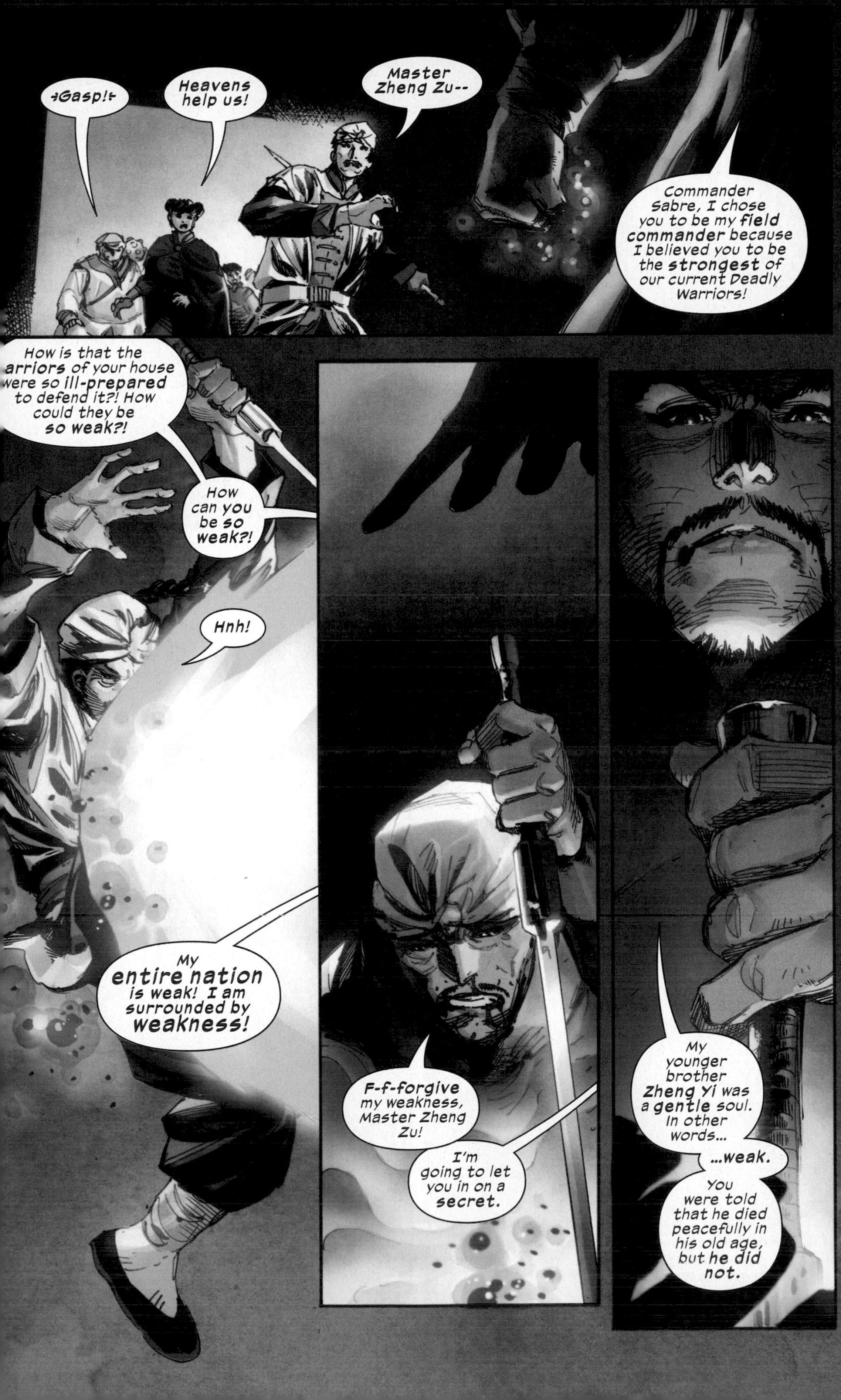

⊰Gasp!⊱
Heavens help us!
Master Zheng Zu--
Commander Sabre, I chose you to be my field commander because I believed you to be the strongest of our current Deadly Warriors!
How is that the arriors of your house were so ill-prepared to defend it?! How could they be so weak?!
How can you be so weak?!
Hnh!
My entire nation is weak! I am surrounded by weakness!
F-f-forgive my weakness, Master Zheng Zu!
I'm going to let you in on a secret.
My younger brother Zheng Yi was a gentle soul. In other words...
...weak.
You were told that he died peacefully in his old age, but he did not.

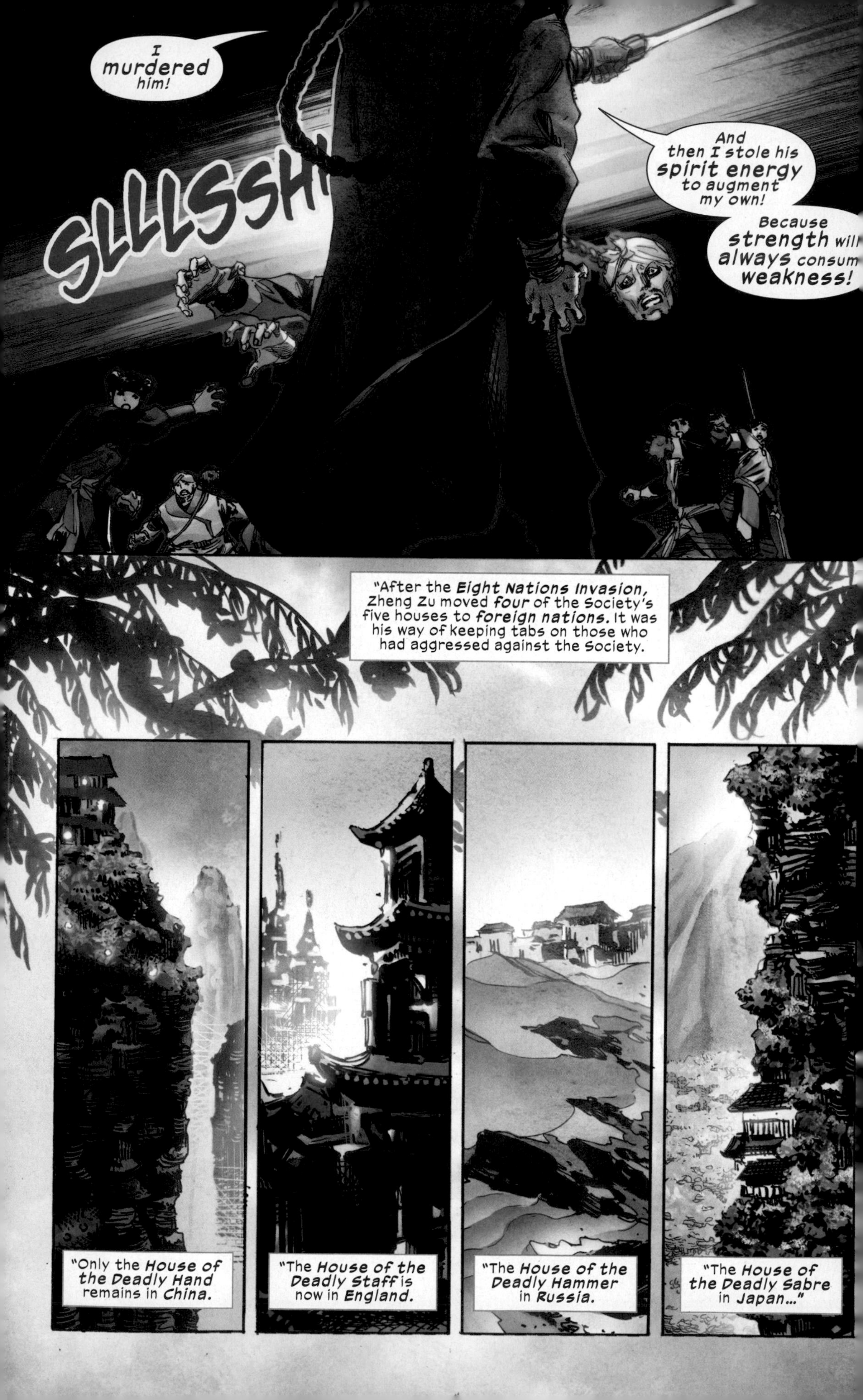
I murdered him!
SLLLSSH
And then I stole his spirit energy to augment my own!
Because strength wil always consum weakness!
"After the Eight Nations Invasion, Zheng Zu moved four of the Society's five houses to foreign nations. It was his way of keeping tabs on those who had aggressed against the Society.
"Only the House of the Deadly Hand remains in China.
"The House of the Deadly Staff is now in England.
"The House of the Deadly Hammer in Russia.
"The House of the Deadly Sabre in Japan..."

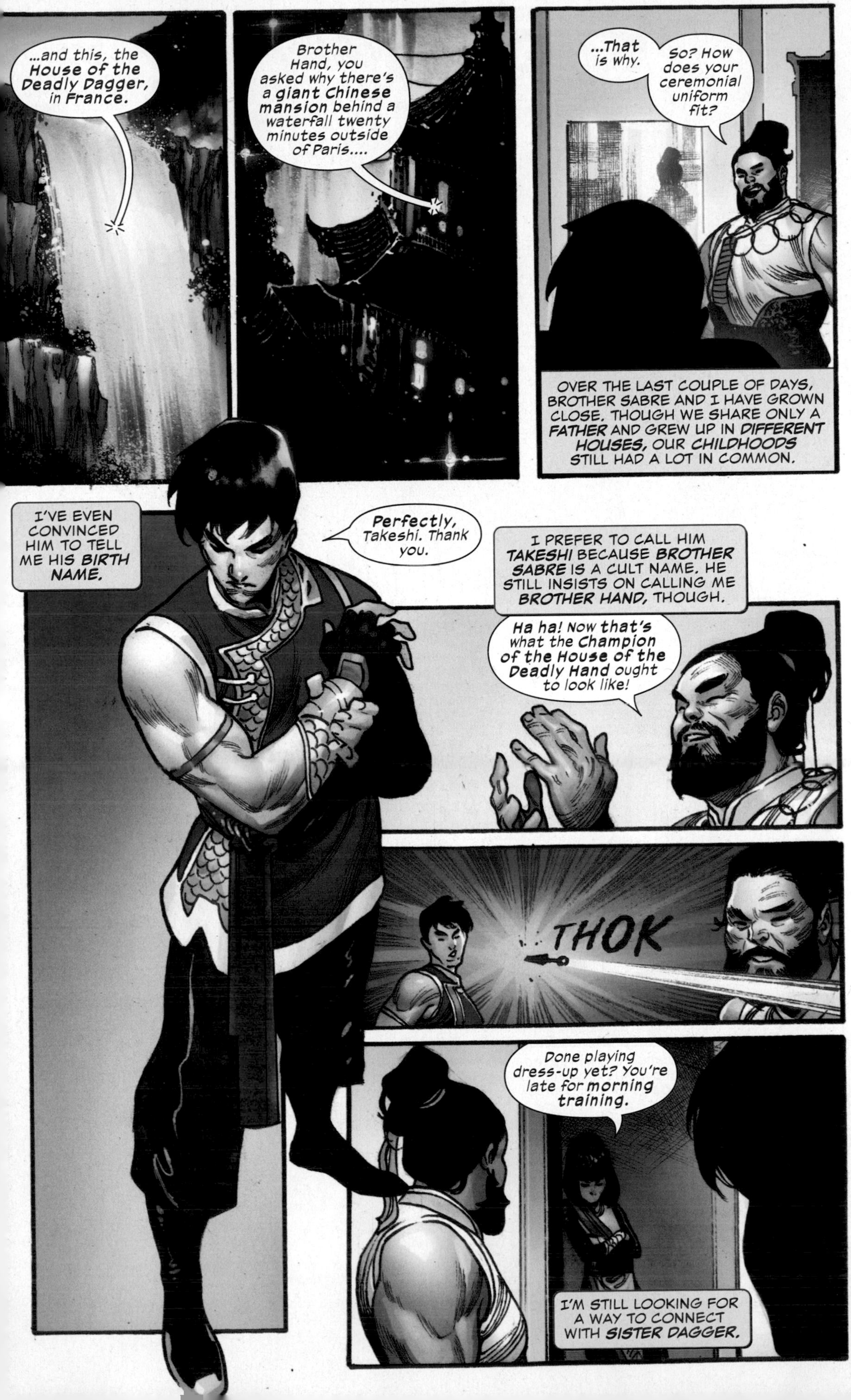

...and this, the House of the Deadly Dagger, in France.
Brother Hand, you asked why there's a giant Chinese mansion behind a waterfall twenty minutes outside of Paris....
...That is why.
So? How does your ceremonial uniform fit?
OVER THE LAST COUPLE OF DAYS, BROTHER SABRE AND I HAVE GROWN CLOSE. THOUGH WE SHARE ONLY A FATHER AND GREW UP IN DIFFERENT HOUSES, OUR CHILDHOODS STILL HAD A LOT IN COMMON.
I'VE EVEN CONVINCED HIM TO TELL ME HIS BIRTH NAME.
Perfectly, Takeshi. Thank you.
I PREFER TO CALL HIM TAKESHI BECAUSE BROTHER SABRE IS A CULT NAME. HE STILL INSISTS ON CALLING ME BROTHER HAND, THOUGH.
Ha ha! Now that's what the Champion of the House of the Deadly Hand ought to look like!
THOK
Done playing dress-up yet? You're late for morning training.
I'M STILL LOOKING FOR A WAY TO CONNECT WITH SISTER DAGGER.

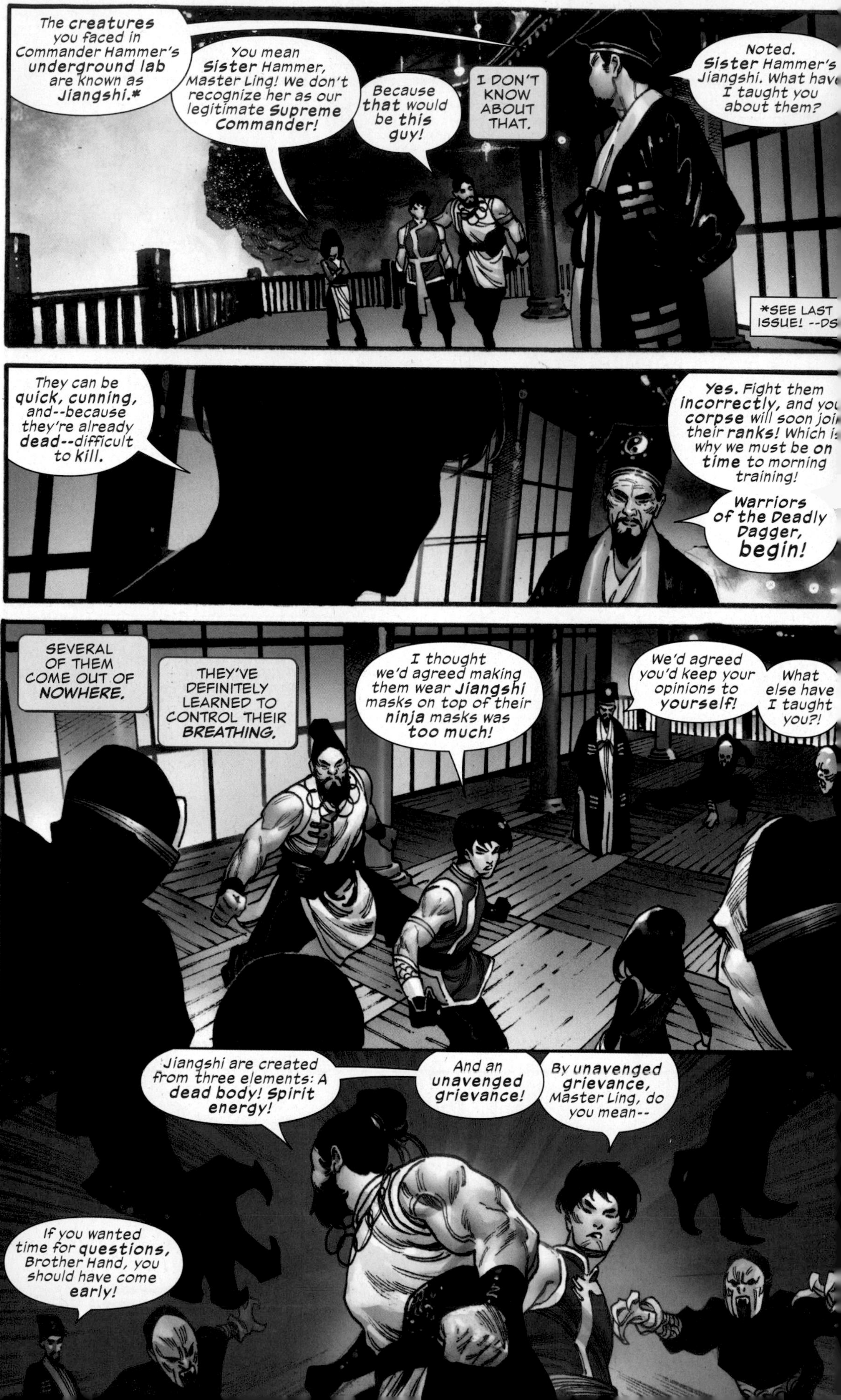

The creatures you faced in Commander Hammer's underground lab are known as Jiangshi.*
You mean Sister Hammer, Master Ling! We don't recognize her as our legitimate Supreme Commander!
Because that would be this guy!
I DON'T KNOW ABOUT THAT.
Noted. Sister Hammer's Jiangshi. What have I taught you about them?
*SEE LAST ISSUE! --DS
They can be quick, cunning, and--because they're already dead--difficult to kill.
Yes. Fight them incorrectly, and your corpse will soon join their ranks! Which is why we must be on time to morning training!
Warriors of the Deadly Dagger, begin!
SEVERAL OF THEM COME OUT OF NOWHERE.
THEY'VE DEFINITELY LEARNED TO CONTROL THEIR BREATHING.
I thought we'd agreed making them wear Jiangshi masks on top of their ninja masks was too much!
We'd agreed you'd keep your opinions to yourself!
What else have I taught you?!
Jiangshi are created from three elements: A dead body! Spirit energy!
And an unavenged grievance!
By unavenged grievance, Master Ling, do you mean--
If you wanted time for questions, Brother Hand, you should have come early!

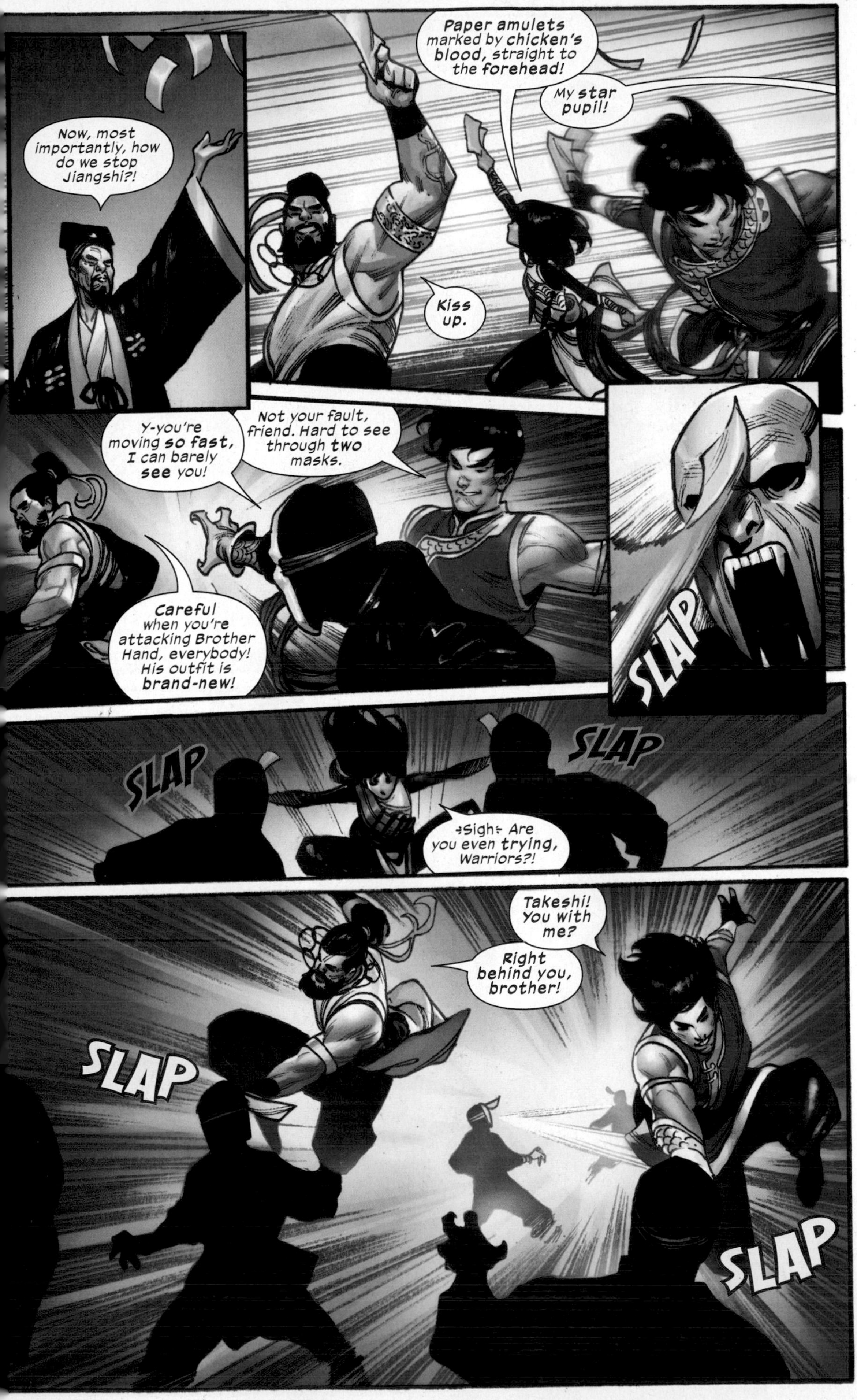
Now, most importantly, how do we stop Jiangshi?!
Paper amulets marked by chicken's blood, straight to the forehead!
My star pupil!
Kiss up.
Y-you're moving so fast, I can barely see you!
Not your fault, friend. Hard to see through two masks.
Careful when you're attacking Brother Hand, everybody! His outfit is brand-new!
SLAP
SLAP
SLAP
-Sigh- Are you even trying, Warriors?!
Takeshi! You with me?
Right behind you, brother!
SLAP
SLAP

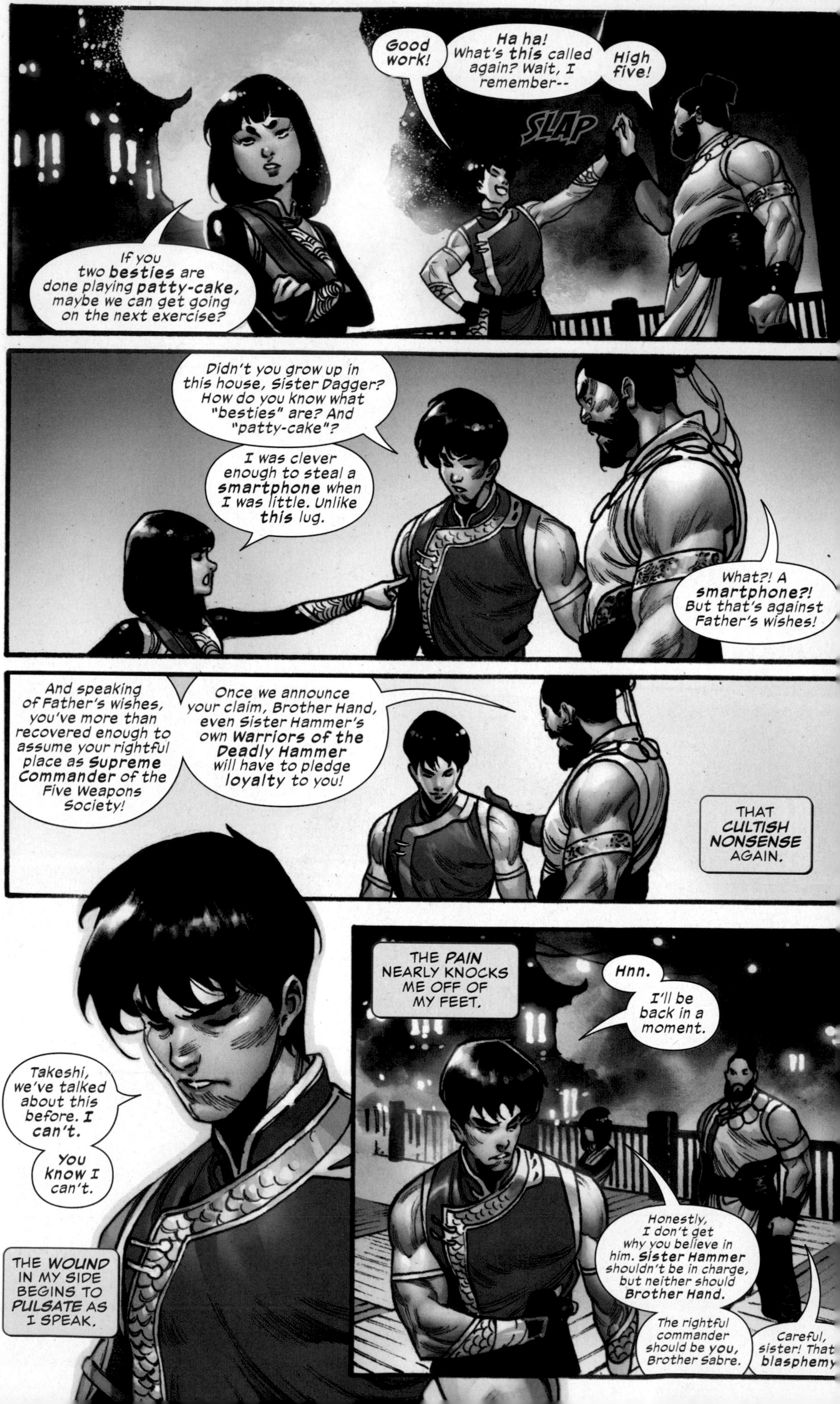

Good work!
Ha ha! What's this called again? Wait, I remember--
High five!
SLAP
If you two besties are done playing patty-cake, maybe we can get going on the next exercise?
Didn't you grow up in this house, Sister Dagger? How do you know what "besties" are? And "patty-cake"?
I was clever enough to steal a smartphone when I was little. Unlike this lug.
What?! A smartphone?! But that's against Father's wishes!
And speaking of Father's wishes, you've more than recovered enough to assume your rightful place as Supreme Commander of the Five Weapons Society!
Once we announce your claim, Brother Hand, even Sister Hammer's own Warriors of the Deadly Hammer will have to pledge loyalty to you!
THAT CULTISH NONSENSE AGAIN.
Takeshi, we've talked about this before. I can't.
You know I can't.
THE WOUND IN MY SIDE BEGINS TO PULSATE AS I SPEAK.
THE PAIN NEARLY KNOCKS ME OFF OF MY FEET.
Hnn.
I'll be back in a moment.
Honestly, I don't get why you believe in him. Sister Hammer shouldn't be in charge, but neither should Brother Hand.
The rightful commander should be you, Brother Sabre.
Careful, sister! That blasphemy

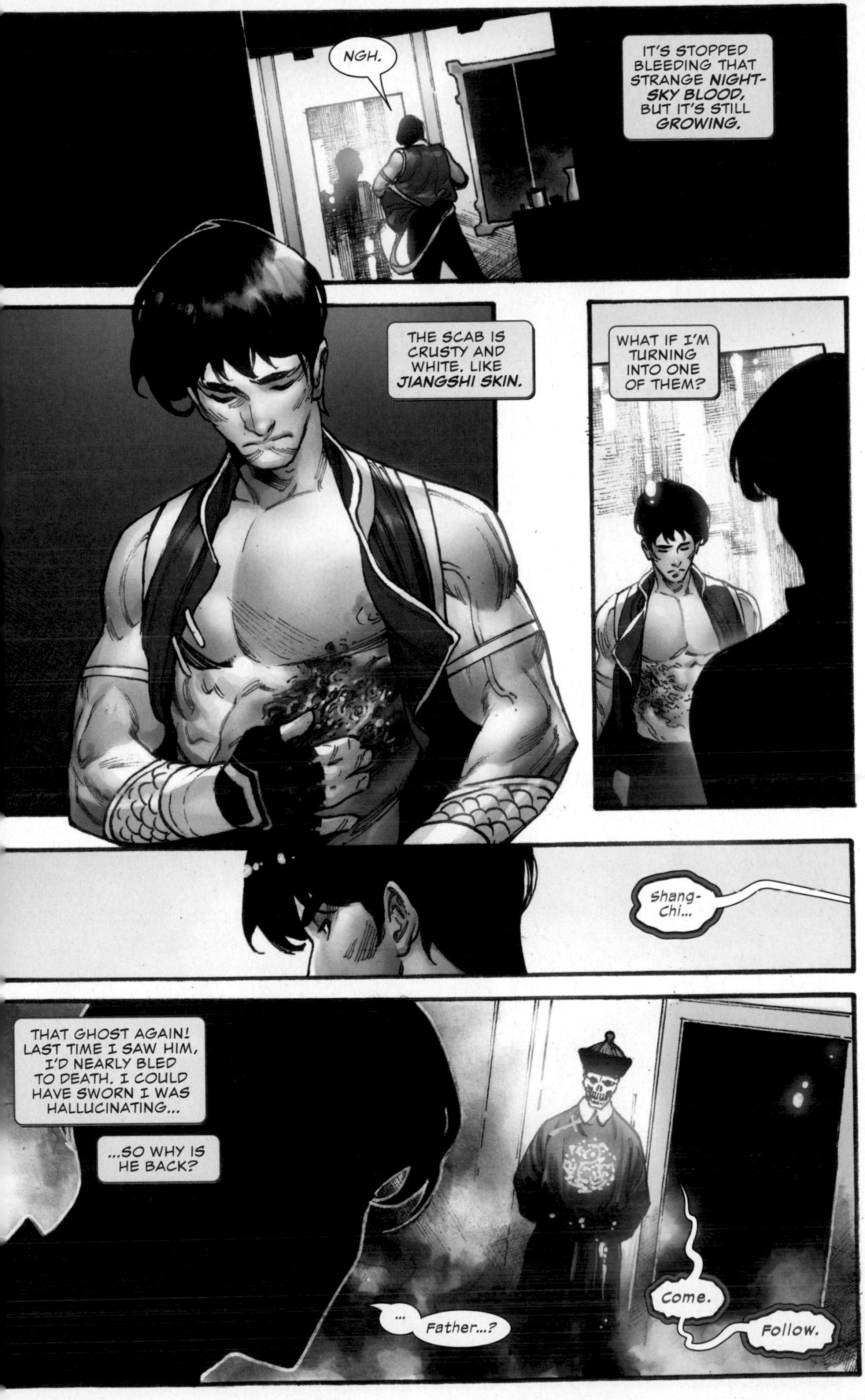
NGH.
IT'S STOPPED BLEEDING THAT STRANGE NIGHT-SKY BLOOD, BUT IT'S STILL GROWING.
THE SCAB IS CRUSTY AND WHITE. LIKE JIANGSHI SKIN.
WHAT IF I'M TURNING INTO ONE OF THEM?
Shang-Chi...
THAT GHOST AGAIN! LAST TIME I SAW HIM, I'D NEARLY BLED TO DEATH. I COULD HAVE SWORN I WAS HALLUCINATING...
...SO WHY IS HE BACK?
... Father...?
Come.
Follow.

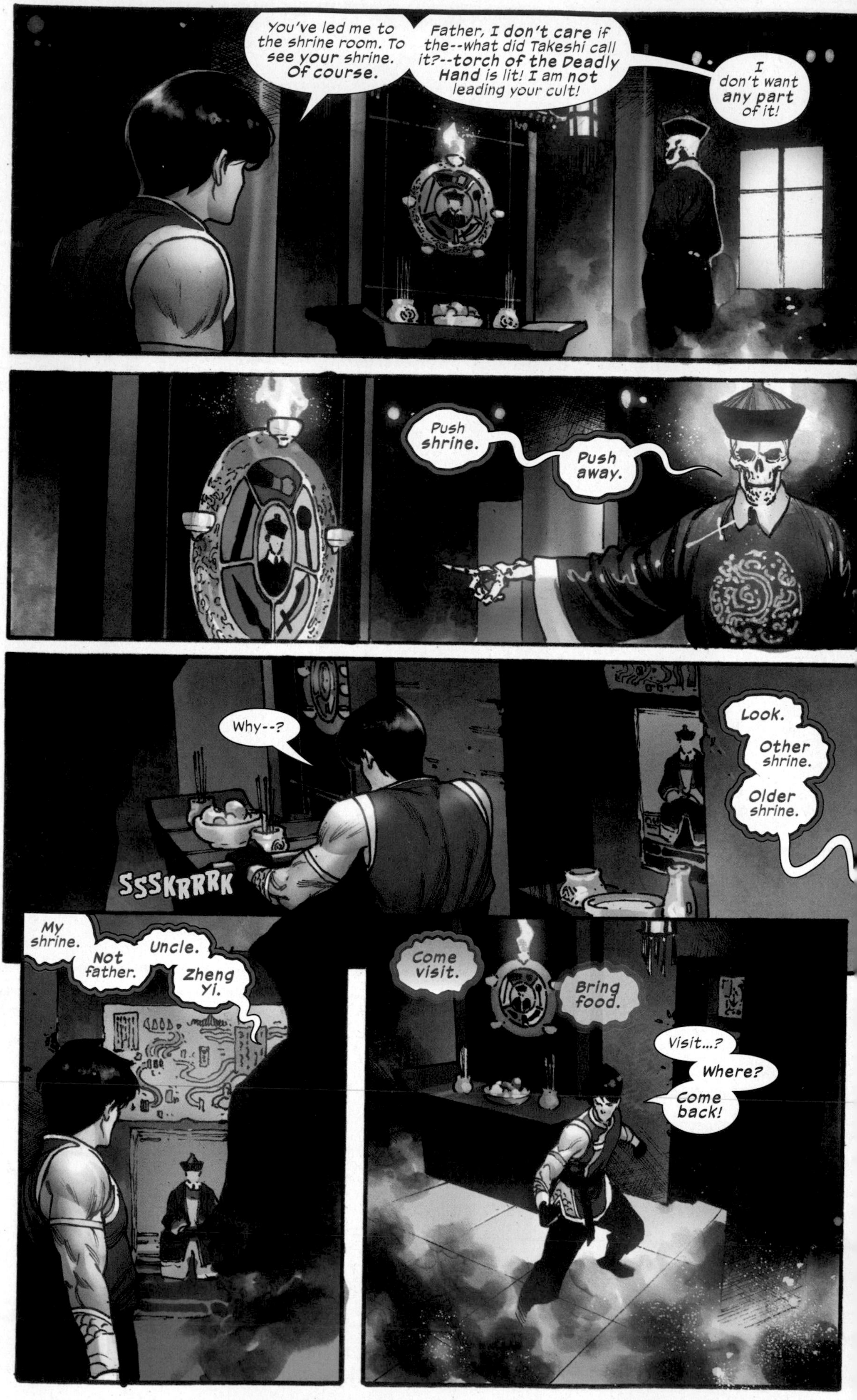
You've led me to the shrine room. To see your shrine. Of course.
Father, I don't care if the--what did Takeshi call it?--torch of the Deadly Hand is lit! I am not leading your cult!
I don't want any part of it!
Push shrine.
Push away.
Why--?
SSSKRRRK
Look.
Other shrine.
Older shrine.
My shrine.
Not father.
Uncle.
Zheng Yi.
Come visit.
Bring food.
Visit...?
Where?
Come back!

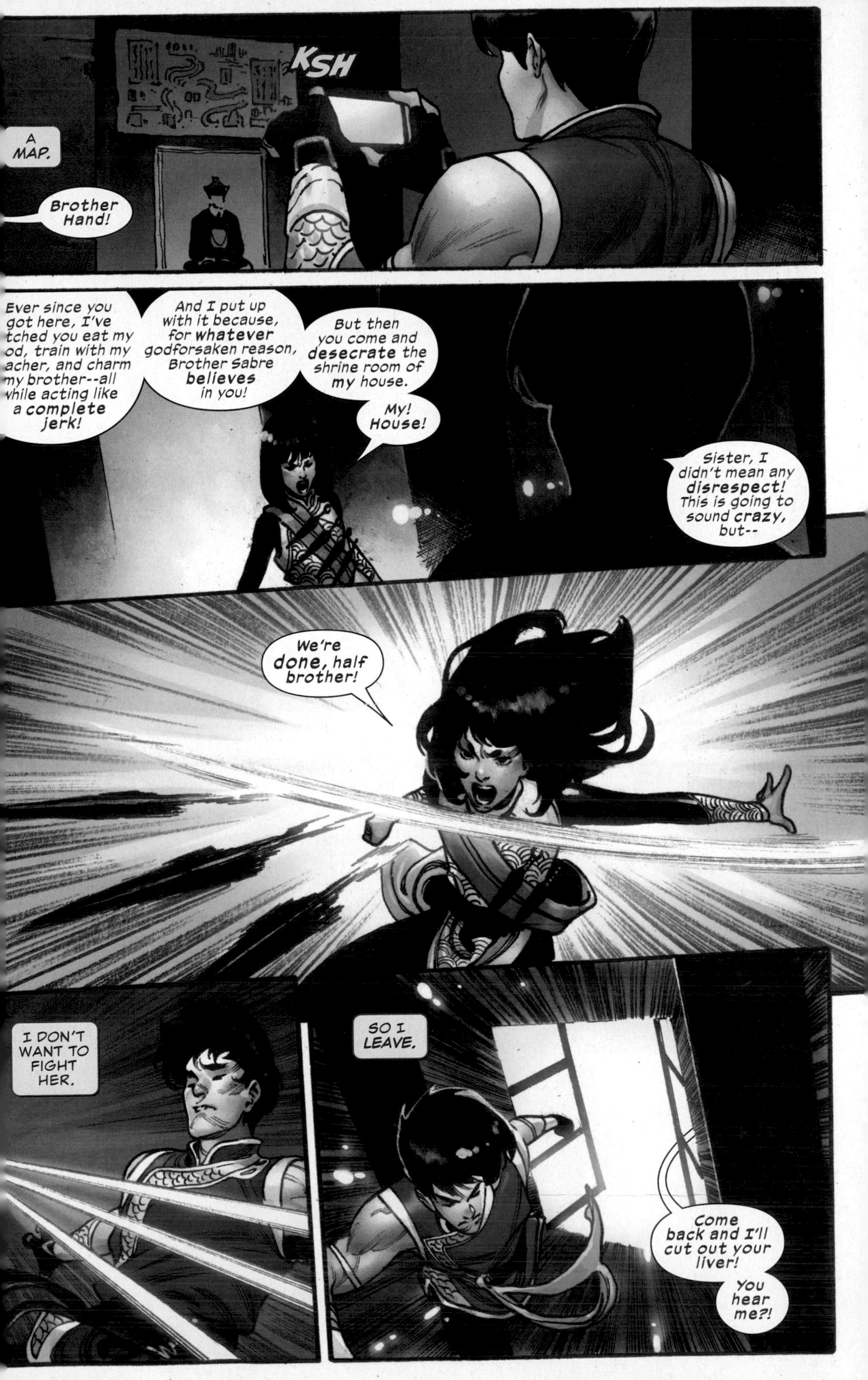

KSH
A MAP.
Brother Hand!
Ever since you got here, I've tched you eat my od, train with my acher, and charm my brother--all while acting like a complete jerk!
And I put up with it because, for whatever godforsaken reason, Brother Sabre believes in you!
But then you come and desecrate the shrine room of my house.
My! House!
Sister, I didn't mean any disrespect! This is going to sound crazy, but--
We're done, half brother!
I DON'T WANT TO FIGHT HER.
SO I LEAVE.
Come back and I'll cut out your liver!
You hear me?!

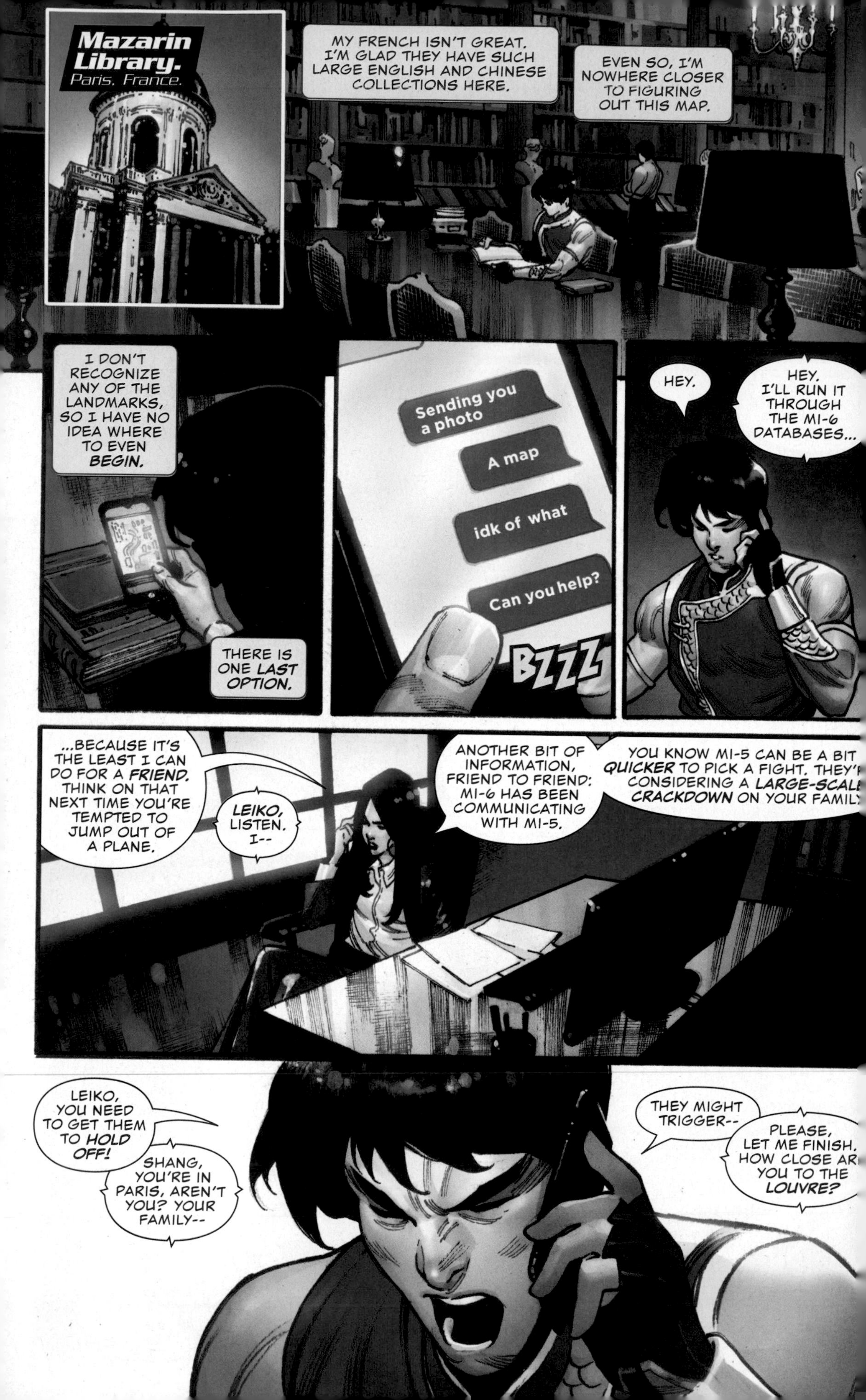

Mazarin Library.
Paris, France.
MY FRENCH ISN'T GREAT. I'M GLAD THEY HAVE SUCH LARGE ENGLISH AND CHINESE COLLECTIONS HERE.
EVEN SO, I'M NOWHERE CLOSER TO FIGURING OUT THIS MAP.
I DON'T RECOGNIZE ANY OF THE LANDMARKS, SO I HAVE NO IDEA WHERE TO EVEN BEGIN.
THERE IS ONE LAST OPTION.
Sending you a photo
A map
idk of what
Can you help?
BZZZ
HEY.
HEY. I'LL RUN IT THROUGH THE MI-6 DATABASES...
...BECAUSE IT'S THE LEAST I CAN DO FOR A FRIEND. THINK ON THAT NEXT TIME YOU'RE TEMPTED TO JUMP OUT OF A PLANE.
LEIKO, LISTEN. I--
ANOTHER BIT OF INFORMATION, FRIEND TO FRIEND: MI-6 HAS BEEN COMMUNICATING WITH MI-5.
YOU KNOW MI-5 CAN BE A BIT QUICKER TO PICK A FIGHT. THEY'R CONSIDERING A LARGE-SCALE CRACKDOWN ON YOUR FAMILY
LEIKO, YOU NEED TO GET THEM TO HOLD OFF!
SHANG, YOU'RE IN PARIS, AREN'T YOU? YOUR FAMILY--
THEY MIGHT TRIGGER--
PLEASE, LET ME FINISH. HOW CLOSE AR YOU TO THE LOUVRE?

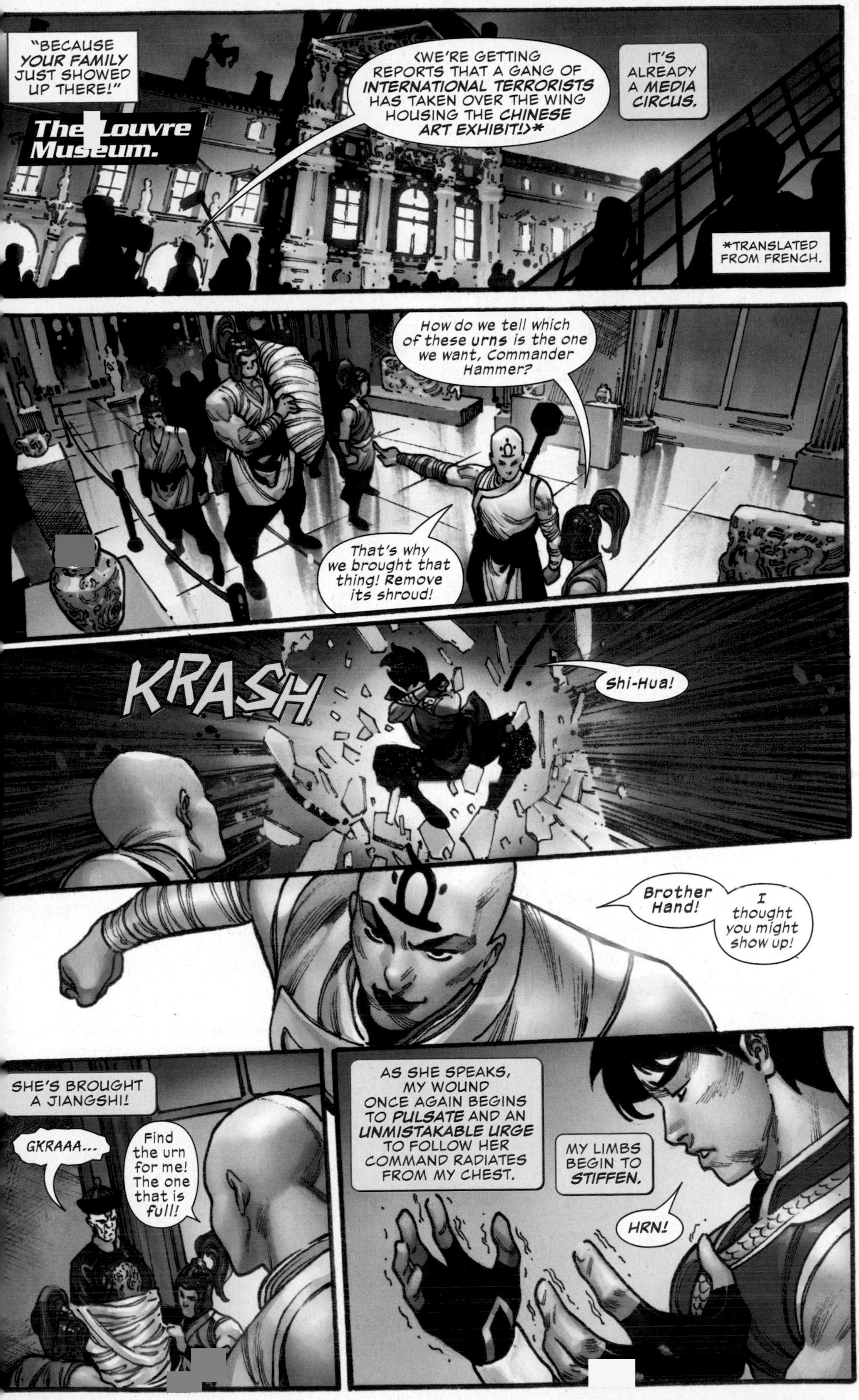

"BECAUSE YOUR FAMILY JUST SHOWED UP THERE!"
The Louvre Museum.
‹WE'RE GETTING REPORTS THAT A GANG OF INTERNATIONAL TERRORISTS HAS TAKEN OVER THE WING HOUSING THE CHINESE ART EXHIBIT!›*
IT'S ALREADY A MEDIA CIRCUS.
*TRANSLATED FROM FRENCH.
How do we tell which of these urns is the one we want, Commander Hammer?
That's why we brought that thing! Remove its shroud!
KRASH
Shi-Hua!
Brother Hand!
I thought you might show up!
SHE'S BROUGHT A JIANGSHI!
GKRAAA...
Find the urn for me! The one that is full!
AS SHE SPEAKS, MY WOUND ONCE AGAIN BEGINS TO PULSATE AND AN UNMISTAKABLE URGE TO FOLLOW HER COMMAND RADIATES FROM MY CHEST.
MY LIMBS BEGIN TO STIFFEN.
HRN!

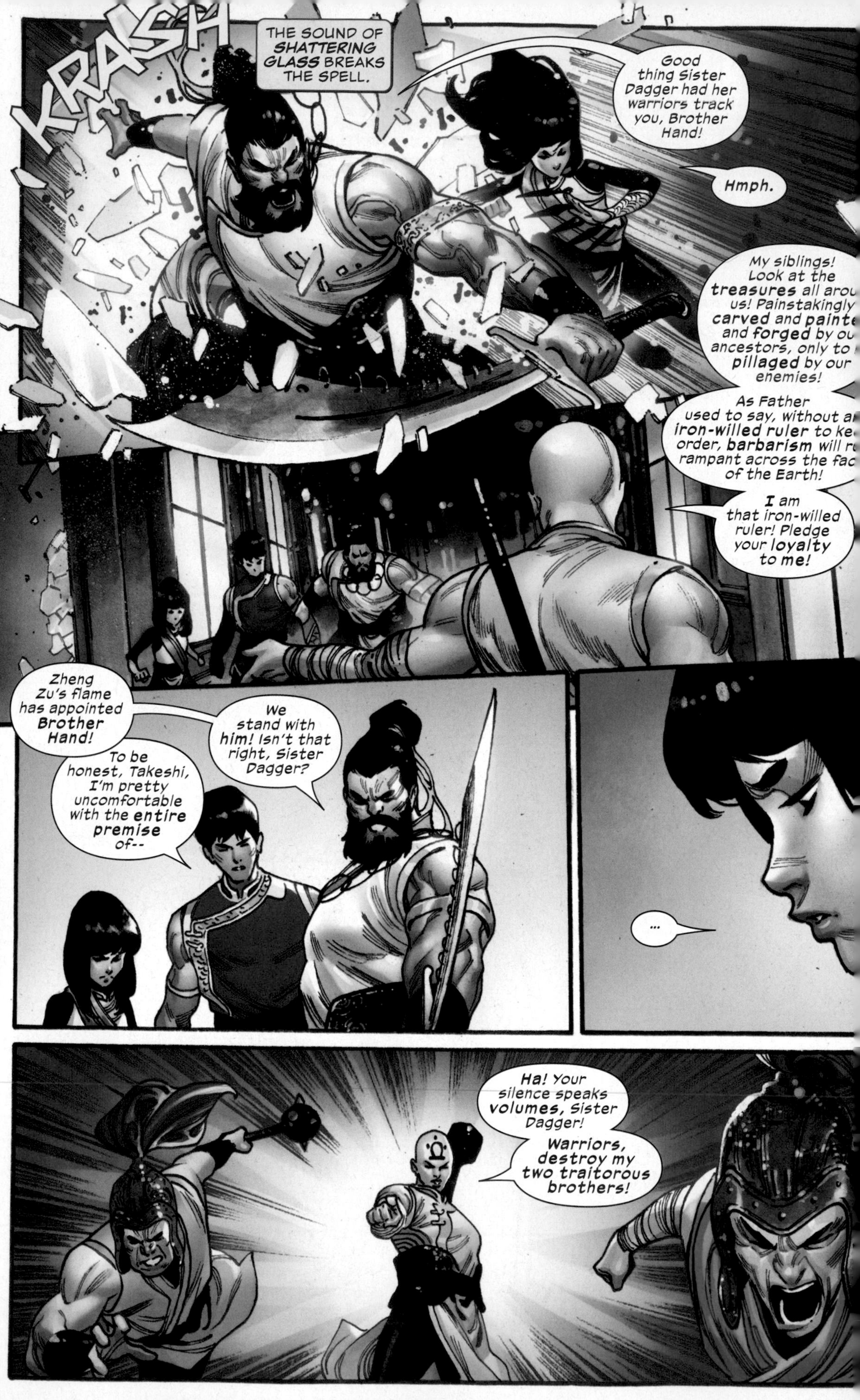
KRASH
THE SOUND OF SHATTERING GLASS BREAKS THE SPELL.
Good thing Sister Dagger had her warriors track you, Brother Hand!
Hmph.
My siblings! Look at the treasures all arou us! Painstakingly carved and painte and forged by ou ancestors, only to pillaged by our enemies!
As Father used to say, without a iron-willed ruler to ke order, barbarism will r rampant across the fac of the Earth!
I am that iron-willed ruler! Pledge your loyalty to me!
Zheng Zu's flame has appointed Brother Hand!
We stand with him! Isn't that right, Sister Dagger?
To be honest, Takeshi, I'm pretty uncomfortable with the entire premise of--
...
Ha! Your silence speaks volumes, Sister Dagger!
Warriors, destroy my two traitorous brothers!

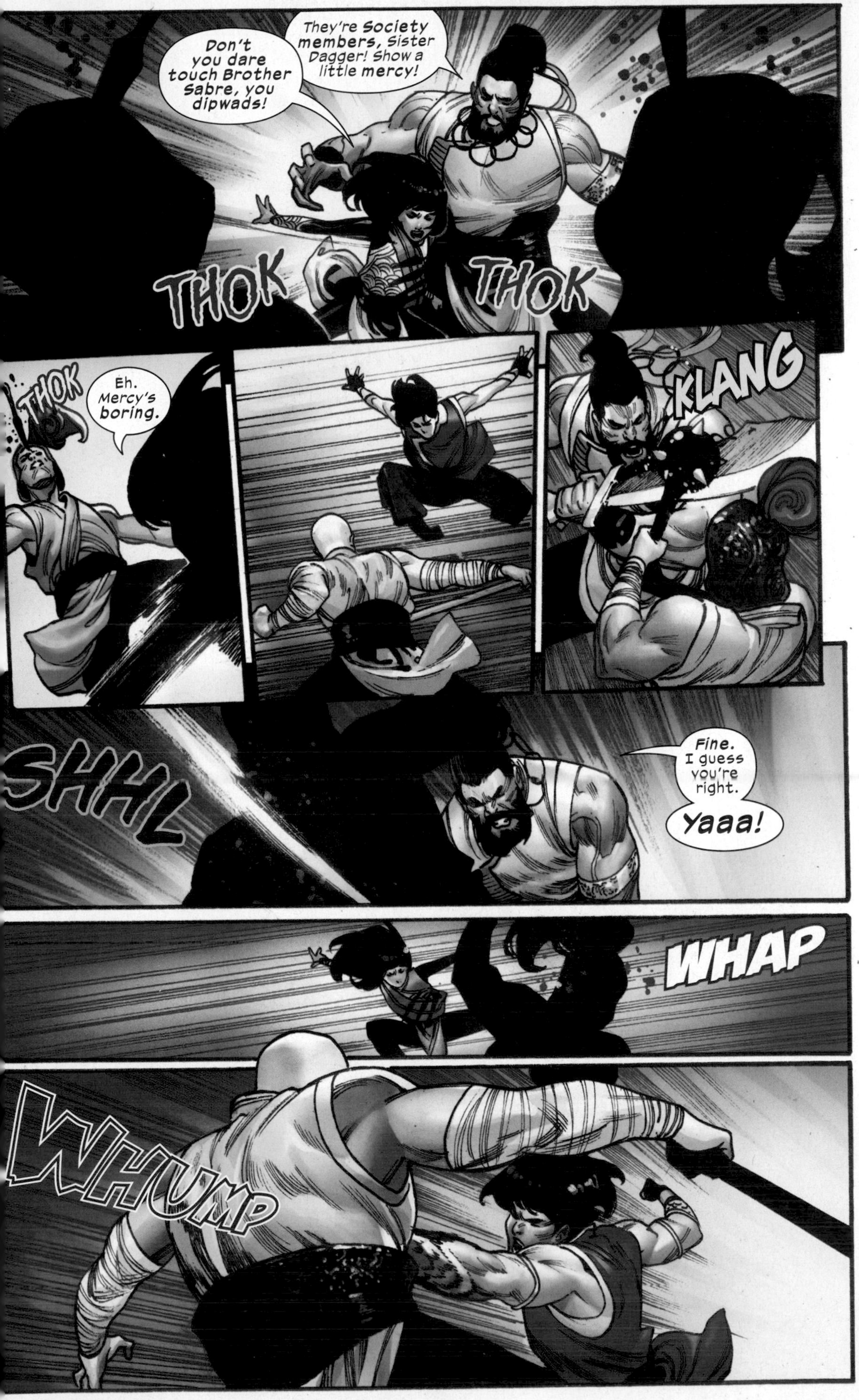
They're Society members, Sister Dagger! Show a little mercy!
Don't you dare touch Brother Sabre, you dipwads!
THOK
THOK
THOK
Eh. Mercy's boring.
KLANG
SHHL
Fine. I guess you're right.
Yaaa!
WHAP
WHUMP

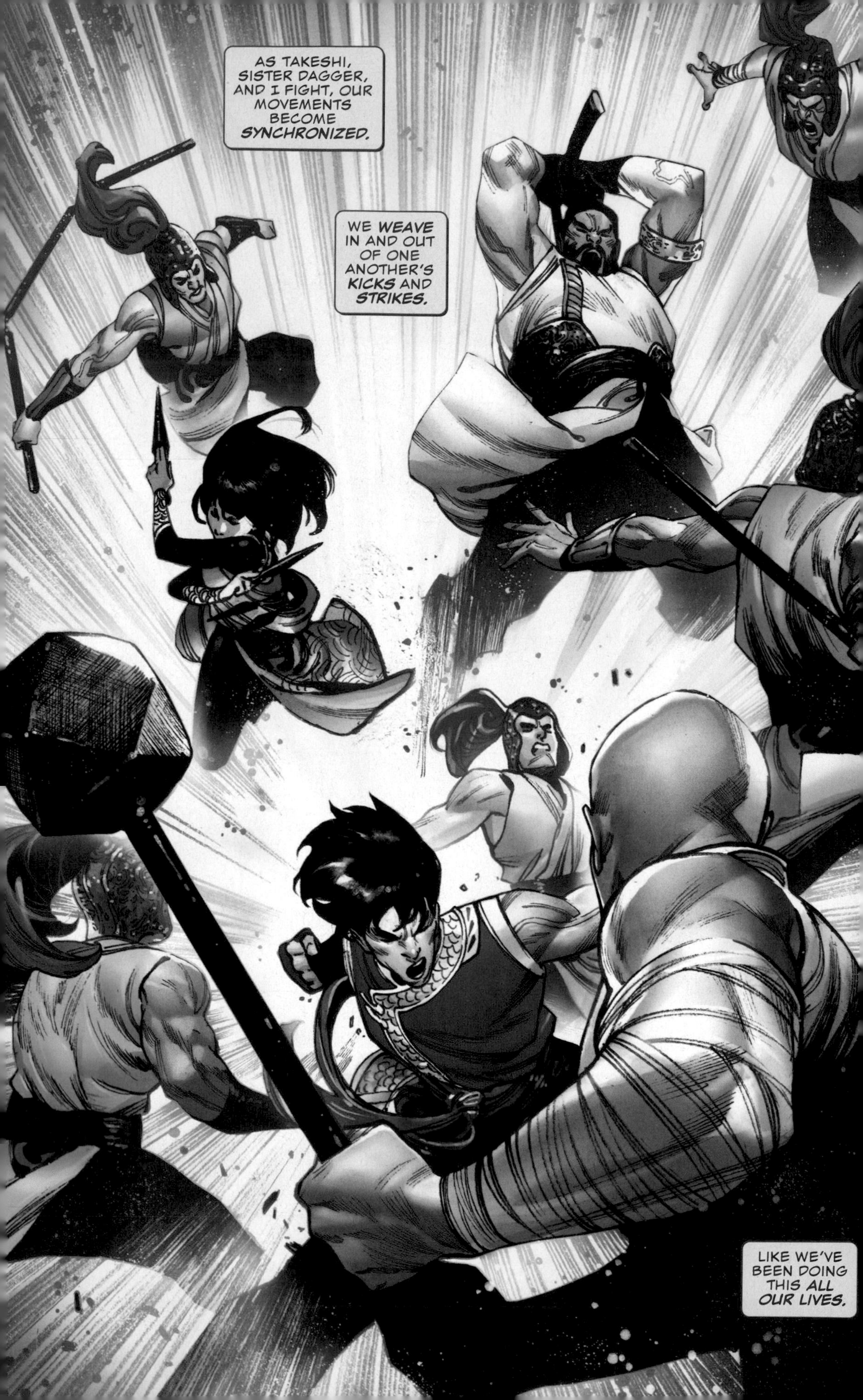
AS TAKESHI, SISTER DAGGER, AND I FIGHT, OUR MOVEMENTS BECOME SYNCHRONIZED.
WE WEAVE IN AND OUT OF ONE ANOTHER'S KICKS AND STRIKES.
LIKE WE'VE BEEN DOING THIS ALL OUR LIVES.

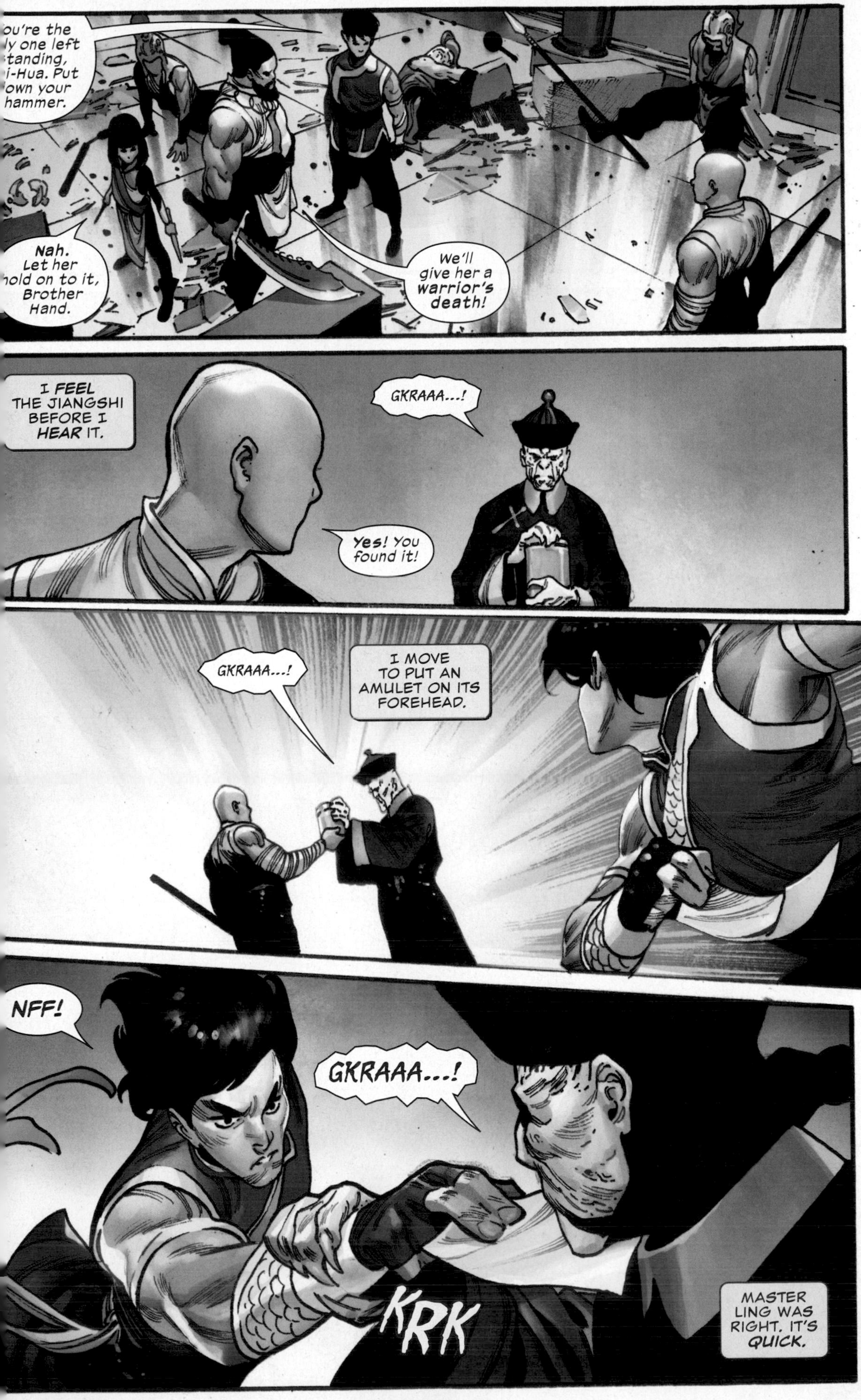

ou're the
ly one left
tanding,
i-Hua. Put
own your
hammer.
Nah. Let her
hold on to it, Brother Hand.
We'll give her a warrior's death!
I FEEL THE JIANGSHI BEFORE I HEAR IT.
GKRAAA...!
Yes! You found it!
GKRAAA...!
I MOVE TO PUT AN AMULET ON ITS FOREHEAD.
NFF!
GKRAAA...!
KRK
MASTER LING WAS RIGHT. IT'S QUICK.

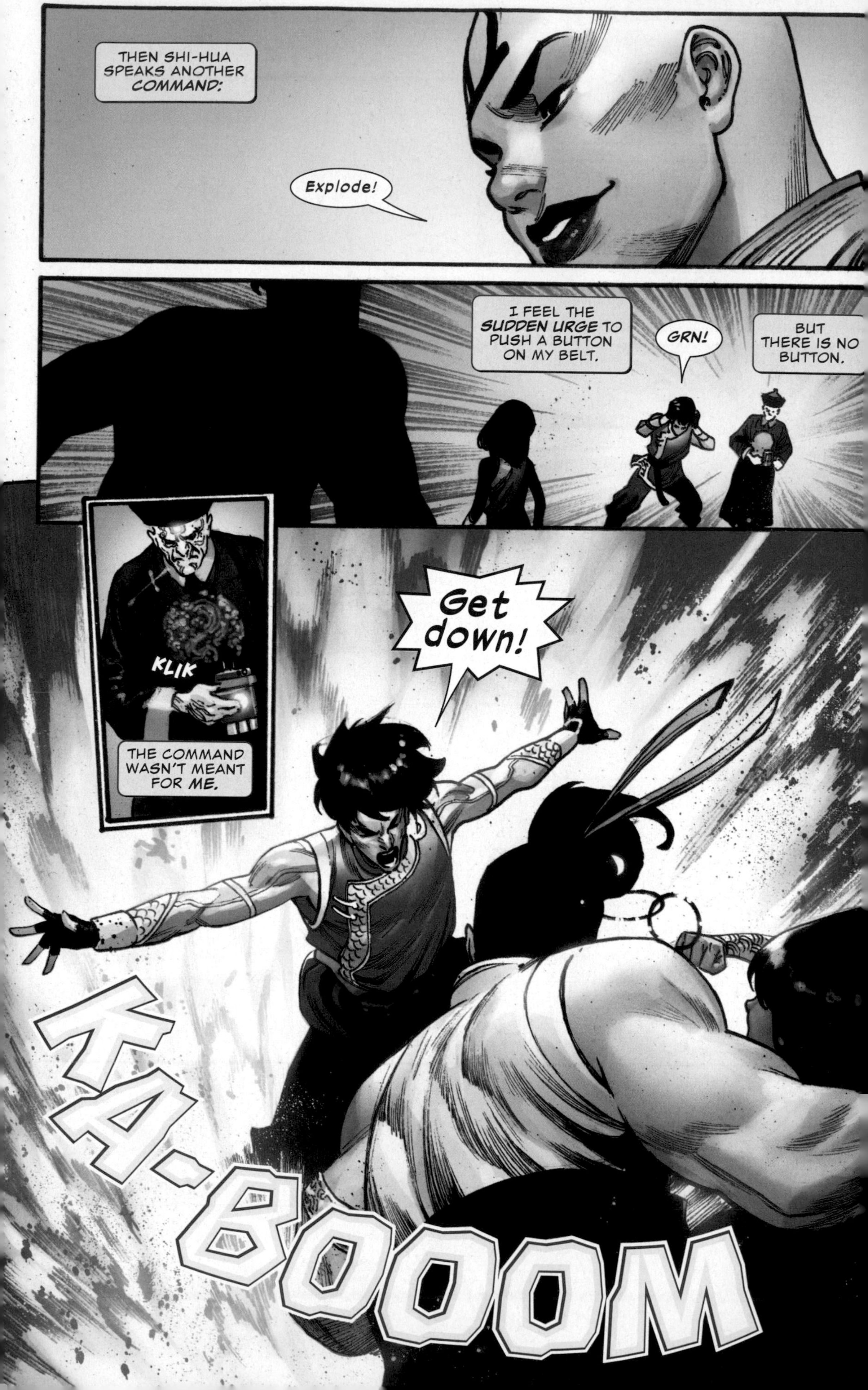
THEN SHI-HUA SPEAKS ANOTHER COMMAND:
Explode!
I FEEL THE SUDDEN URGE TO PUSH A BUTTON ON MY BELT.
GRN!
BUT THERE IS NO BUTTON.
KLIK
THE COMMAND WASN'T MEANT FOR ME.
Get down!
KA-BOOOM

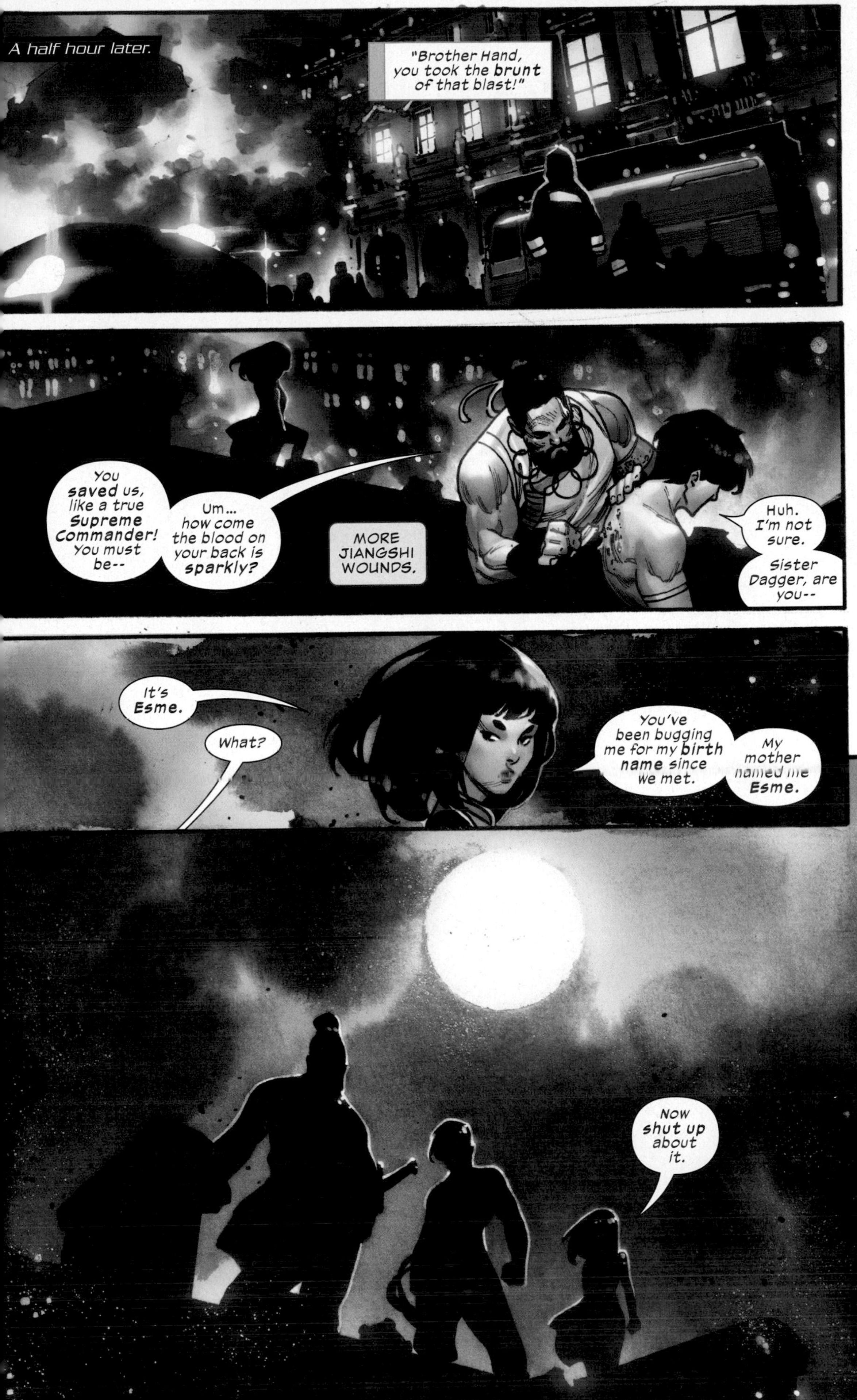
A half hour later.
"Brother Hand, you took the brunt of that blast!"
You saved us, like a true Supreme Commander! You must be--
Um... how come the blood on your back is sparkly?
MORE JIANGSHI WOUNDS.
Huh. I'm not sure.
Sister Dagger, are you--
It's Esme.
What?
You've been bugging me for my birth name since we met.
My mother named me Esme.
Now shut up about it.

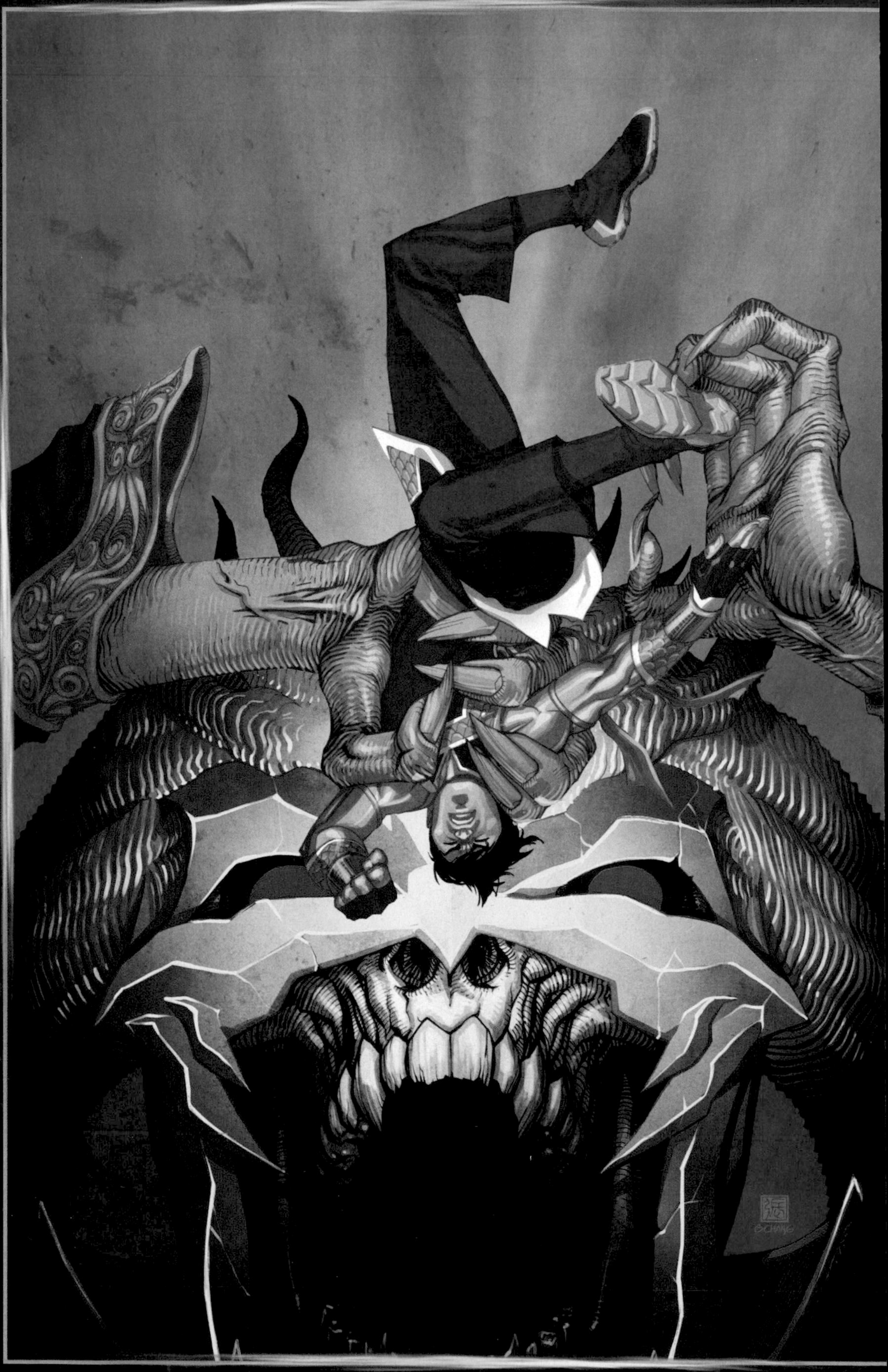

FOUR

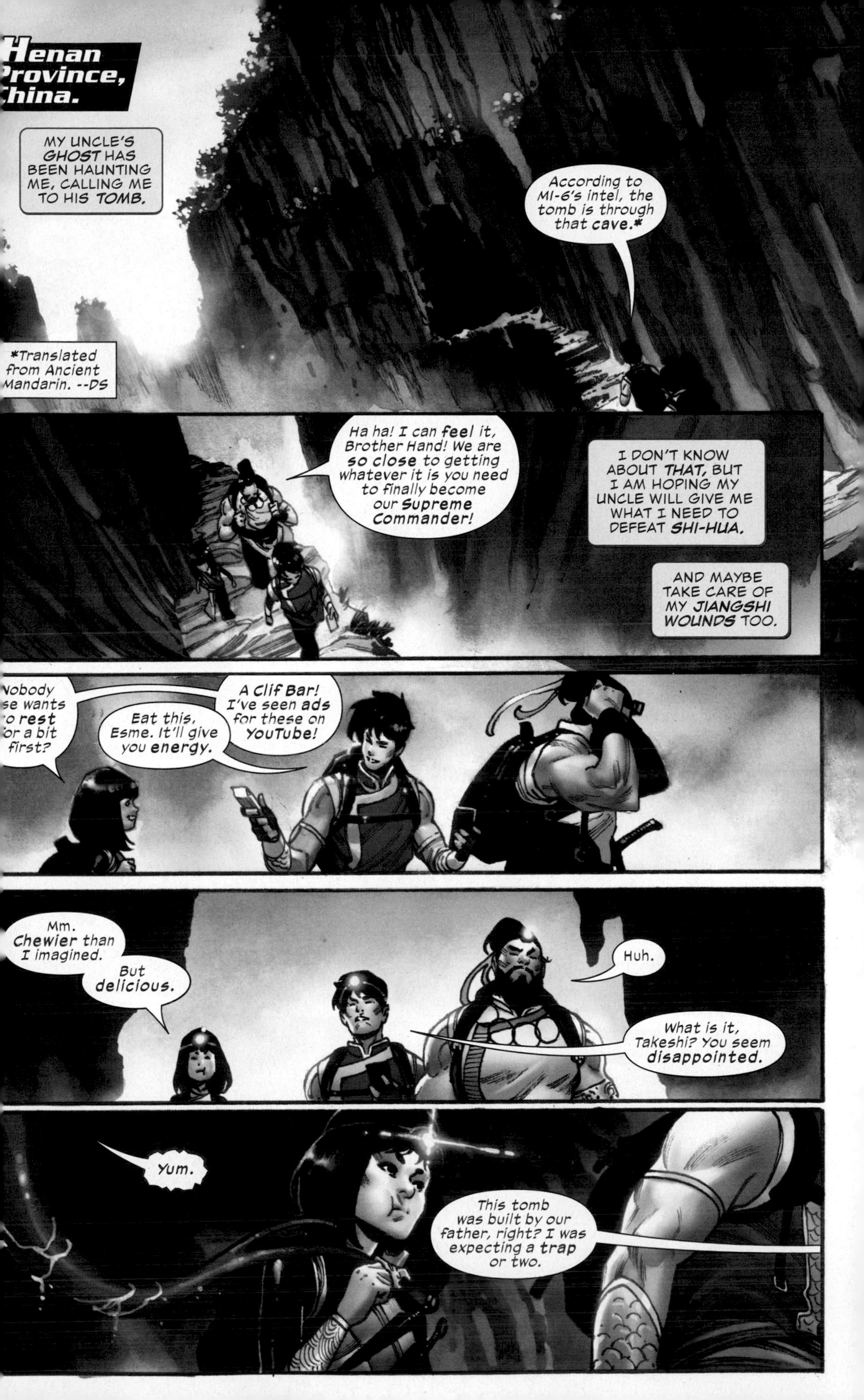
Henan Province, China.
MY UNCLE'S GHOST HAS BEEN HAUNTING ME, CALLING ME TO HIS TOMB.
According to MI-6's intel, the tomb is through that cave.*
*Translated from Ancient Mandarin. --DS
Ha ha! I can feel it, Brother Hand! We are so close to getting whatever it is you need to finally become our Supreme Commander!
I DON'T KNOW ABOUT THAT, BUT I AM HOPING MY UNCLE WILL GIVE ME WHAT I NEED TO DEFEAT SHI-HUA.
AND MAYBE TAKE CARE OF MY JIANGSHI WOUNDS TOO.
Nobody else wants to rest for a bit first?
A Clif Bar! I've seen ads for these on YouTube!
Eat this, Esme. It'll give you energy.
Mm. Chewier than I imagined.
But delicious.
Huh.
What is it, Takeshi? You seem disappointed.
Yum.
This tomb was built by our father, right? I was expecting a trap or two.

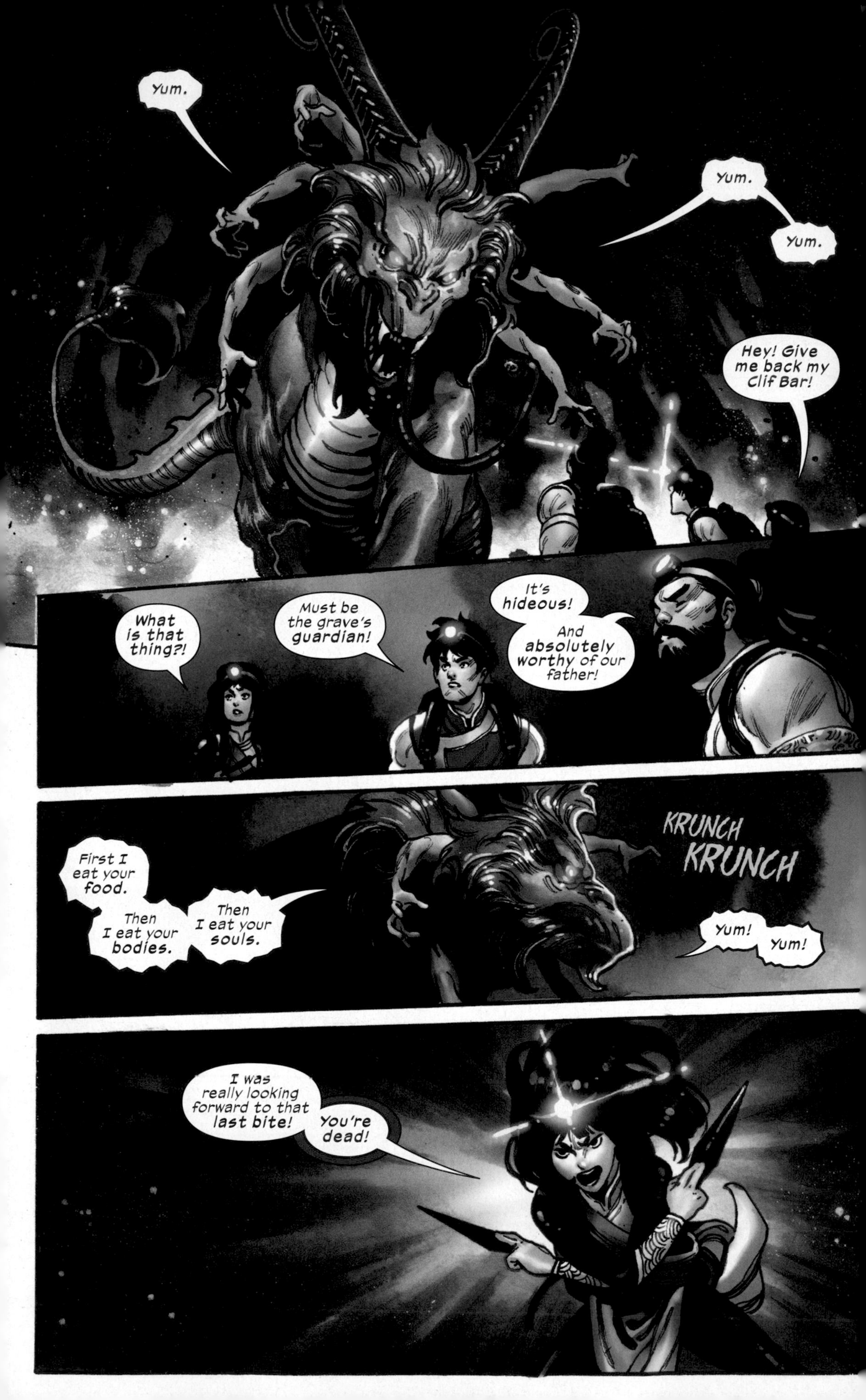
Yum.
Yum.
Yum.
Hey! Give me back my Clif Bar!
What is that thing?!
Must be the grave's guardian!
It's hideous!
And absolutely worthy of our father!
KRUNCH KRUNCH
First I eat your food.
Then I eat your bodies.
Then I eat your souls.
Yum!
Yum!
I was really looking forward to that last bite!
You're dead!

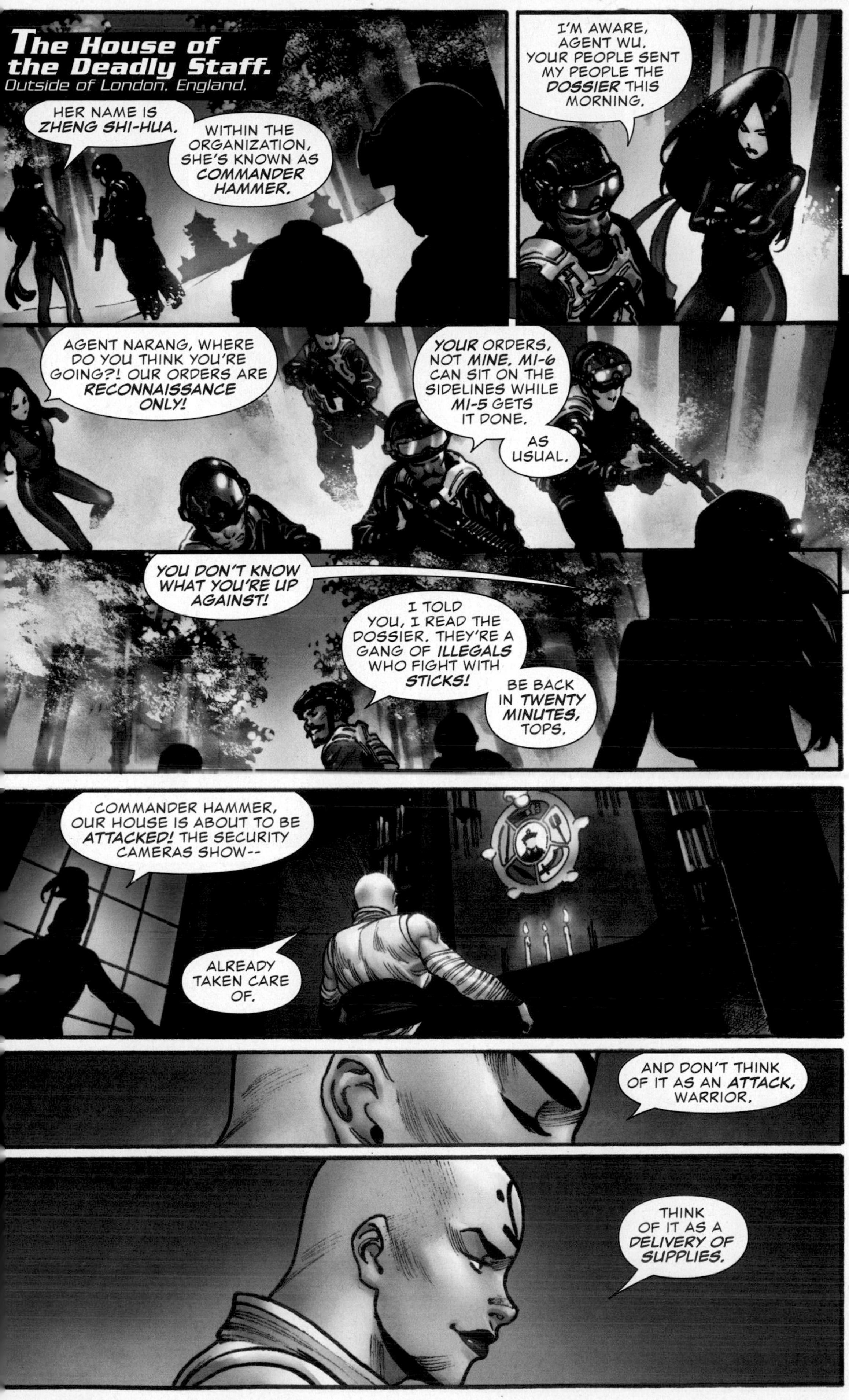
The House of the Deadly Staff.
Outside of London, England.
HER NAME IS ZHENG SHI-HUA.
WITHIN THE ORGANIZATION, SHE'S KNOWN AS COMMANDER HAMMER.
I'M AWARE, AGENT WU. YOUR PEOPLE SENT MY PEOPLE THE DOSSIER THIS MORNING.
AGENT NARANG, WHERE DO YOU THINK YOU'RE GOING?! OUR ORDERS ARE RECONNAISSANCE ONLY!
YOUR ORDERS, NOT MINE. MI-6 CAN SIT ON THE SIDELINES WHILE MI-5 GETS IT DONE.
AS USUAL.
YOU DON'T KNOW WHAT YOU'RE UP AGAINST!
I TOLD YOU, I READ THE DOSSIER. THEY'RE A GANG OF ILLEGALS WHO FIGHT WITH STICKS!
BE BACK IN TWENTY MINUTES, TOPS.
COMMANDER HAMMER, OUR HOUSE IS ABOUT TO BE ATTACKED! THE SECURITY CAMERAS SHOW--
ALREADY TAKEN CARE OF.
AND DON'T THINK OF IT AS AN ATTACK, WARRIOR.
THINK OF IT AS A DELIVERY OF SUPPLIES.

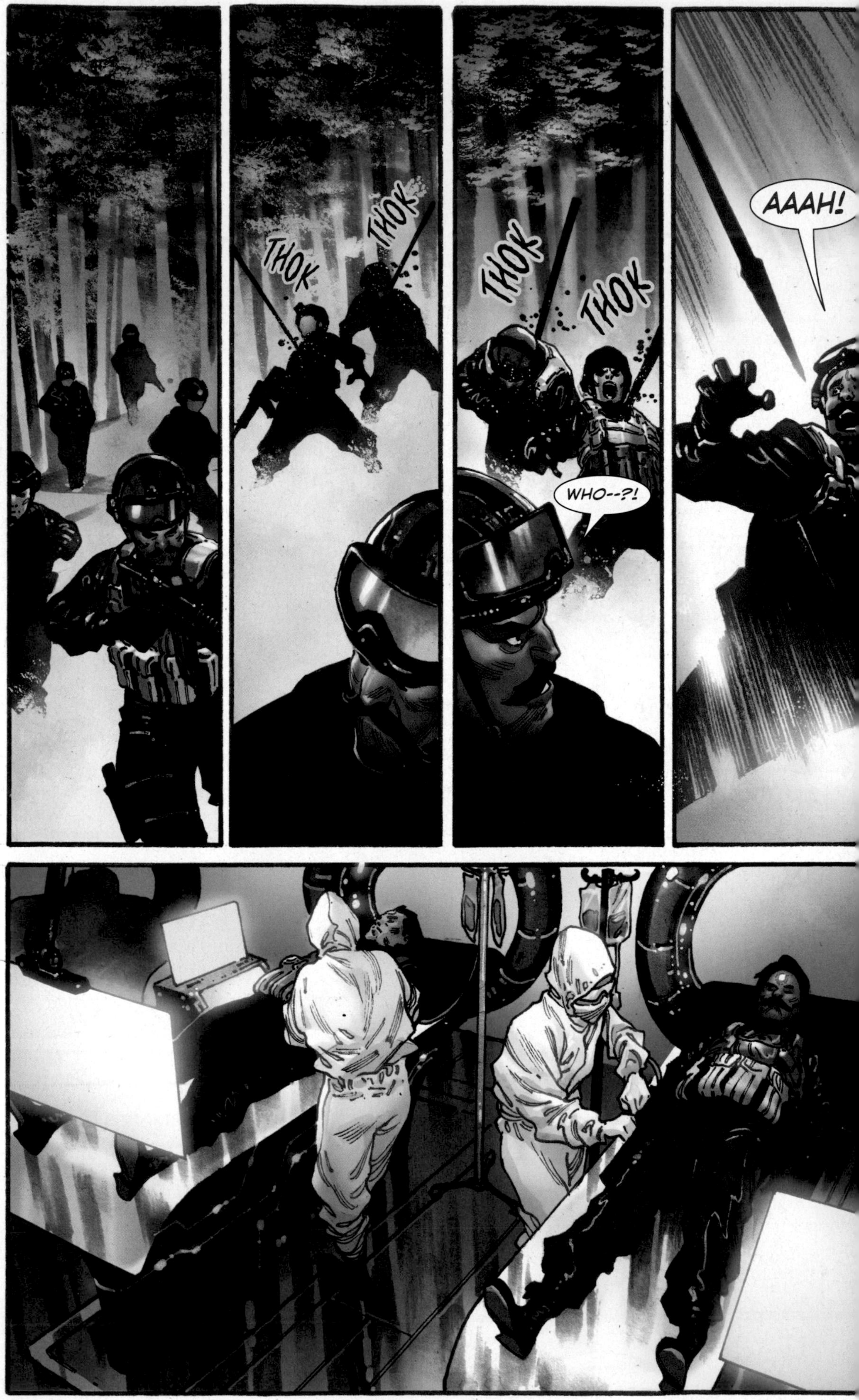
THOK
THOK
THOK
THOK
WHO--?!
AAAH!

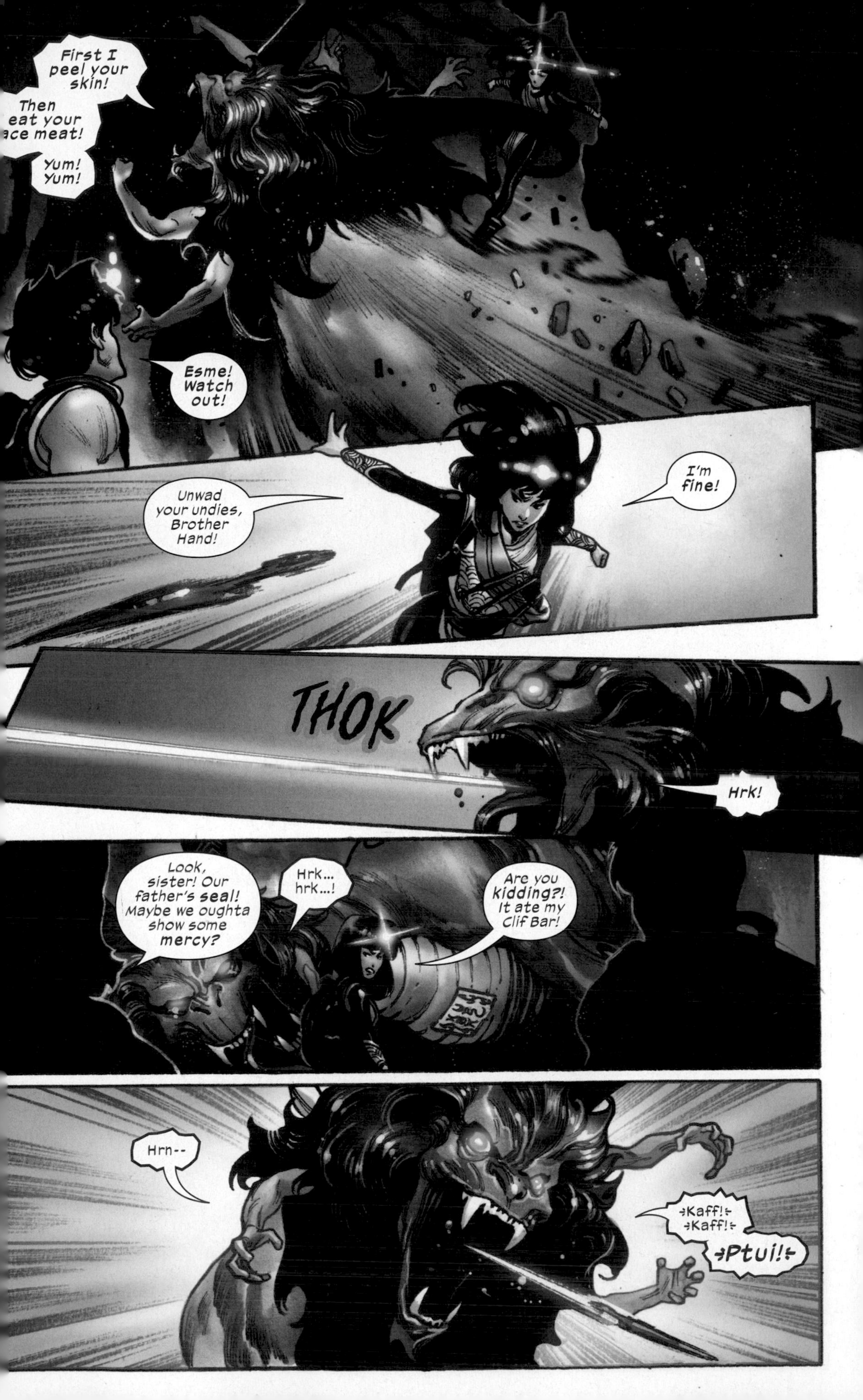
First I peel your skin!
Then eat your ace meat!
Yum! Yum!
Esme! Watch out!
Unwad your undies, Brother Hand!
I'm fine!
THOK
Hrk!
Look, sister! Our father's seal! Maybe we oughta show some mercy?
Hrk... hrk...!
Are you kidding?! It ate my Clif Bar!
Hrn--
Kaff! Kaff!
Ptui!

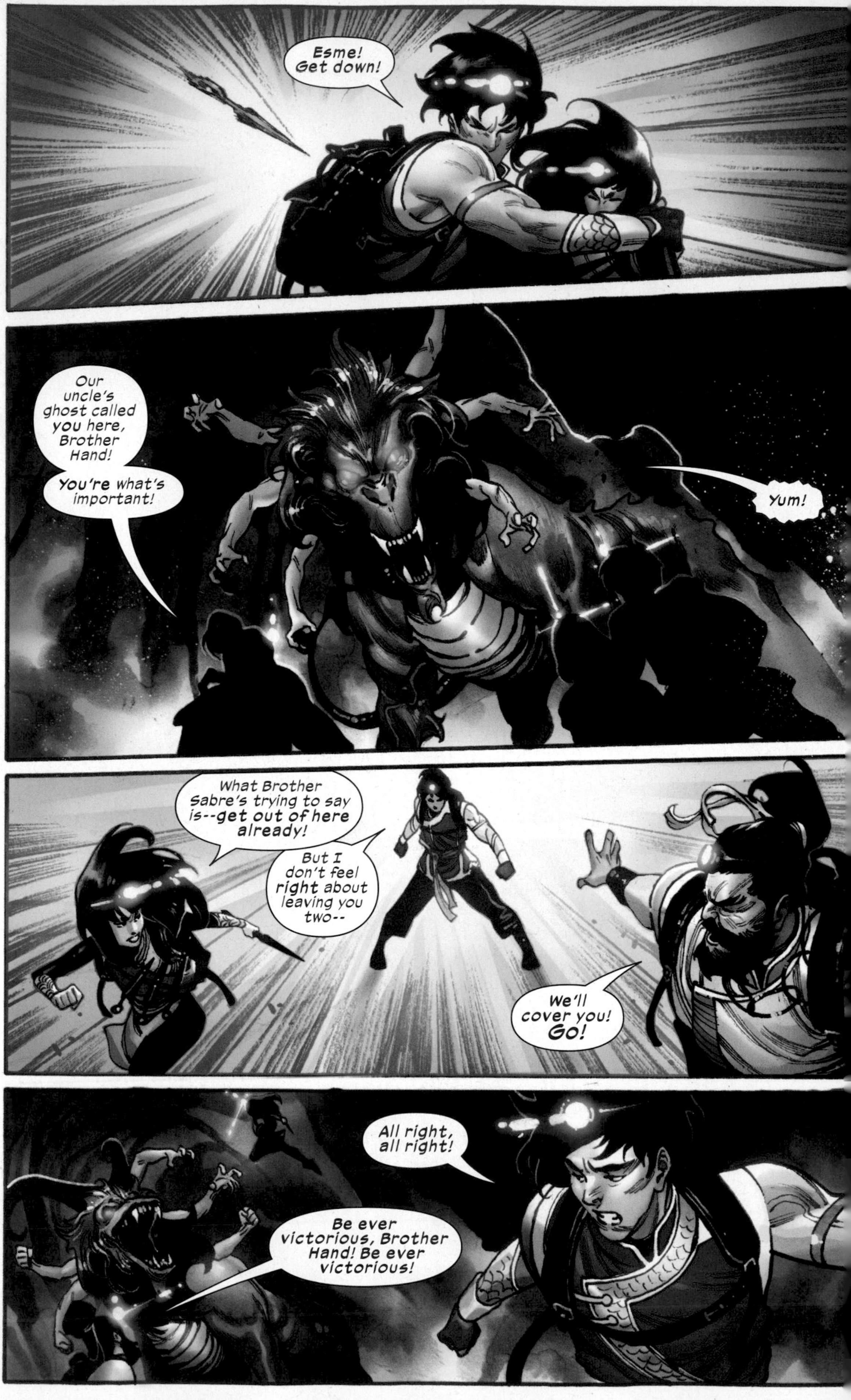

Esme! Get down!
Our uncle's ghost called you here, Brother Hand!
You're what's important!
Yum!
What Brother Sabre's trying to say is--get out of here already!
But I don't feel right about leaving you two--
We'll cover you! GO!
All right, all right!
Be ever victorious, Brother Hand! Be ever victorious!

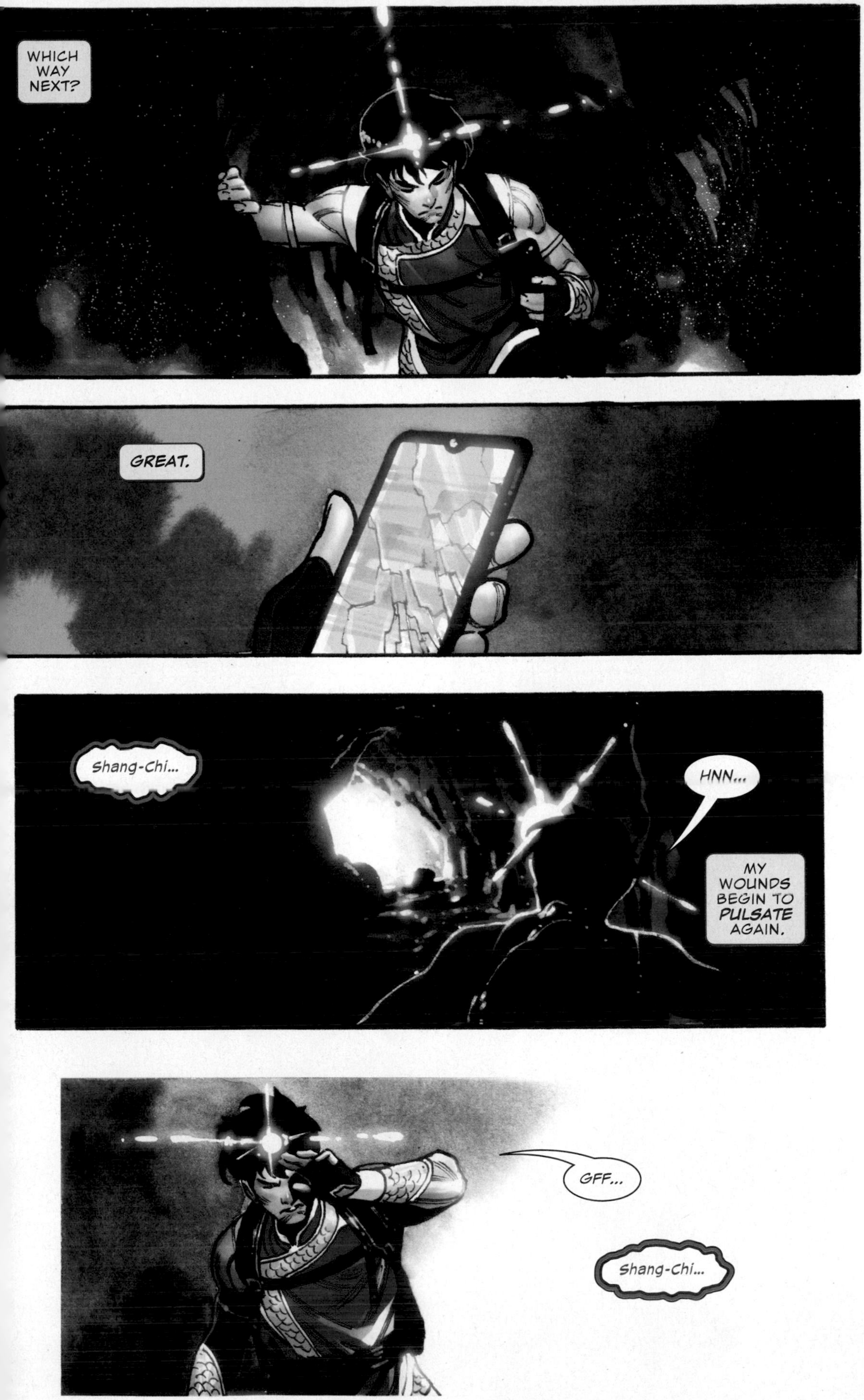
WHICH WAY NEXT?
GREAT.
Shang-Chi...
HNN...
MY WOUNDS BEGIN TO PULSATE AGAIN.
GFF...
Shang-Chi...

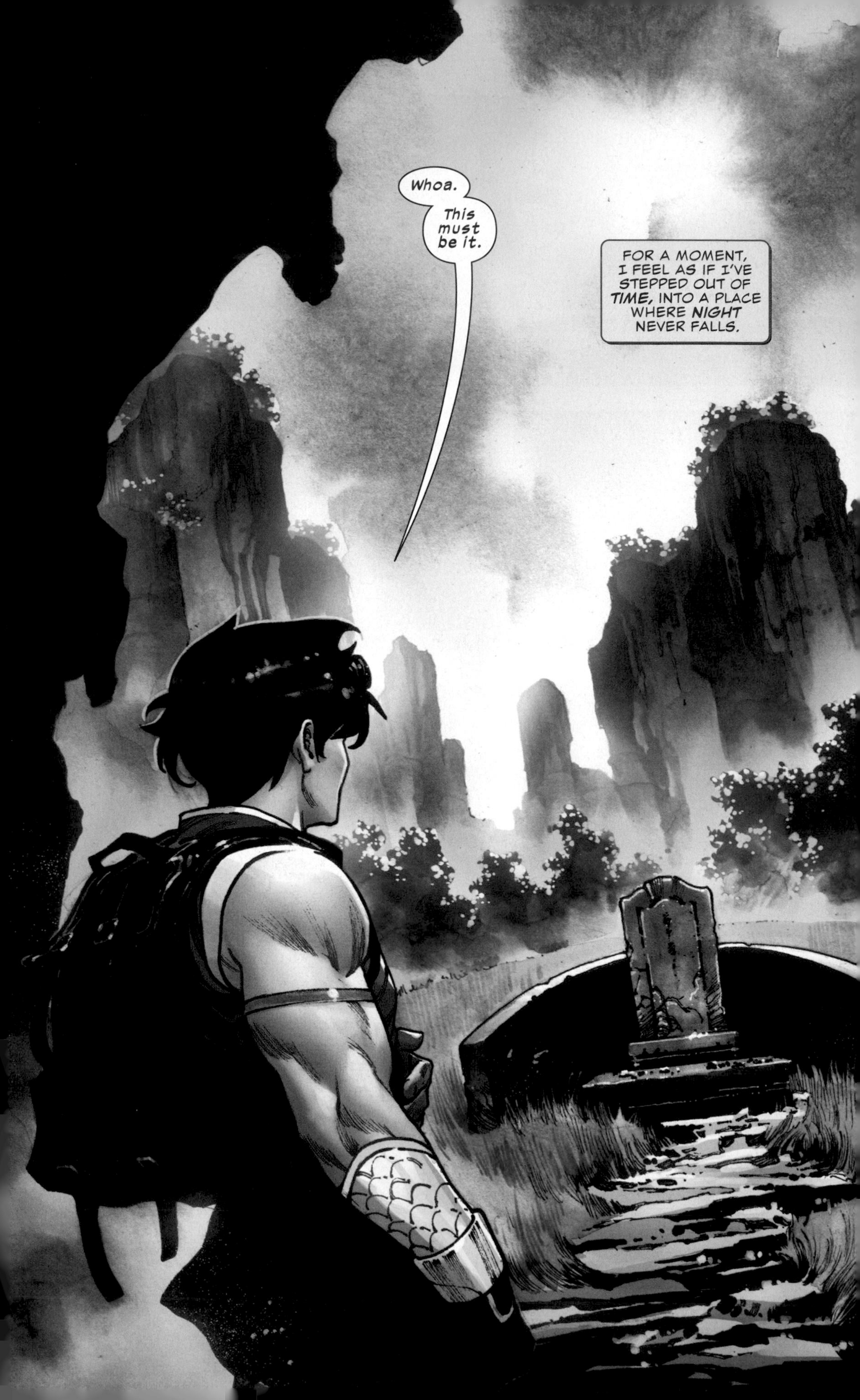
Whoa.
This must be it.
FOR A MOMENT, I FEEL AS IF I'VE STEPPED OUT OF TIME, INTO A PLACE WHERE NIGHT NEVER FALLS.

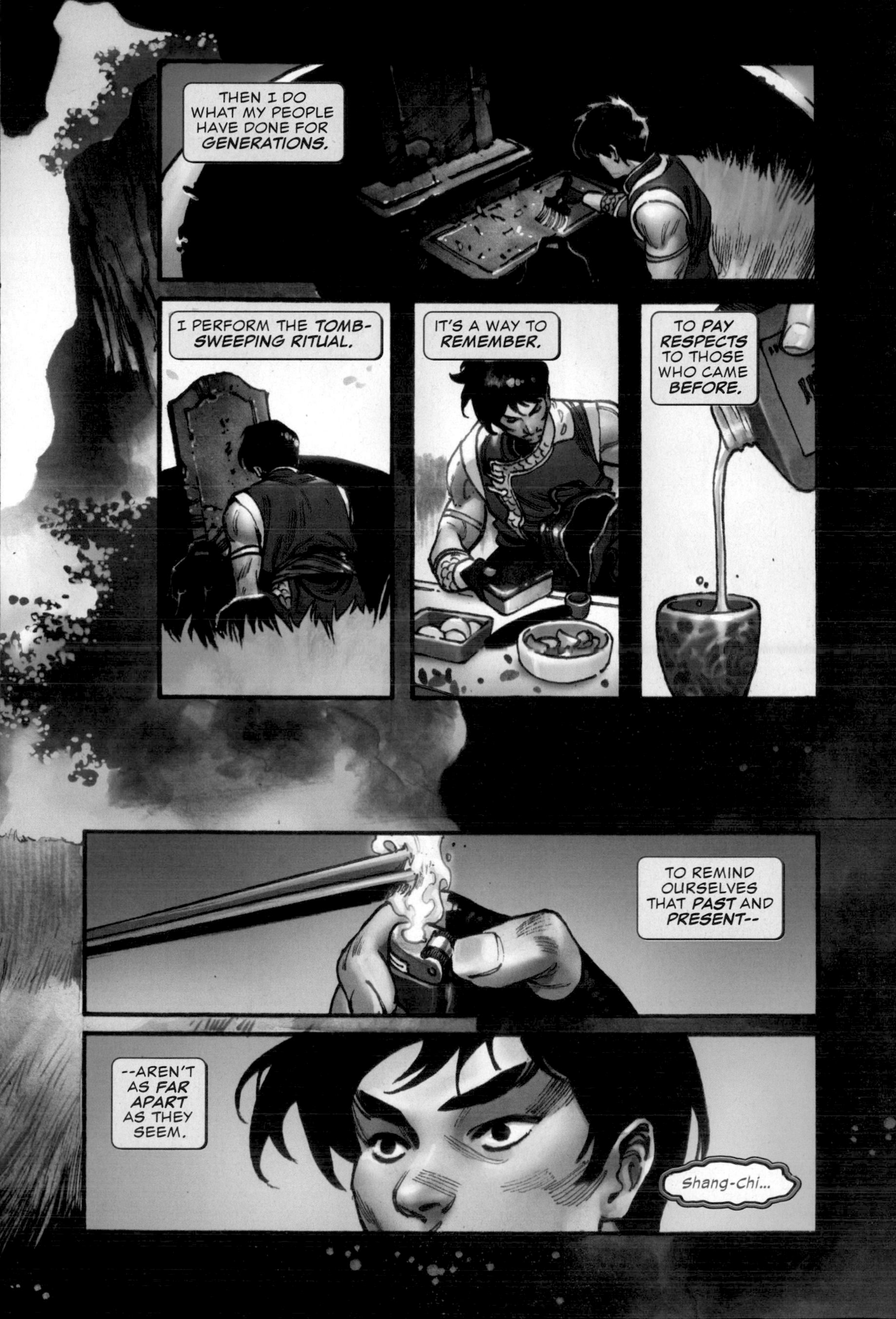
THEN I DO WHAT MY PEOPLE HAVE DONE FOR GENERATIONS.
I PERFORM THE TOMB-SWEEPING RITUAL.
IT'S A WAY TO REMEMBER.
TO PAY RESPECTS TO THOSE WHO CAME BEFORE.
TO REMIND OURSELVES THAT PAST AND PRESENT--
--AREN'T AS FAR APART AS THEY SEEM.
Shang-Chi...

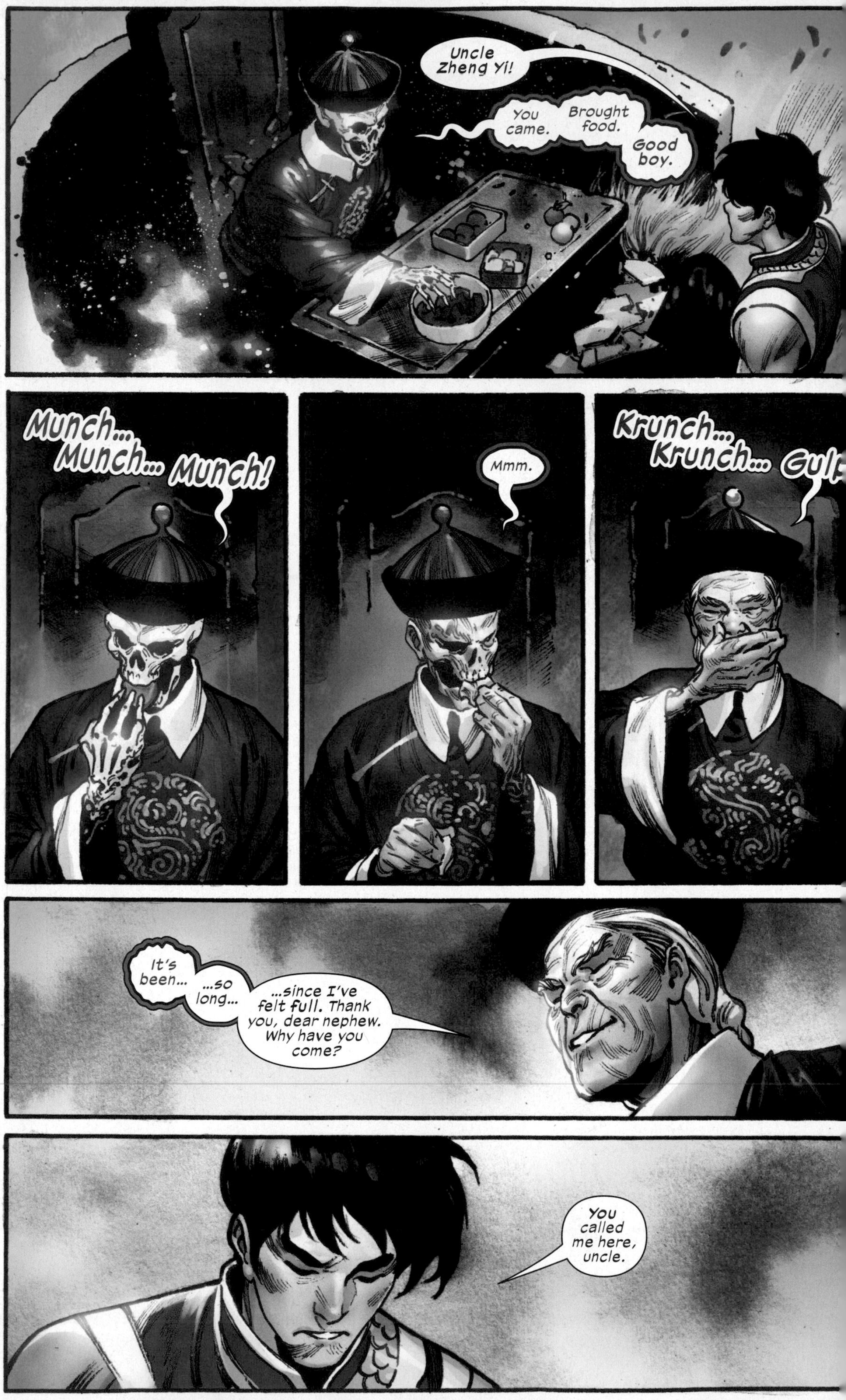

Uncle Zheng Yi!
You came.
Brought food.
Good boy.
Munch... Munch... Munch!
Mmm.
Krunch... Krunch...
It's been...
...so long...
...since I've felt full. Thank you, dear nephew. Why have you come?
You called me here, uncle.

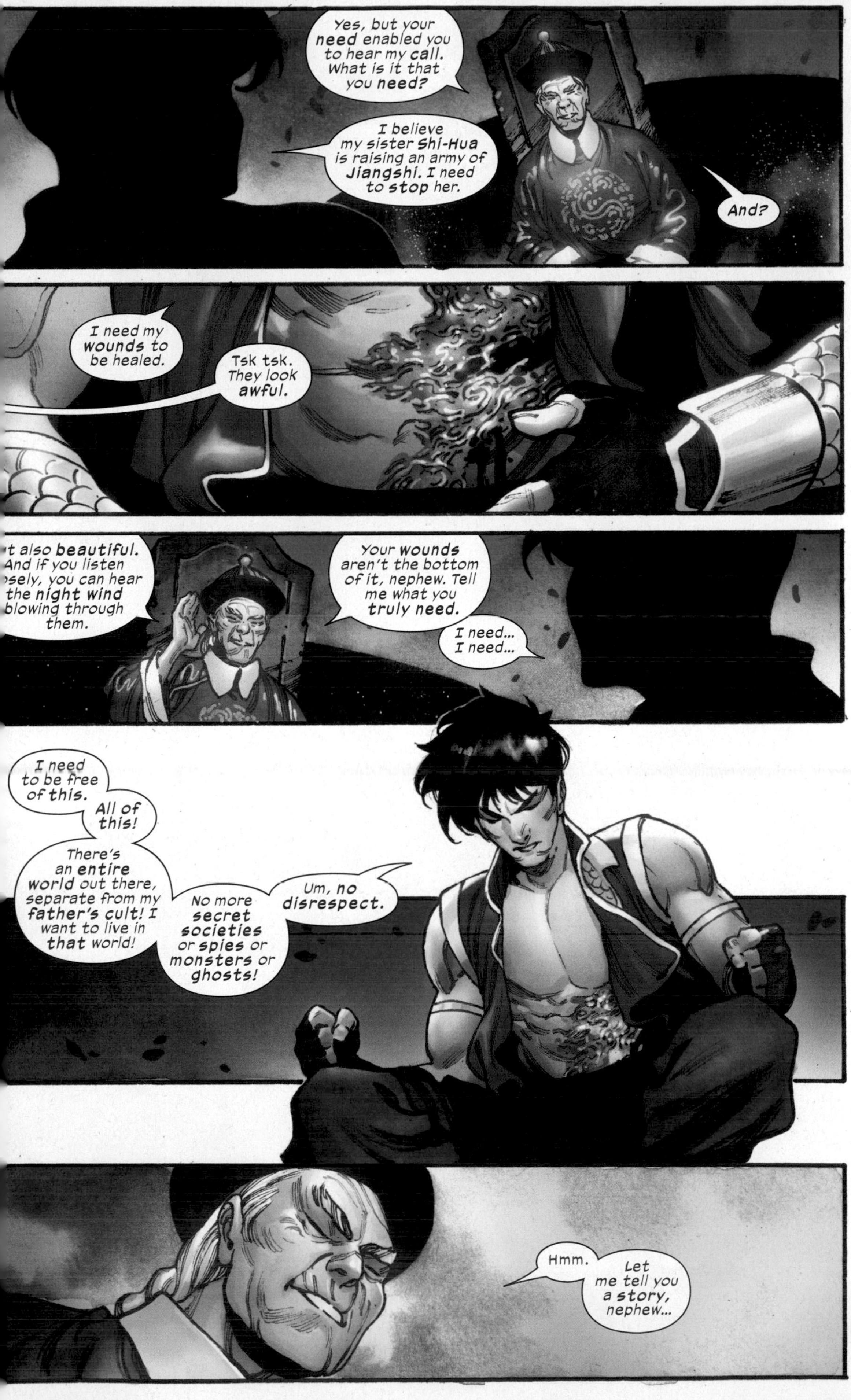

Yes, but your **need** enabled you to hear my **call.** What is it that you **need?**
I believe my sister **Shi-Hua** is raising an army of **Jiangshi.** I need to **stop** her.
And?
I need my **wounds** to be healed.
Tsk tsk. They look **awful.**
t also **beautiful.** And if you listen osely, you can hear the **night wind** blowing through them.
Your **wounds** aren't the bottom of it, nephew. Tell me what you **truly need.**
I need... I need...
I need to be free of **this.**
All of this!
There's an **entire world** out there, separate from my **father's cult!** I want to live in **that** world!
No more **secret societies** or **spies** or **monsters** or **ghosts!**
Um, no **disrespect.**
Hmm.
Let me tell you a **story,** nephew...

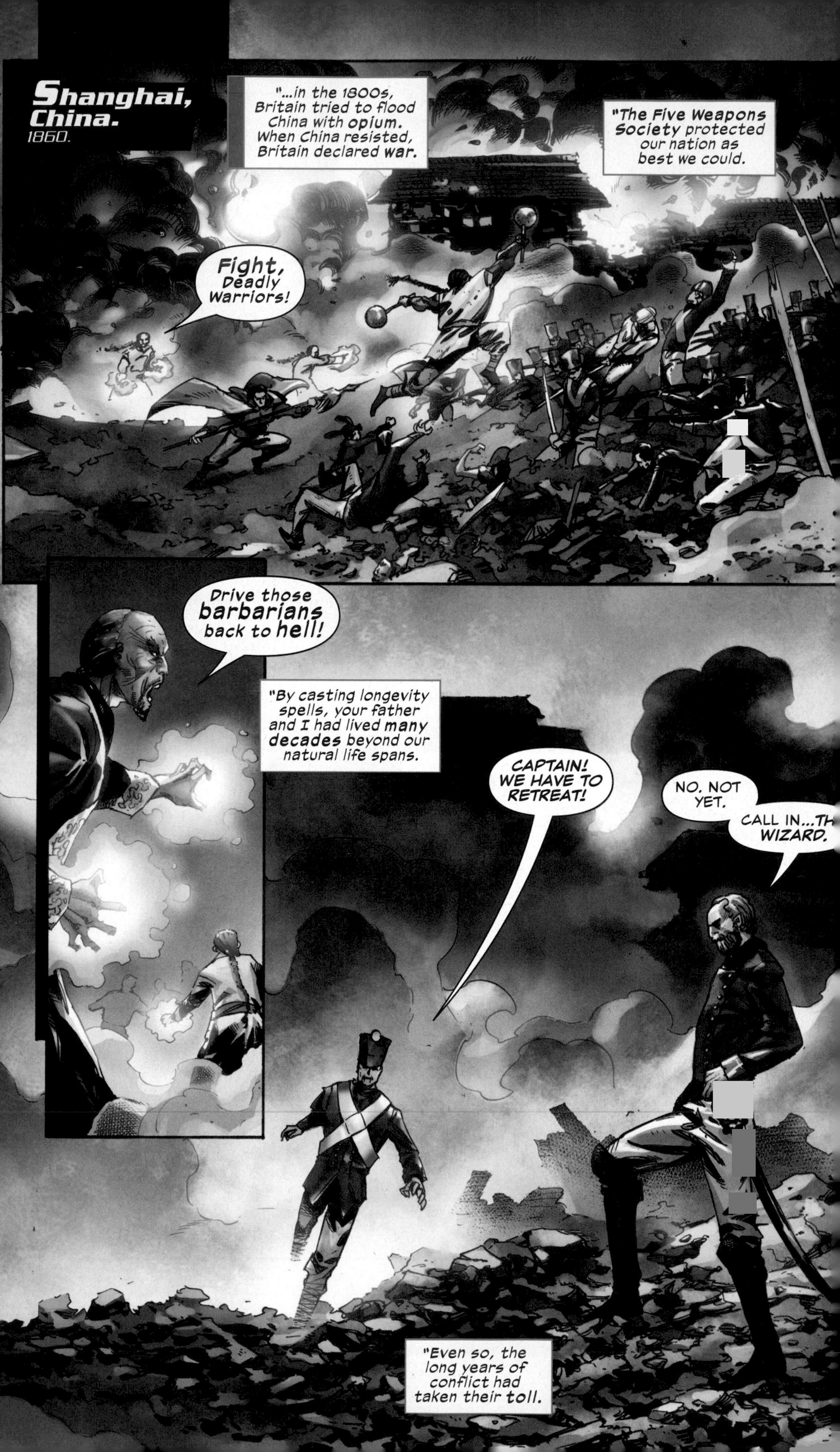
Shanghai, China. 1860.
"...in the 1800s, Britain tried to flood China with opium. When China resisted, Britain declared war.
"The Five Weapons Society protected our nation as best we could.
Fight, Deadly Warriors!
Drive those barbarians back to hell!
"By casting longevity spells, your father and I had lived many decades beyond our natural life spans.
CAPTAIN! WE HAVE TO RETREAT!
NO. NOT YET.
CALL IN...TH WIZARD.
"Even so, the long years of conflict had taken their toll.

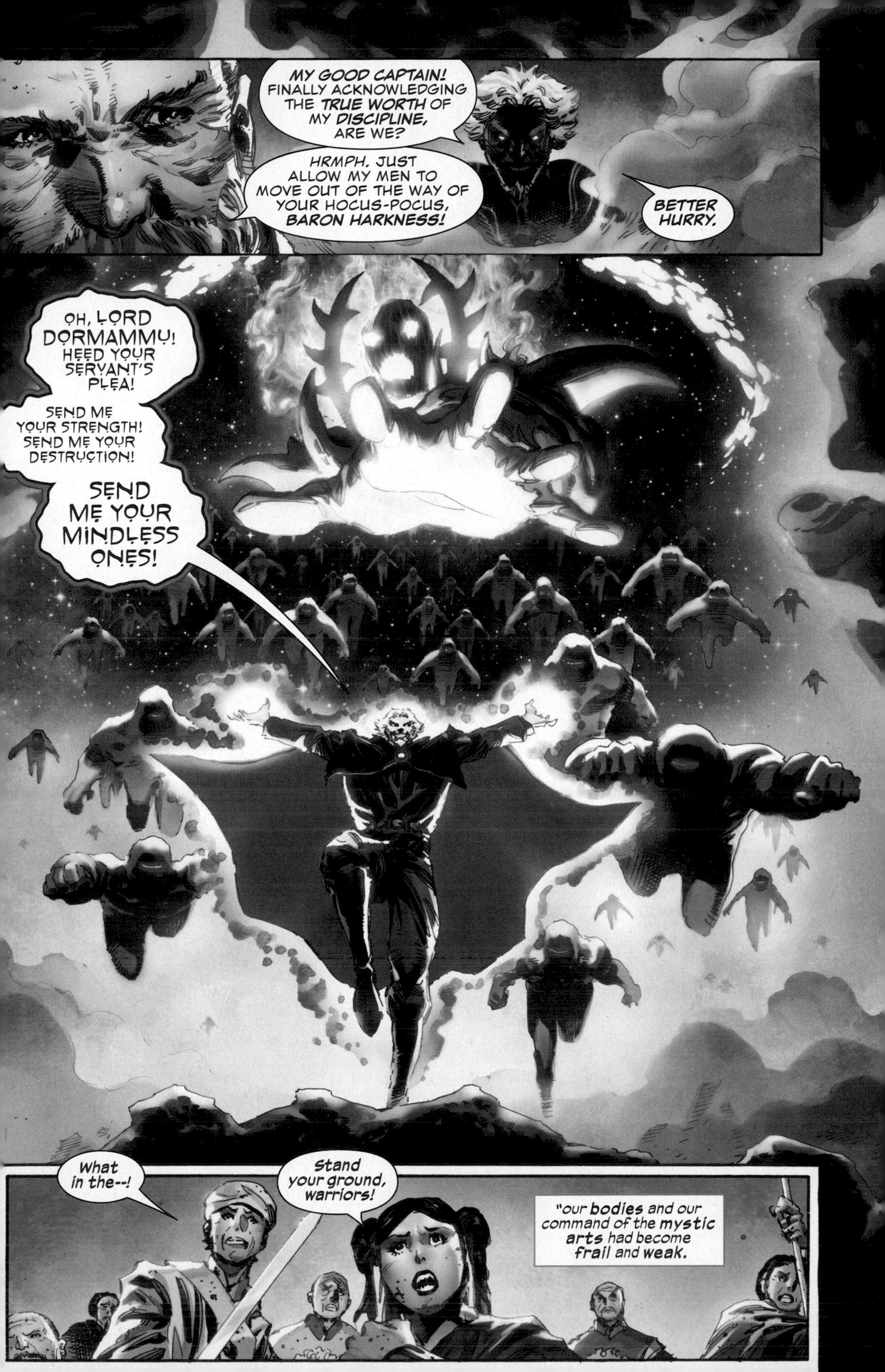
MY GOOD CAPTAIN! FINALLY ACKNOWLEDGING THE TRUE WORTH OF MY DISCIPLINE, ARE WE?
HRMPH. JUST ALLOW MY MEN TO MOVE OUT OF THE WAY OF YOUR HOCUS-POCUS, BARON HARKNESS!
BETTER HURRY.
OH, LORD DORMAMMU! HEED YOUR SERVANT'S PLEA!
SEND ME YOUR STRENGTH! SEND ME YOUR DESTRUCTION!
SEND ME YOUR MINDLESS ONES!
What in the--!
Stand your ground, warriors!
"our bodies and our command of the mystic arts had become frail and weak.

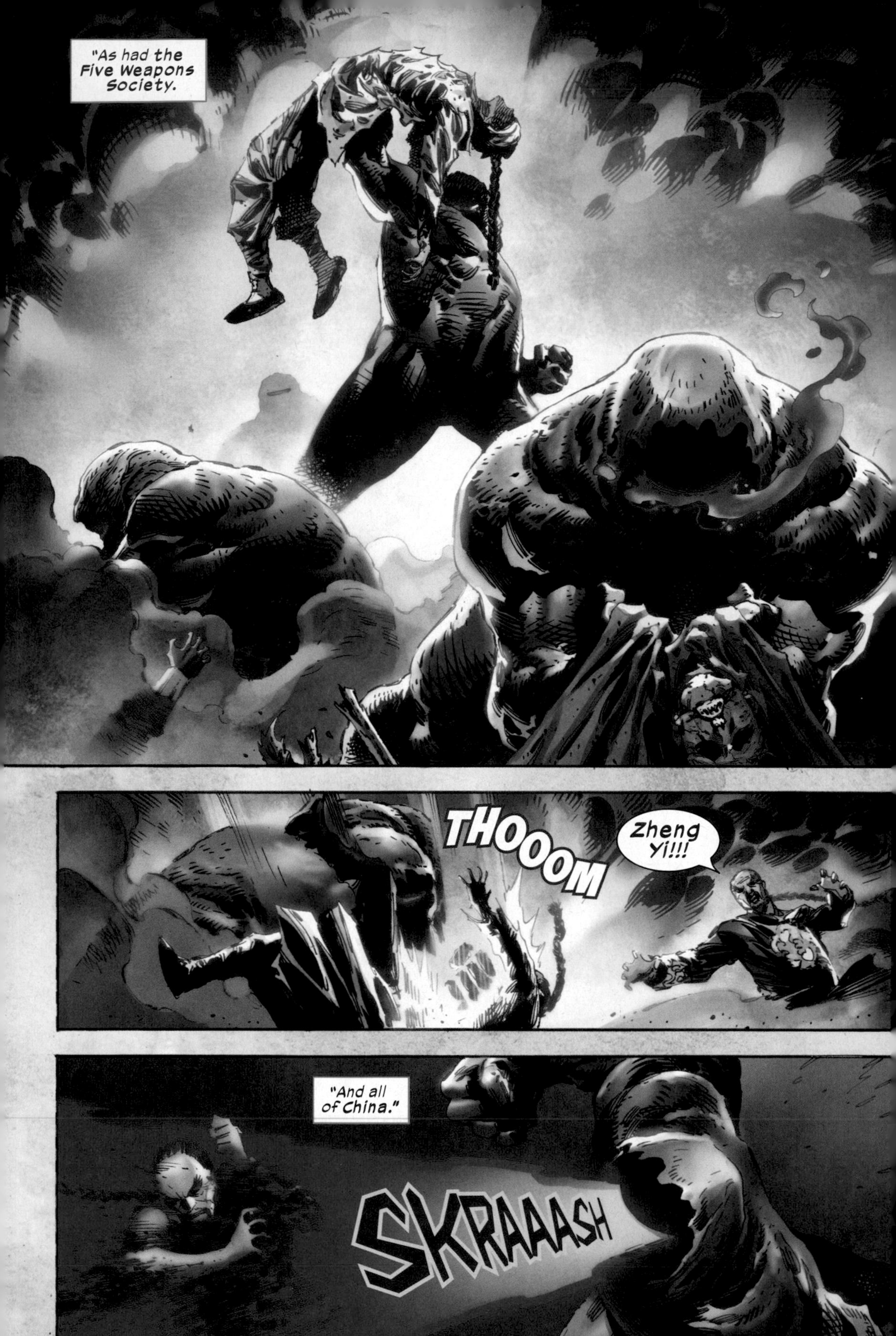
"As had the Five Weapons Society.
THOOOM
Zheng Yi!!!
"And all of China."
SKRAAASH

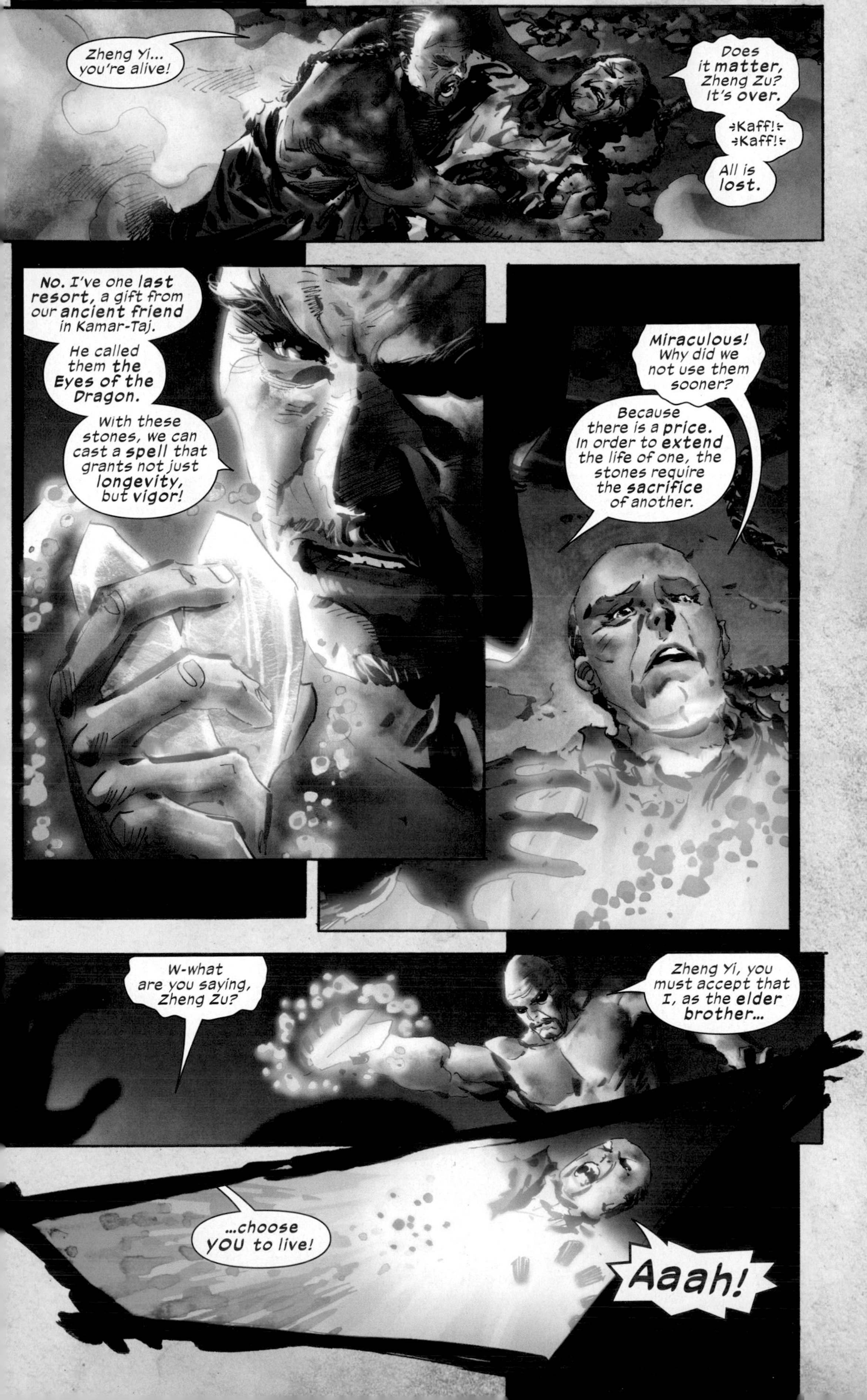
Zheng Yi... you're alive!
Does it matter, Zheng Zu? It's over.
Kaff! Kaff!
All is lost.
No. I've one last resort, a gift from our ancient friend in Kamar-Taj.
He called them the Eyes of the Dragon.
With these stones, we can cast a spell that grants not just longevity, but vigor!
Miraculous! Why did we not use them sooner?
Because there is a price. In order to extend the life of one, the stones require the sacrifice of another.
W-what are you saying, Zheng Zu?
Zheng Yi, you must accept that I, as the elder brother...
...choose YOU to live!
Aaah!

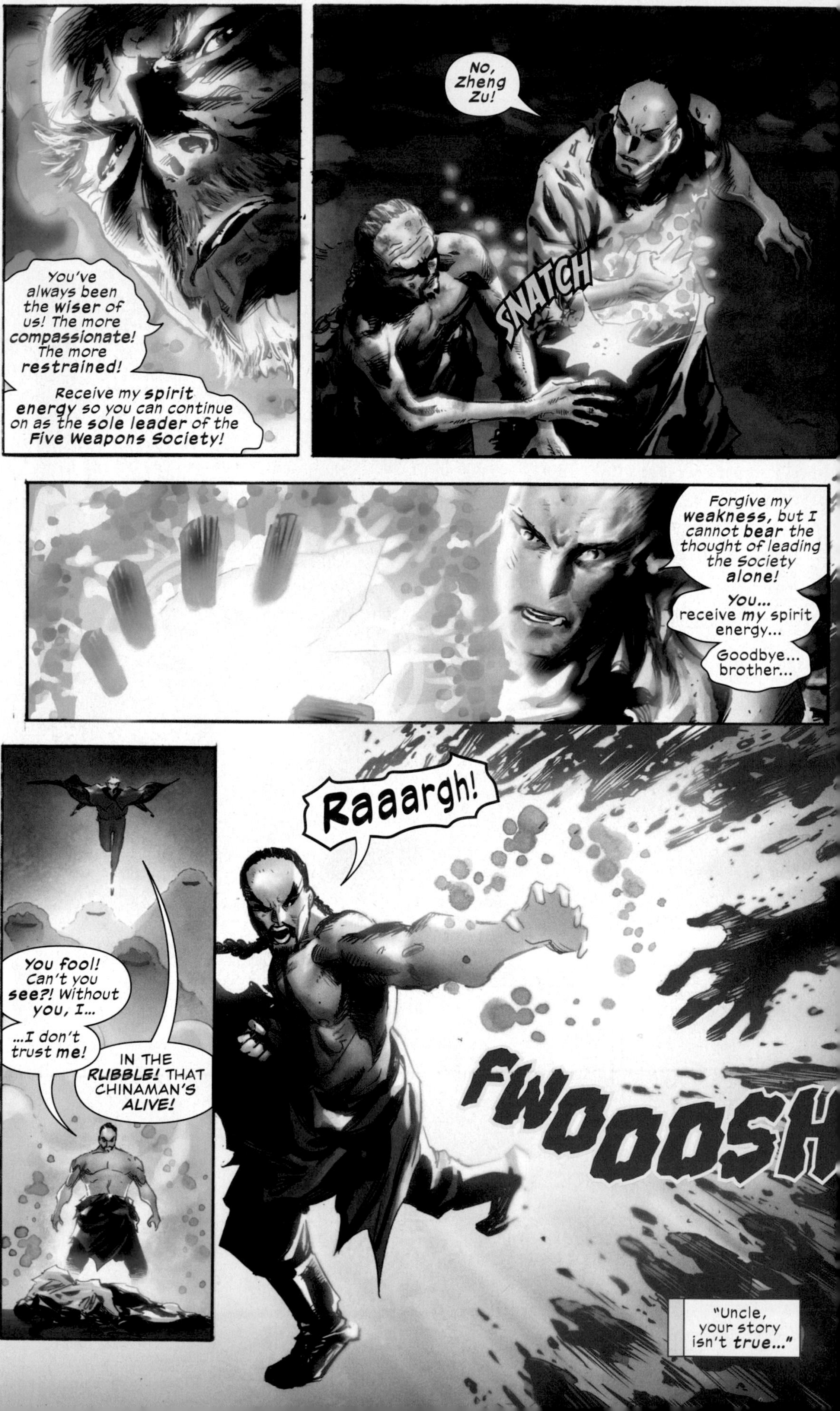
You've always been the wiser of us! The more compassionate! The more restrained!
Receive my spirit energy so you can continue on as the sole leader of the Five Weapons Society!
No, Zheng Zu!
SNATCH
Forgive my weakness, but I cannot bear the thought of leading the Society alone!
You... receive my spirit energy...
Goodbye... brother...
You fool! Can't you see?! Without you, I...
...I don't trust me!
IN THE RUBBLE! THAT CHINAMAN'S ALIVE!
Raaargh!
FWOOOSH
"Uncle, your story isn't true..."

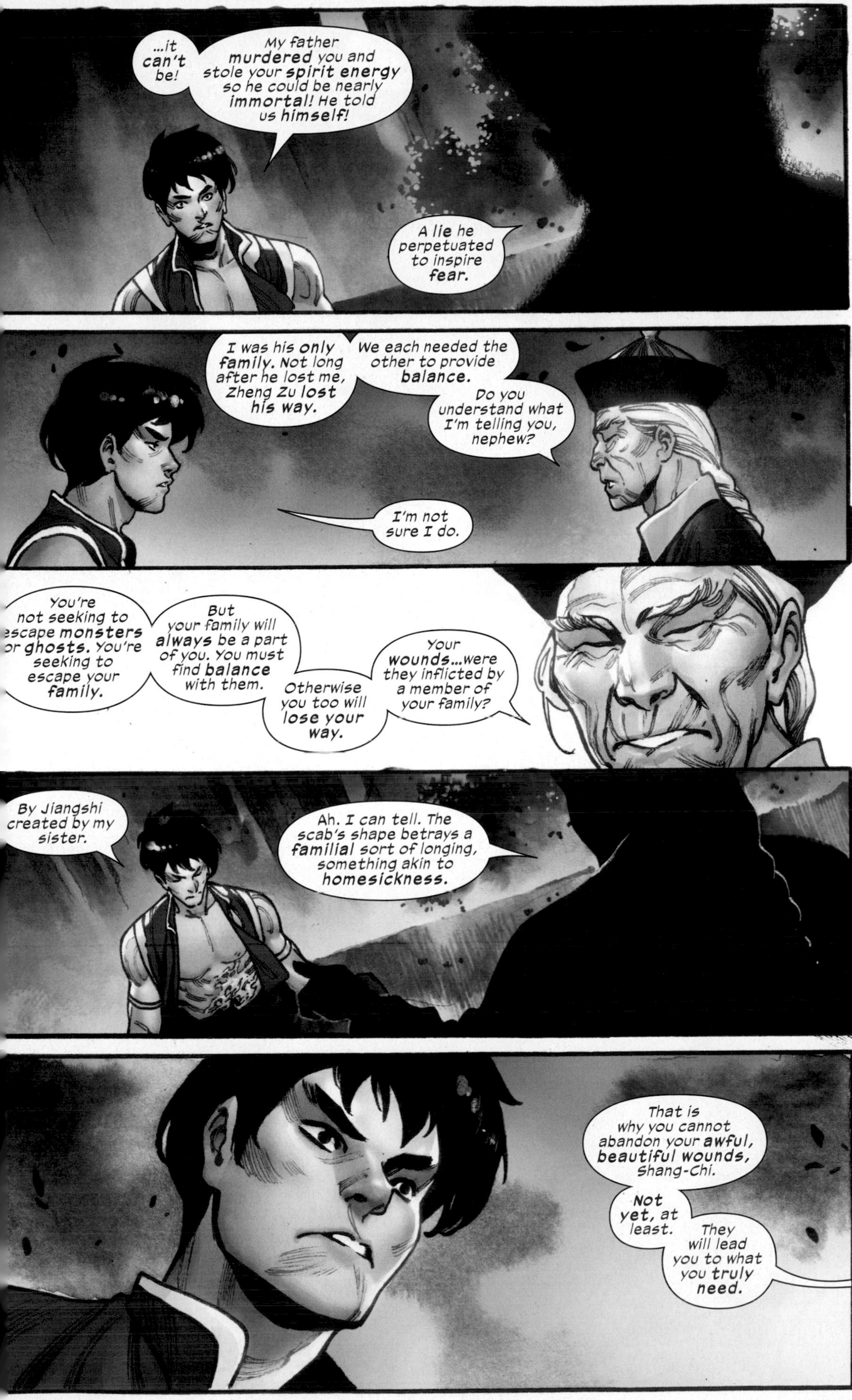

...it can't be!
My father murdered you and stole your spirit energy so he could be nearly immortal! He told us himself!
A lie he perpetuated to inspire fear.
I was his only family. Not long after he lost me, Zheng Zu lost his way.
We each needed the other to provide balance.
Do you understand what I'm telling you, nephew?
I'm not sure I do.
You're not seeking to escape monsters or ghosts. You're seeking to escape your family.
But your family will always be a part of you. You must find balance with them.
Otherwise you too will lose your way.
Your wounds...were they inflicted by a member of your family?
By Jiangshi created by my sister.
Ah. I can tell. The scab's shape betrays a familial sort of longing, something akin to homesickness.
That is why you cannot abandon your awful, beautiful wounds, Shang-Chi.
Not yet, at least.
They will lead you to what you truly need.

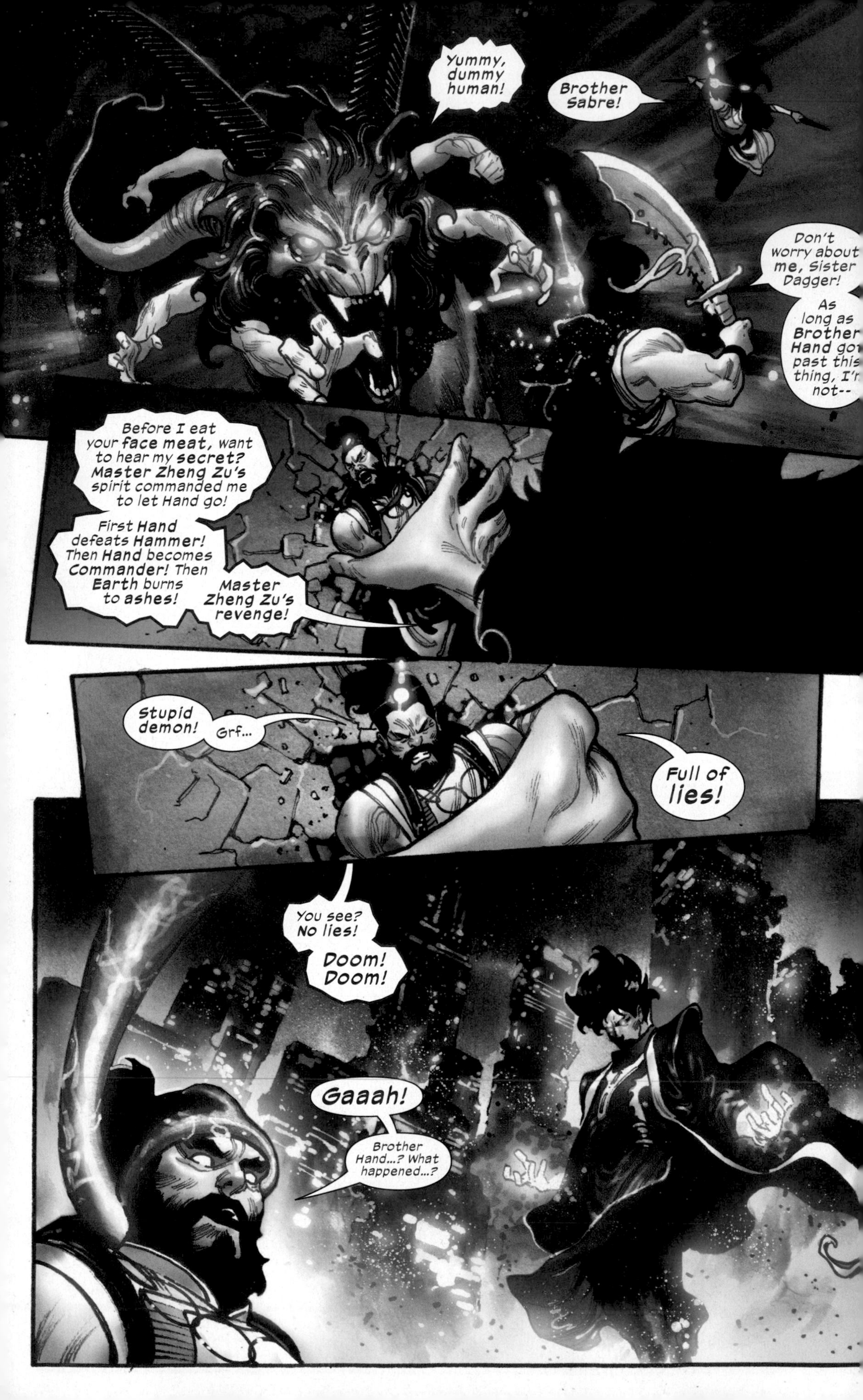
Yummy, dummy human!
Brother Sabre!
Don't worry about me, Sister Dagger!
As long as Brother Hand go past this thing, I'r not--
Before I eat your face meat, want to hear my secret? Master Zheng Zu's spirit commanded me to let Hand go!
First Hand defeats Hammer! Then Hand becomes Commander! Then Earth burns to ashes!
Master Zheng Zu's revenge!
Stupid demon!
Grf...
Full of lies!
You see? No lies!
Doom! Doom!
Gaaah!
Brother Hand...? What happened...?

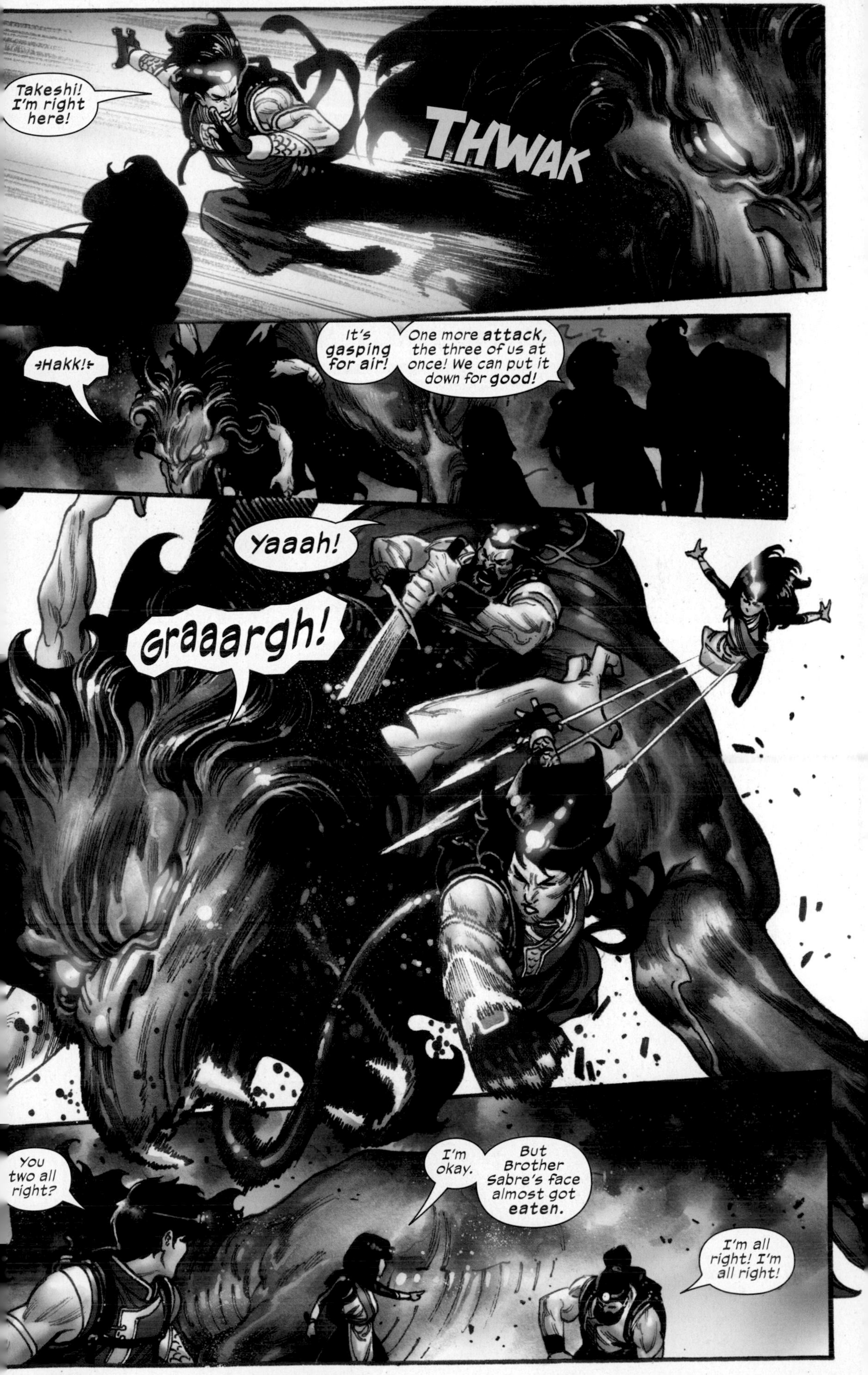
Takeshi! I'm right here!
THWAK
-Hakk!-
It's gasping for air!
One more attack, the three of us at once! We can put it down for good!
Yaaah!
Graaargh!
You two all right?
I'm okay.
But Brother Sabre's face almost got eaten.
I'm all right! I'm all right!

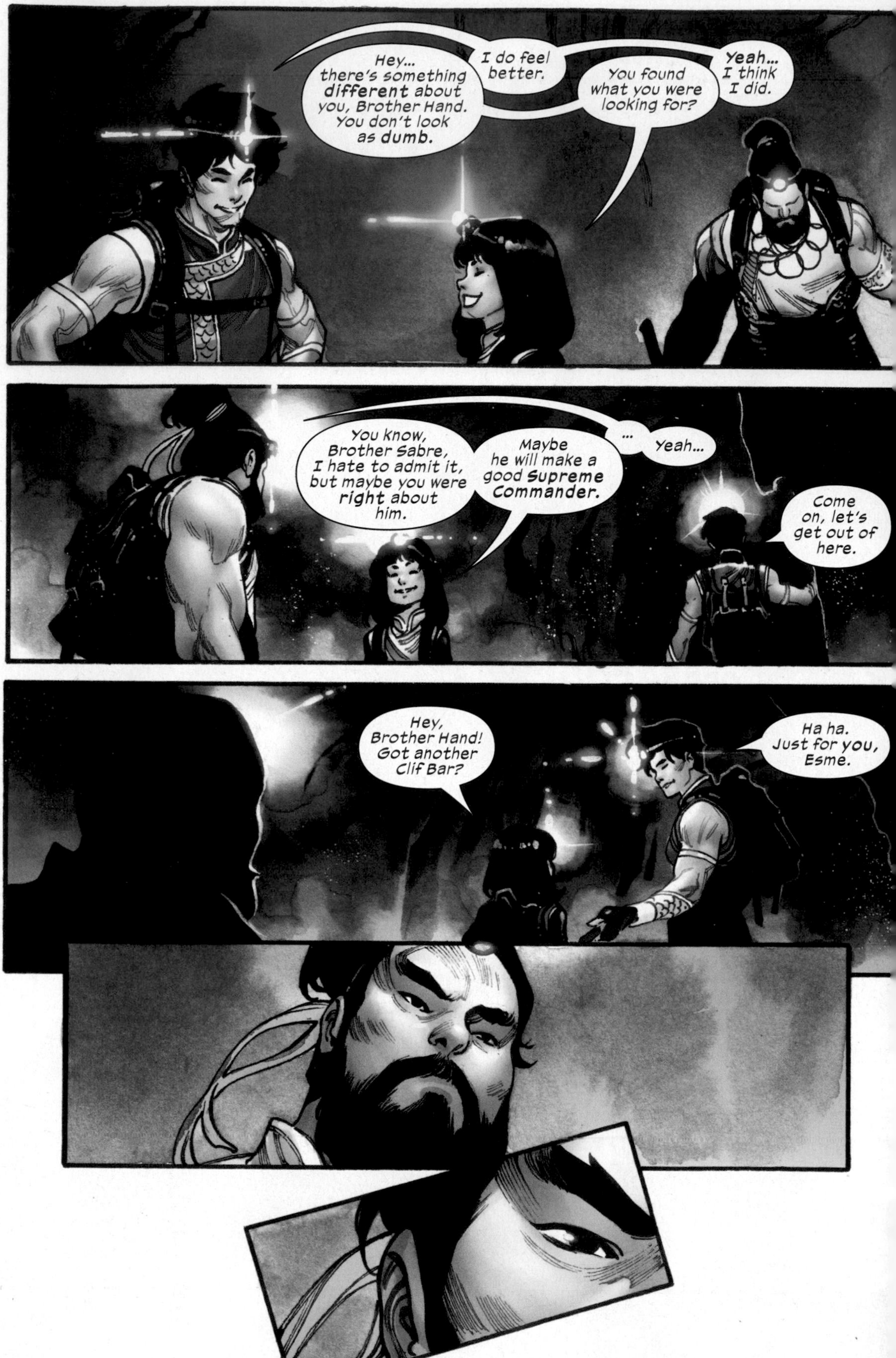
Hey... there's something different about you, Brother Hand. You don't look as dumb.
I do feel better.
You found what you were looking for?
Yeah... I think I did.
You know, Brother Sabre, I hate to admit it, but maybe you were right about him.
Maybe he will make a good Supreme Commander.
...
Yeah...
Come on, let's get out of here.
Hey, Brother Hand! Got another Clif Bar?
Ha ha. Just for you, Esme.

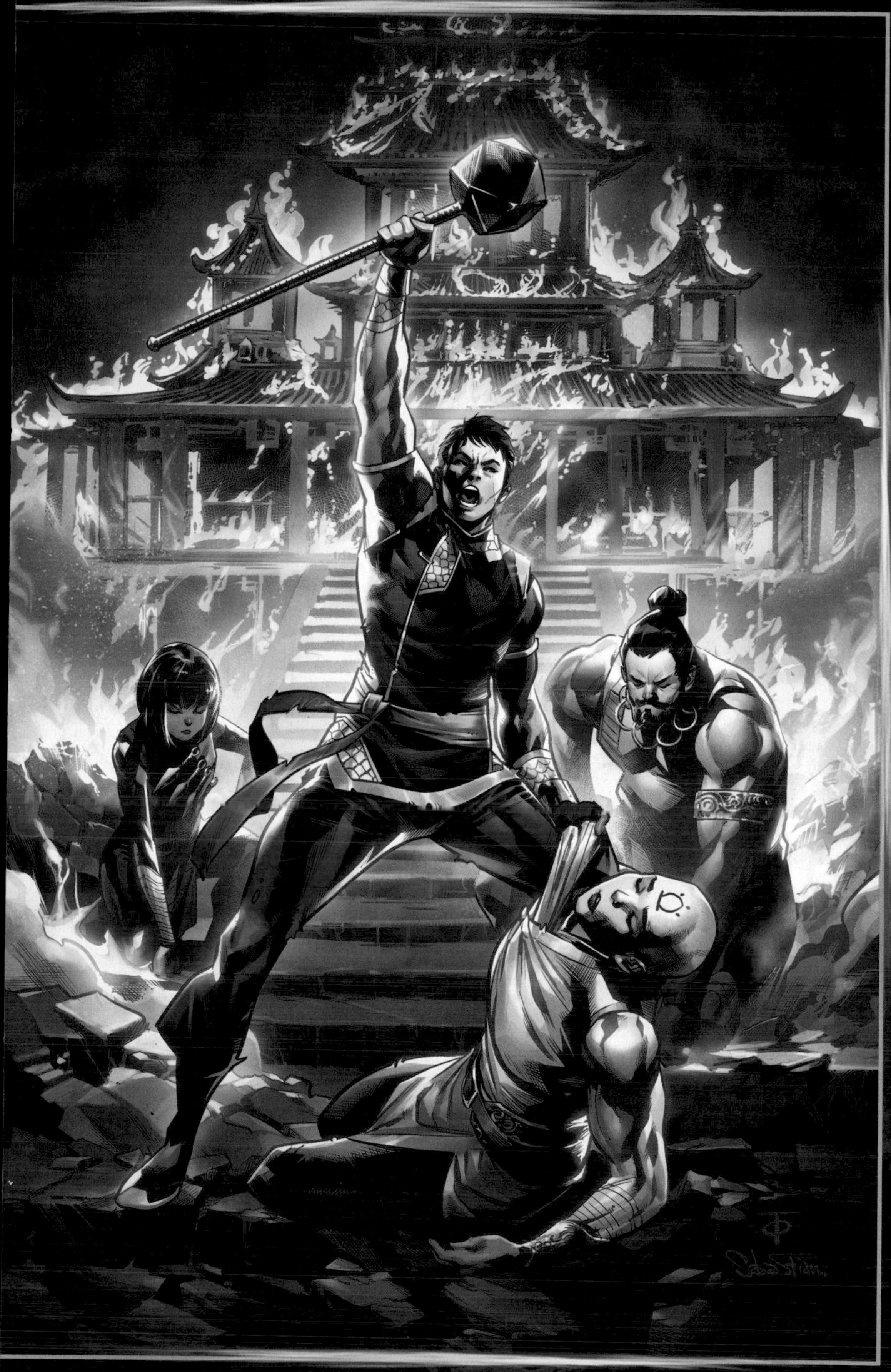

FIVE

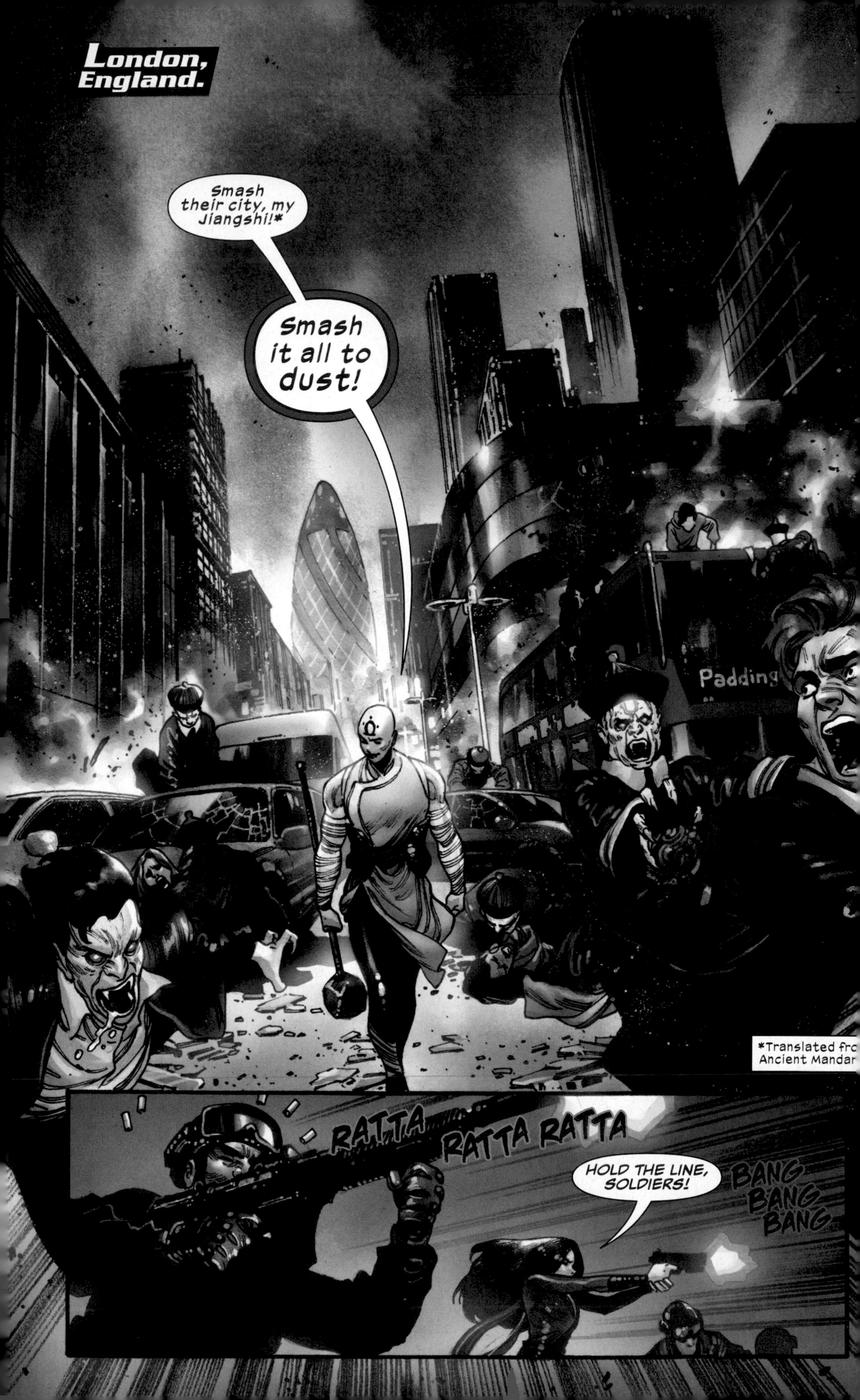
London, England.
Smash their city, my Jiangshi!*
Smash it all to dust!
Padding
*Translated fro
Ancient Mandar
RATTA RATTA RATTA
HOLD THE LINE, SOLDIERS!
BANG BANG BANG

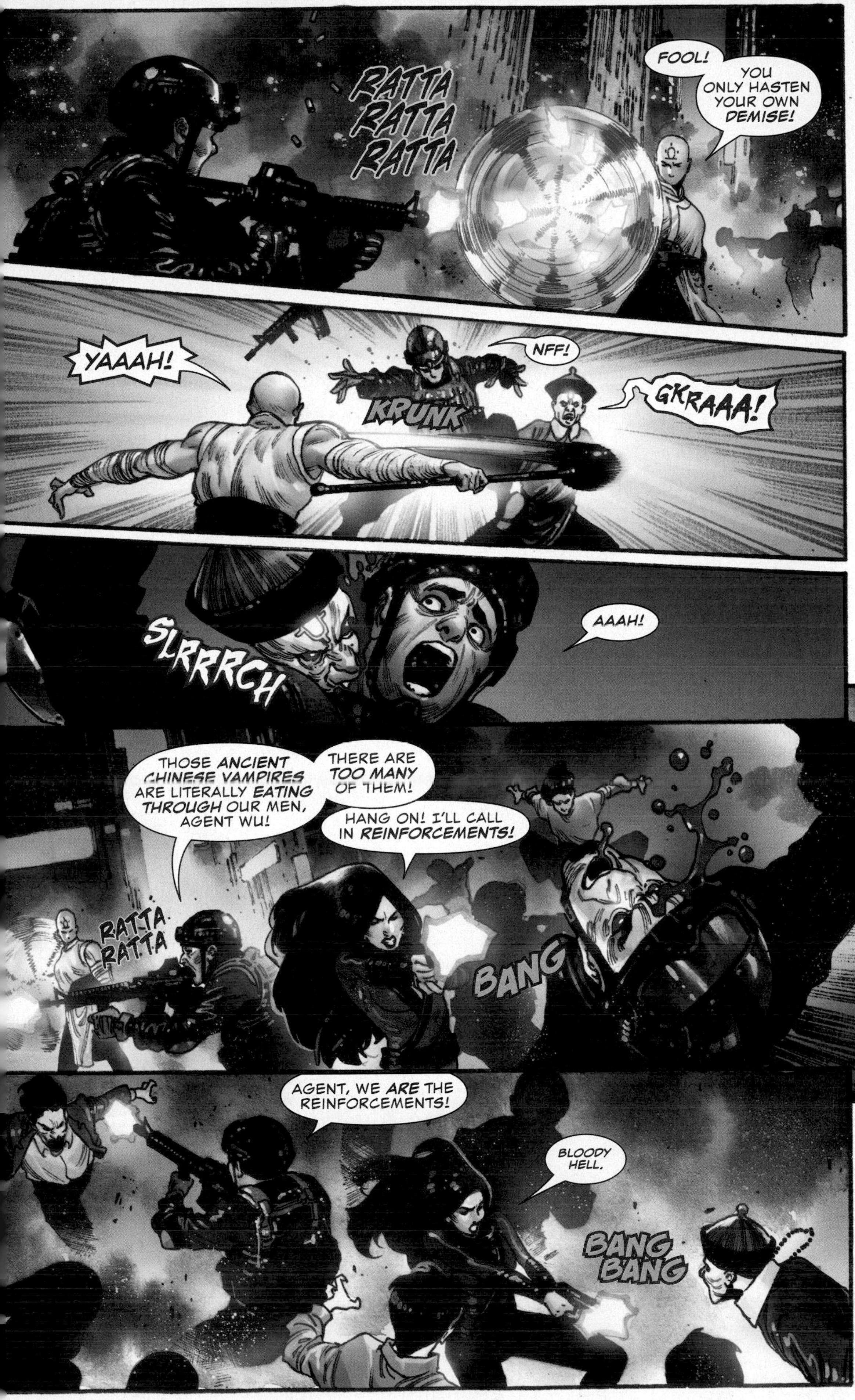
RATTA
RATTA
RATTA
FOOL!
YOU ONLY HASTEN YOUR OWN DEMISE!
YAAAH!
NFF!
KRUNK
GKRAAA!
SLRRRCH
AAAH!
THOSE ANCIENT CHINESE VAMPIRES ARE LITERALLY EATING THROUGH OUR MEN, AGENT WU!
THERE ARE TOO MANY OF THEM!
HANG ON! I'LL CALL IN REINFORCEMENTS!
RATTA
RATTA
BANG
AGENT, WE ARE THE REINFORCEMENTS!
BLOODY HELL.
BANG
BANG

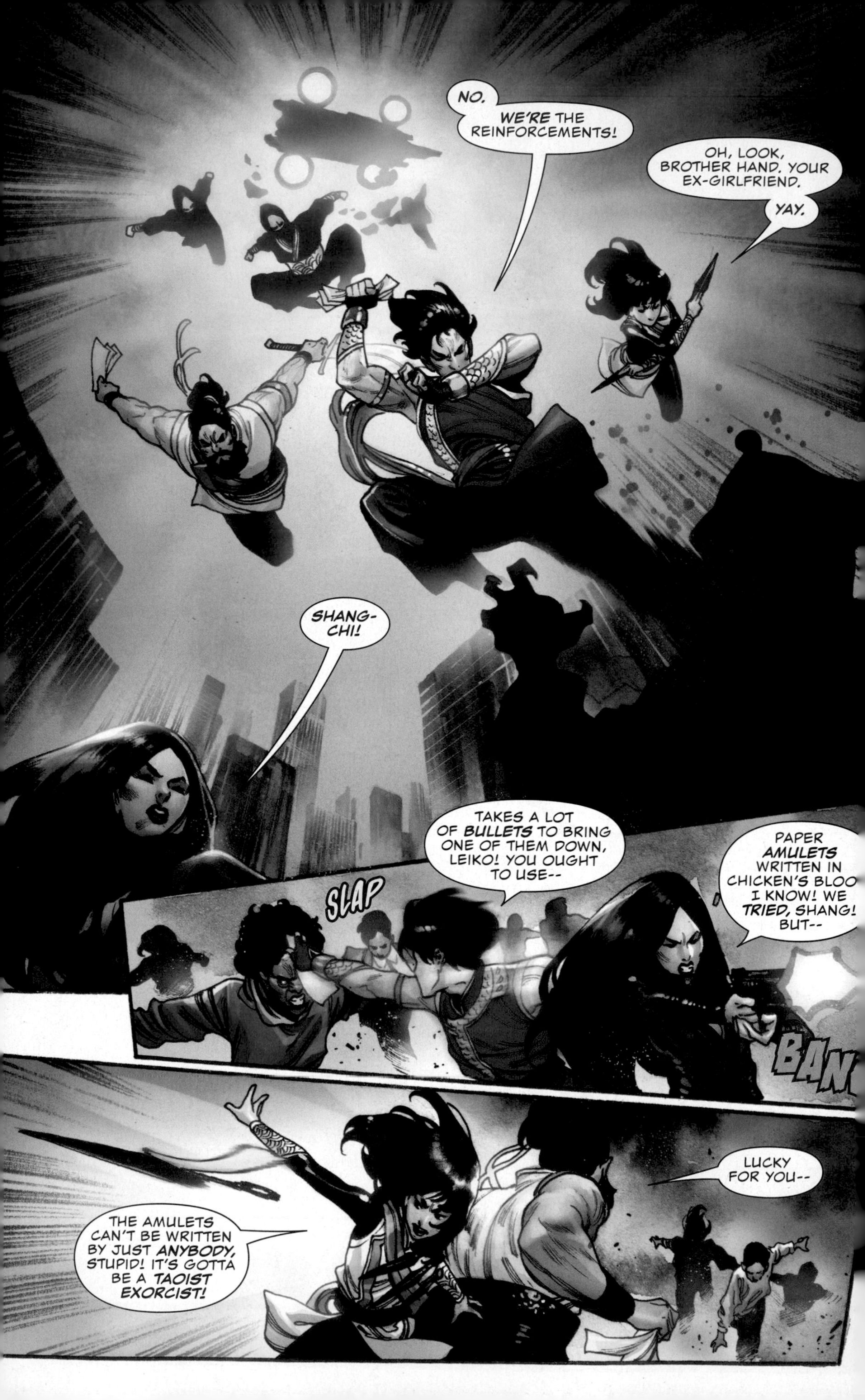
NO.
WE'RE THE REINFORCEMENTS!
OH, LOOK, BROTHER HAND. YOUR EX-GIRLFRIEND.
YAY.
SHANG-CHI!
TAKES A LOT OF BULLETS TO BRING ONE OF THEM DOWN, LEIKO! YOU OUGHT TO USE--
SLAP
PAPER AMULETS WRITTEN IN CHICKEN'S BLOO
I KNOW! WE TRIED, SHANG! BUT--
BAN
LUCKY FOR YOU--
THE AMULETS CAN'T BE WRITTEN BY JUST ANYBODY, STUPID! IT'S GOTTA BE A TAOIST EXORCIST!

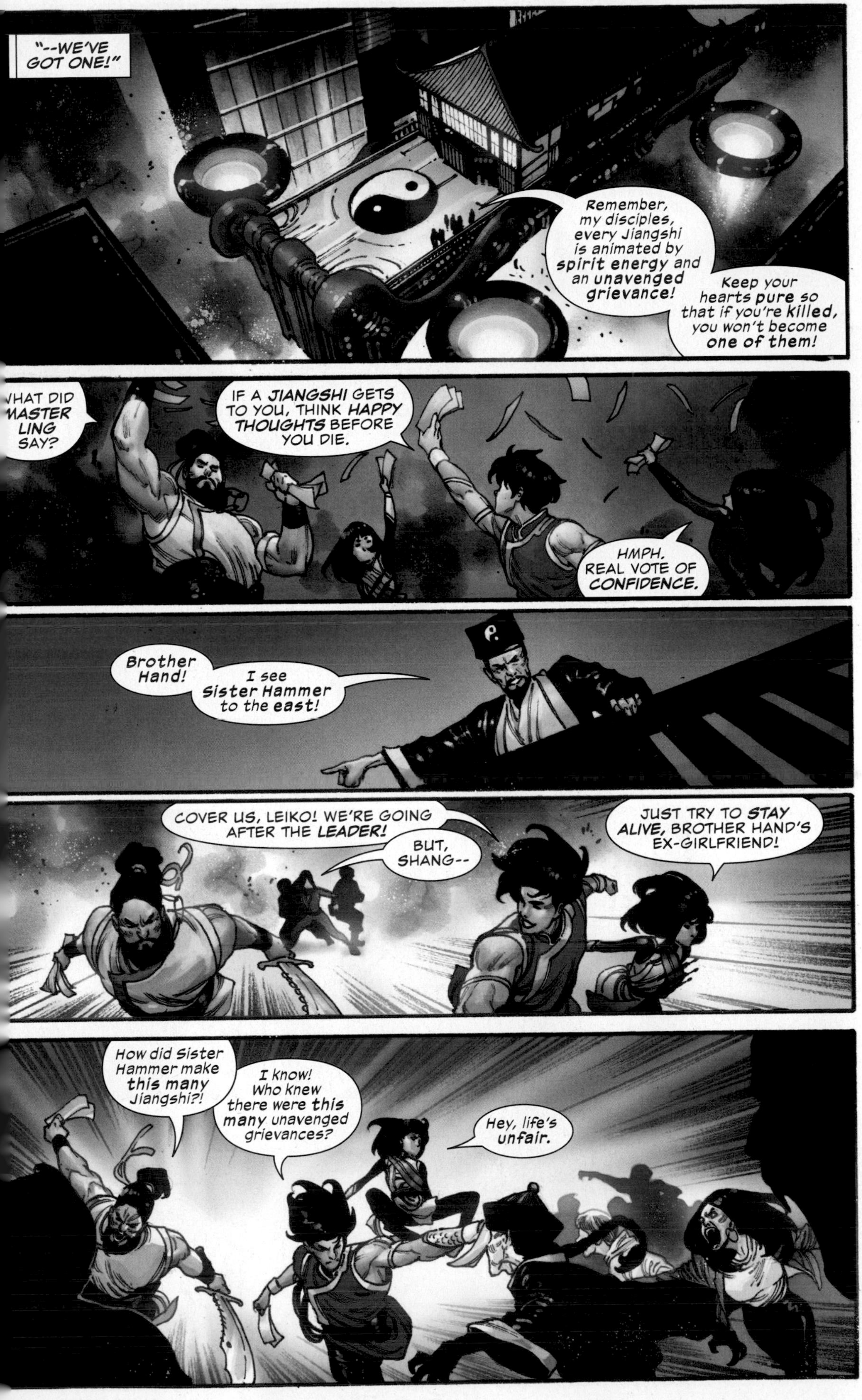
"--WE'VE GOT ONE!"
Remember, my disciples, every Jiangshi is animated by spirit energy and an unavenged grievance!
Keep your hearts pure so that if you're killed, you won't become one of them!
WHAT DID MASTER LING SAY?
IF A JIANGSHI GETS TO YOU, THINK HAPPY THOUGHTS BEFORE YOU DIE.
HMPH. REAL VOTE OF CONFIDENCE.
Brother Hand!
I see Sister Hammer to the east!
COVER US, LEIKO! WE'RE GOING AFTER THE LEADER!
BUT, SHANG--
JUST TRY TO STAY ALIVE, BROTHER HAND'S EX-GIRLFRIEND!
How did Sister Hammer make this many Jiangshi?!
I know! Who knew there were this many unavenged grievances?
Hey, life's unfair.

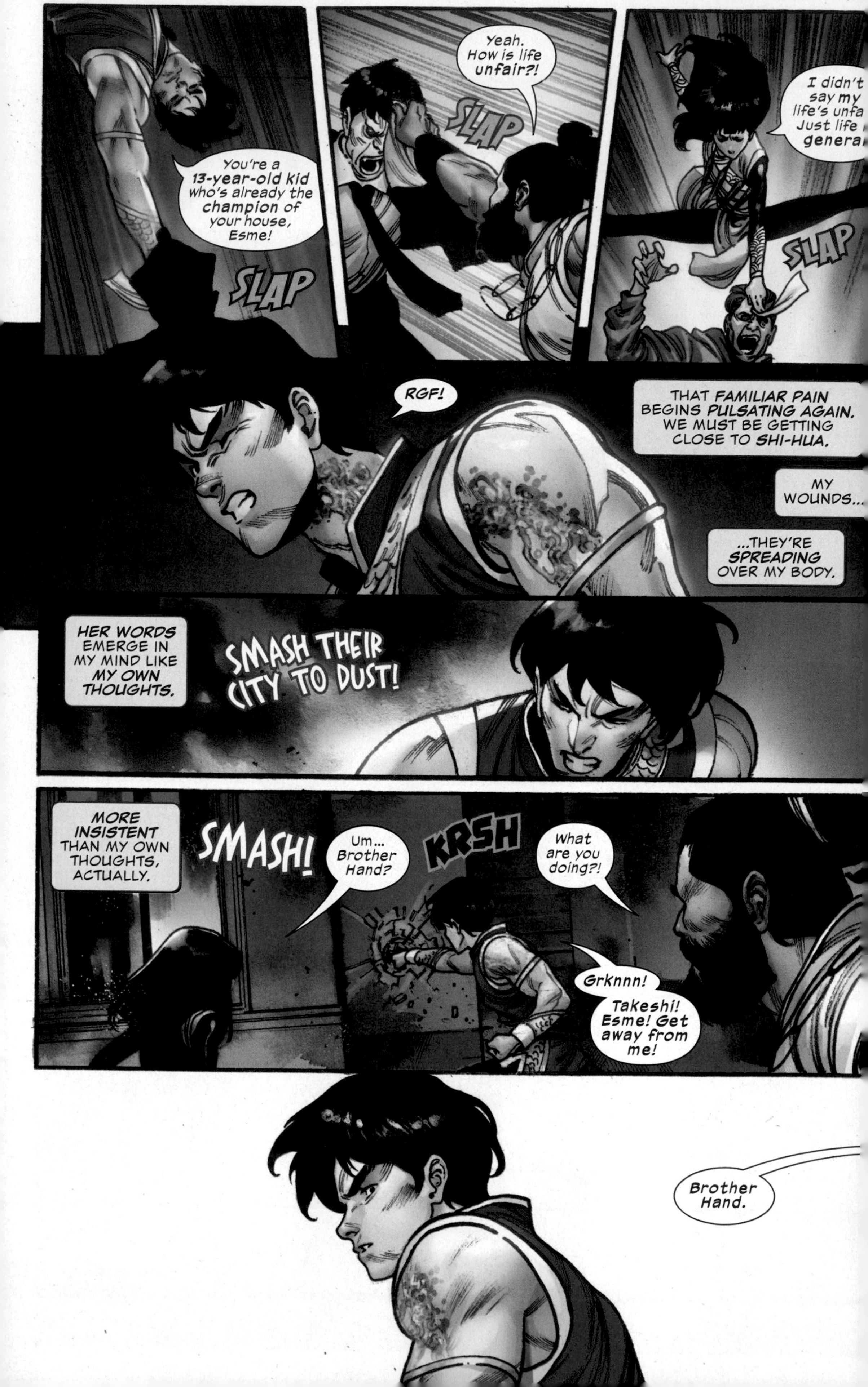
You're a 13-year-old kid who's already the champion of your house, Esme!
SLAP
Yeah. How is life unfair?!
SLAP
I didn't say my life's unfa Just life genera
SLAP
RGF!
THAT FAMILIAR PAIN BEGINS PULSATING AGAIN. WE MUST BE GETTING CLOSE TO SHI-HUA.
MY WOUNDS...
...THEY'RE SPREADING OVER MY BODY.
HER WORDS EMERGE IN MY MIND LIKE MY OWN THOUGHTS.
SMASH THEIR CITY TO DUST!
MORE INSISTENT THAN MY OWN THOUGHTS, ACTUALLY.
SMASH!
Um... Brother Hand?
KRSH
What are you doing?!
Grknnn!
Takeshi! Esme! Get away from me!
Brother Hand.

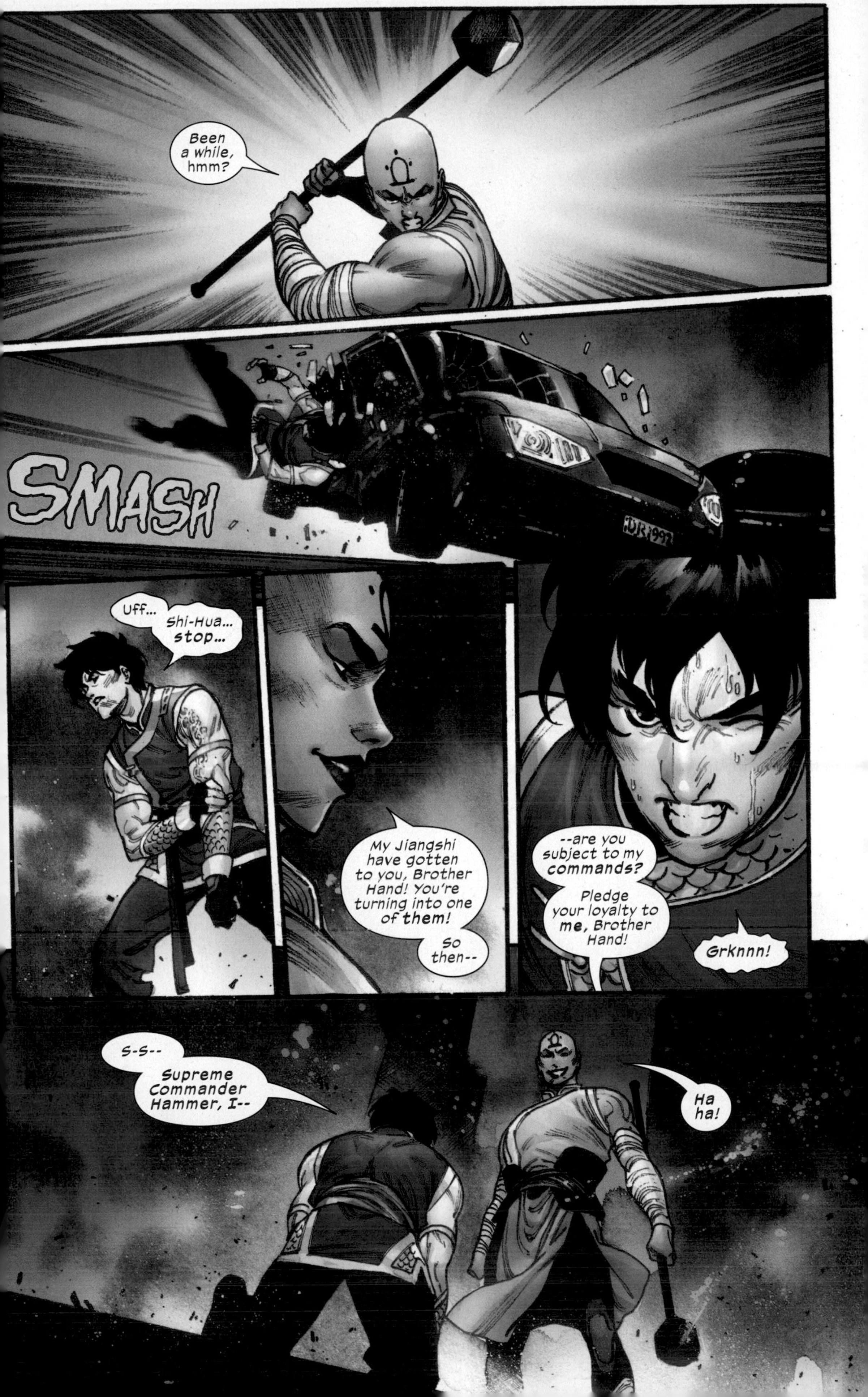

Been a while, hmm?
SMASH
Uff... Shi-Hua... stop...
My Jiangshi have gotten to you, Brother Hand! You're turning into one of them!
So then--
--are you subject to my commands?
Pledge your loyalty to me, Brother Hand!
Grknnn!
S-S--
Supreme Commander Hammer, I--
Ha ha!

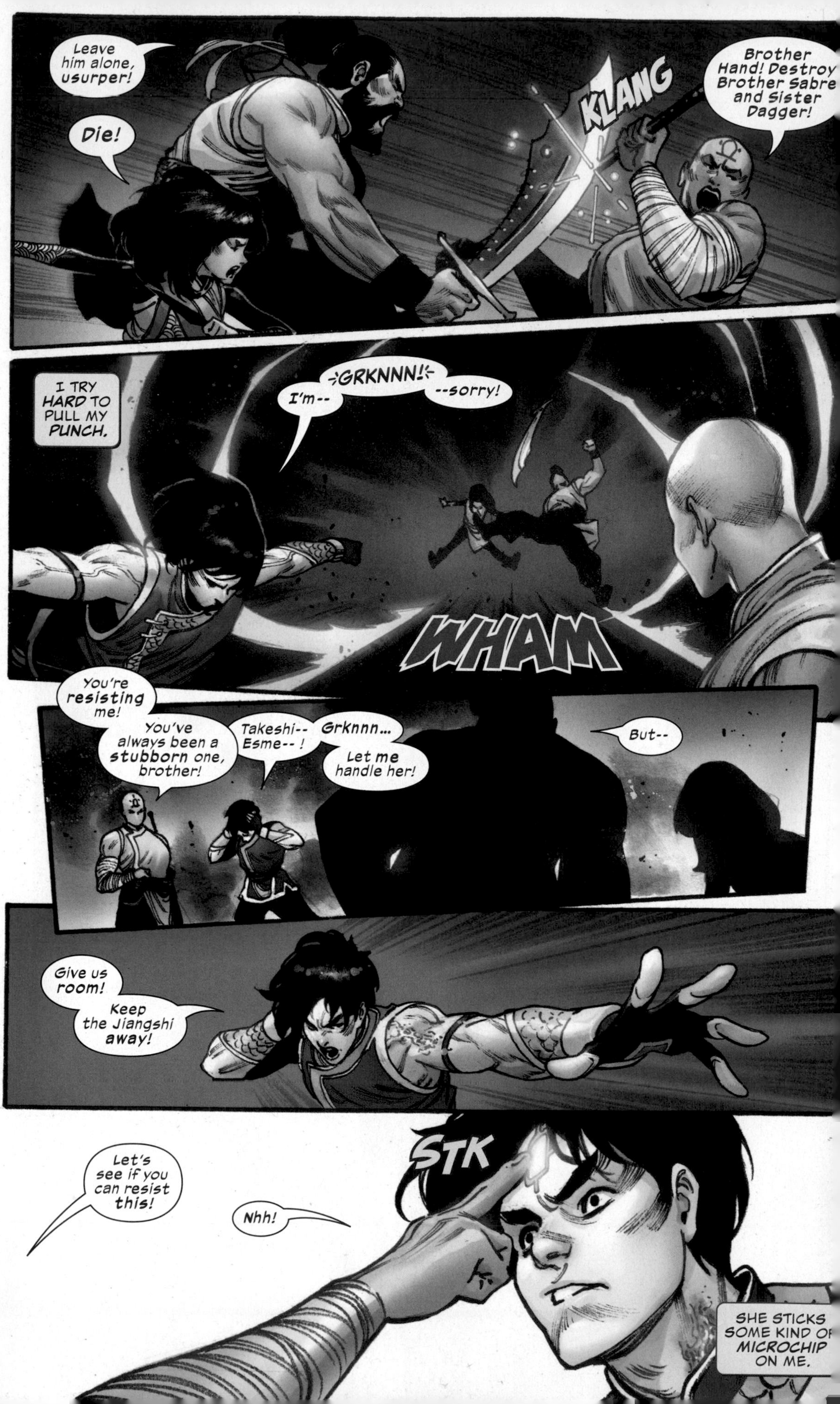
Leave him alone, usurper!
Die!
KLANG
Brother Hand! Destroy Brother Sabre and Sister Dagger!
I TRY HARD TO PULL MY PUNCH.
I'm--
GRKNNN!
--sorry!
WHAM
You're resisting me!
You've always been a stubborn one, brother!
Takeshi-- Esme-- !
Grknnn... Let me handle her!
But--
Give us room!
Keep the Jiangshi away!
STK
Let's see if you can resist this!
Nhh!
SHE STICKS SOME KIND OF MICROCHIP ON ME.

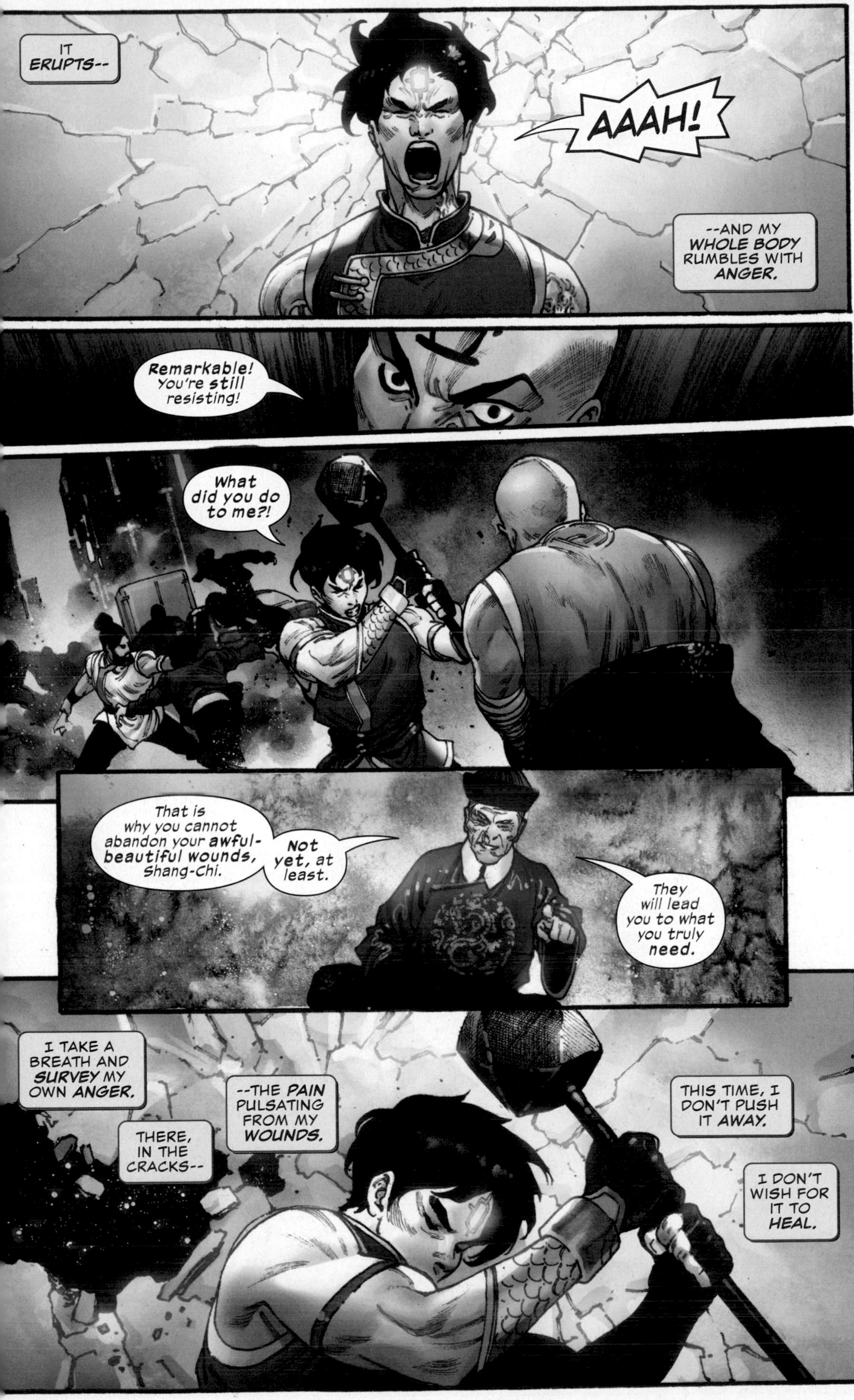
IT ERUPTS--
AAAH!
--AND MY WHOLE BODY RUMBLES WITH ANGER.
Remarkable! You're still resisting!
What did you do to me?!
That is why you cannot abandon your awful-beautiful wounds, Shang-Chi.
Not yet, at least.
They will lead you to what you truly need.
I TAKE A BREATH AND SURVEY MY OWN ANGER.
THERE, IN THE CRACKS--
--THE PAIN PULSATING FROM MY WOUNDS.
THIS TIME, I DON'T PUSH IT AWAY.
I DON'T WISH FOR IT TO HEAL.

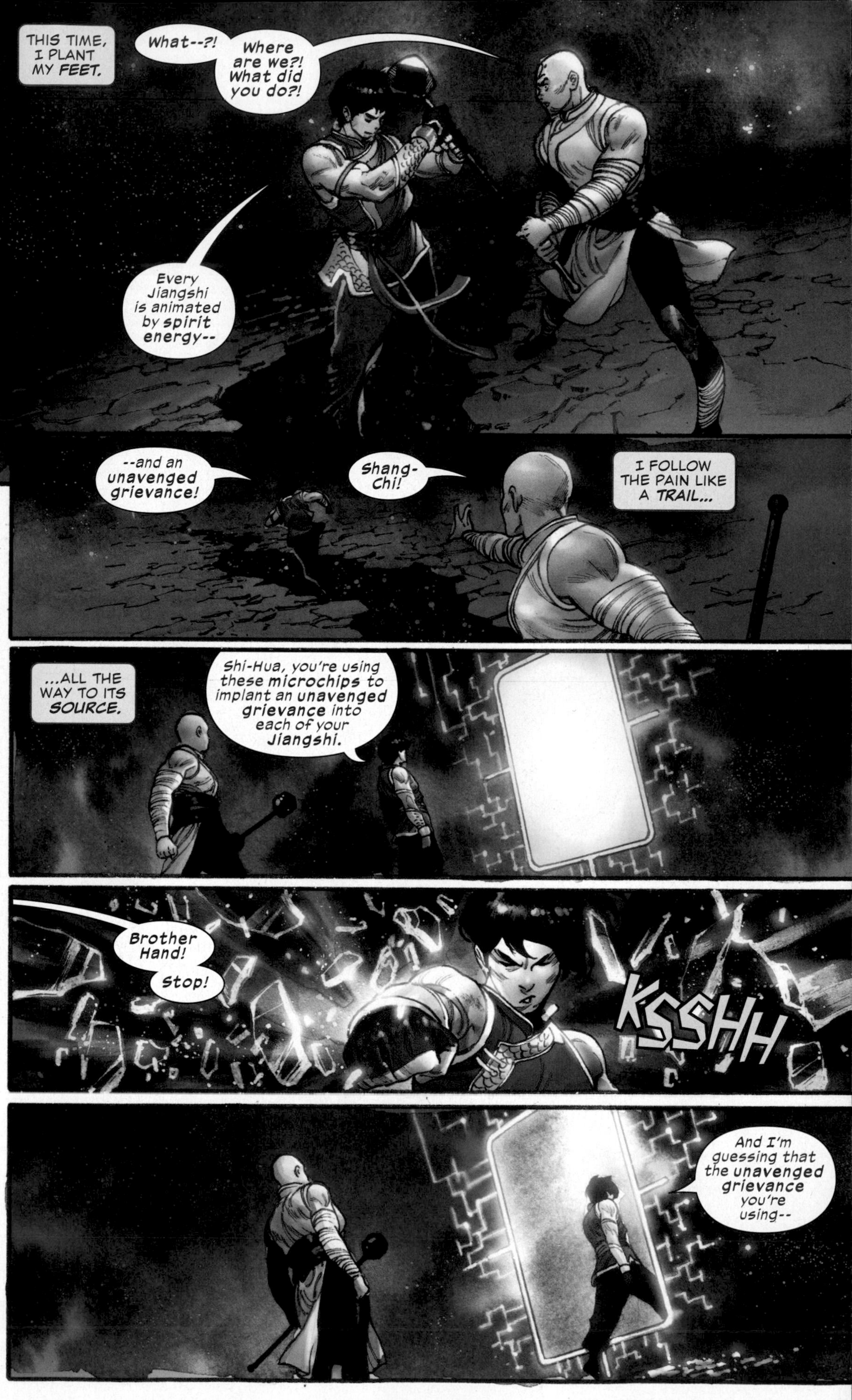
THIS TIME, I PLANT MY FEET.
What--?!
Where are we?! What did you do?!
Every Jiangshi is animated by spirit energy--
--and an unavenged grievance!
Shang-Chi!
I FOLLOW THE PAIN LIKE A TRAIL...
...ALL THE WAY TO ITS SOURCE.
Shi-Hua, you're using these microchips to implant an unavenged grievance into each of your Jiangshi.
Brother Hand!
Stop!
KSSHH
And I'm guessing that the unavenged grievance you're using--

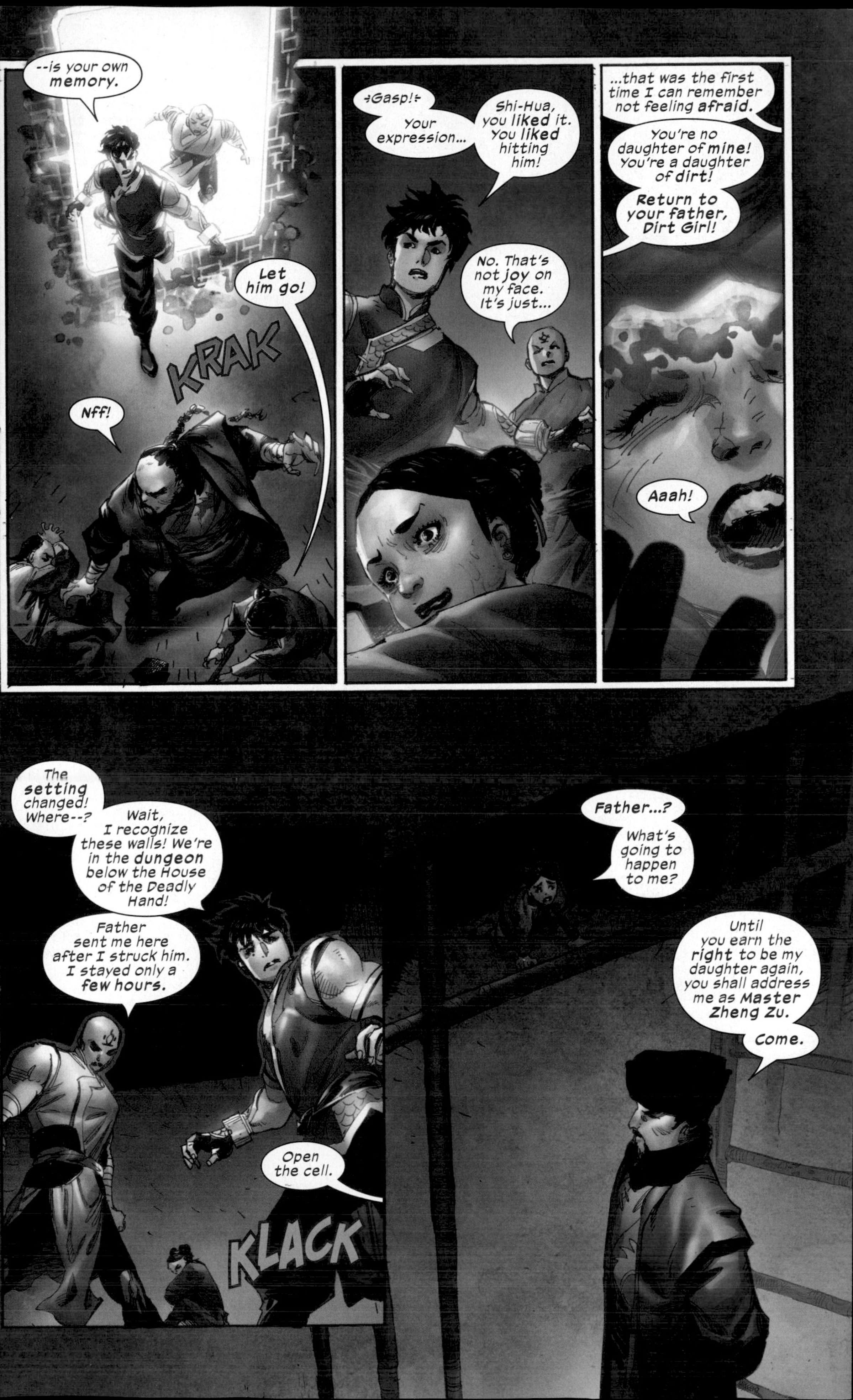

--is your own memory.
Let him go!
KRAK
Nff!
⸗Gasp!⸗
Your expression...
Shi-Hua, you liked it. You liked hitting him!
No. That's not joy on my face. It's just...
...that was the first time I can remember not feeling afraid.
You're no daughter of mine! You're a daughter of dirt!
Return to your father, Dirt Girl!
Aaah!
The setting changed! Where--?
Wait, I recognize these walls! We're in the dungeon below the House of the Deadly Hand!
Father sent me here after I struck him. I stayed only a few hours.
Open the cell.
KLACK
Father...?
What's going to happen to me?
Until you earn the right to be my daughter again, you shall address me as Master Zheng Zu.
Come.

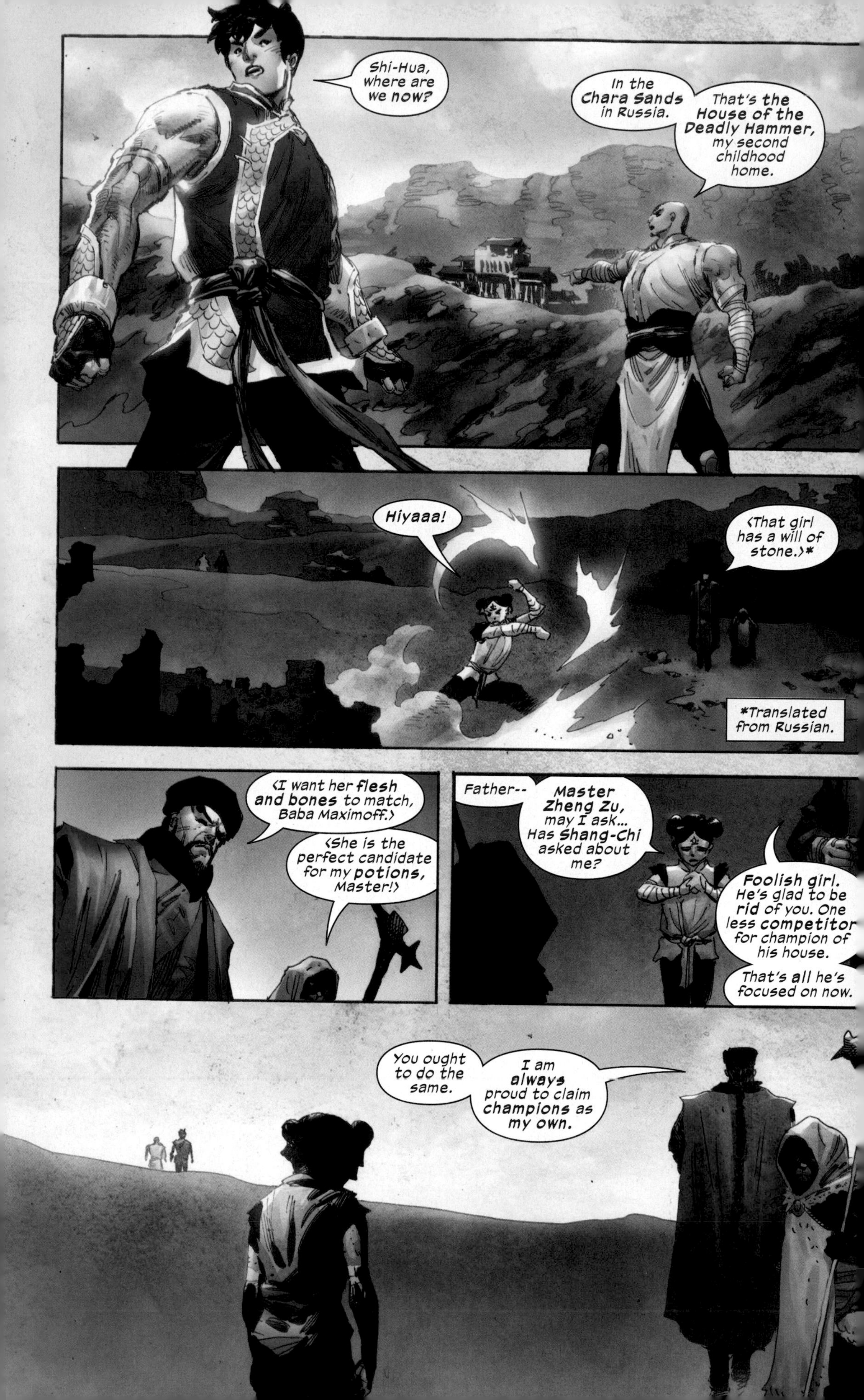
Shi-Hua, where are we now?
In the Chara Sands in Russia.
That's the House of the Deadly Hammer, my second childhood home.
Hiyaaa!
‹That girl has a will of stone.›*
*Translated from Russian.
‹I want her flesh and bones to match, Baba Maximoff.›
‹She is the perfect candidate for my potions, Master!›
Father--
Master Zheng Zu, may I ask... Has Shang-Chi asked about me?
Foolish girl. He's glad to be rid of you. One less competitor for champion of his house.
That's all he's focused on now.
You ought to do the same.
I am always proud to claim champions as my own.

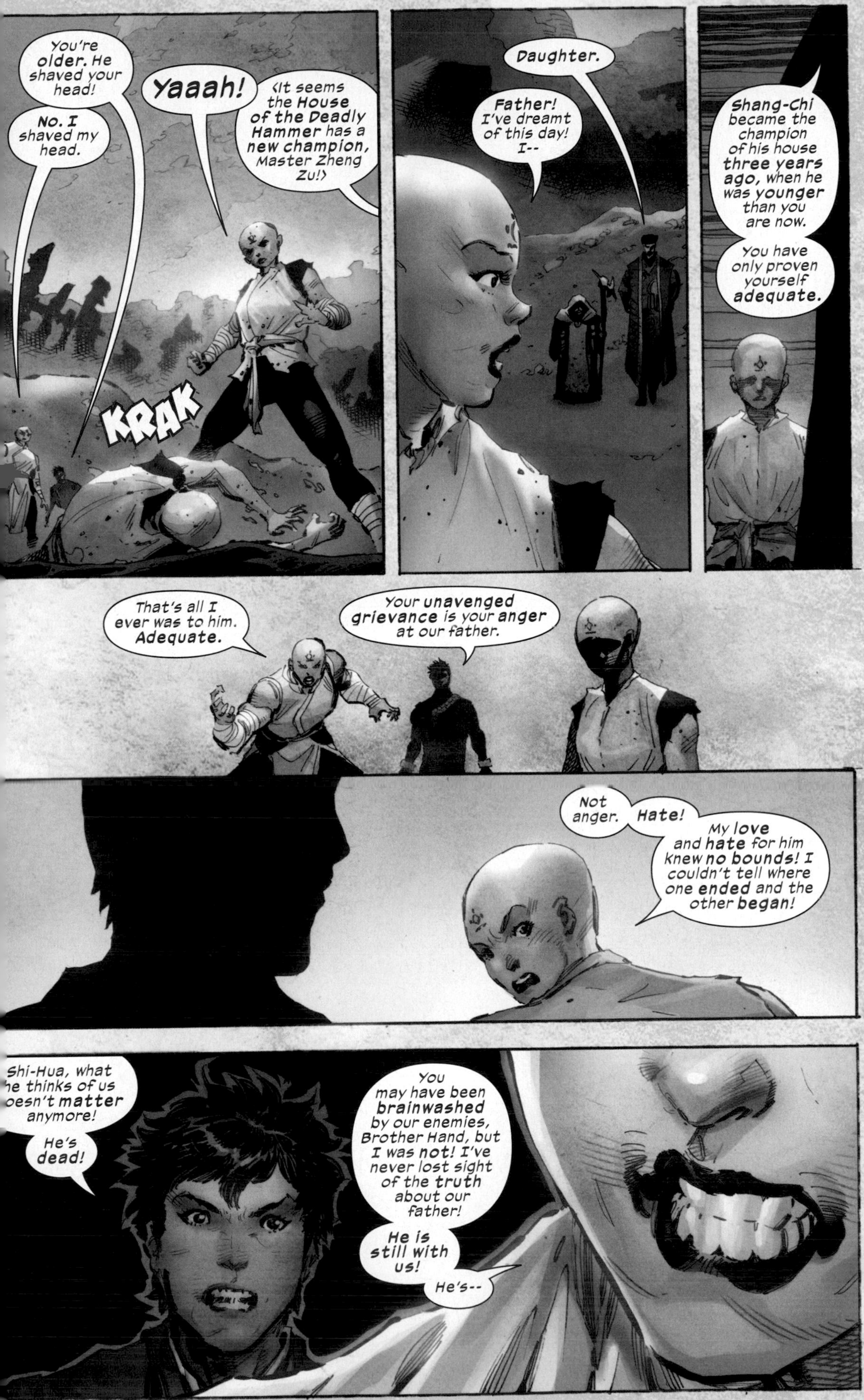
You're older. He shaved your head!
No. I shaved my head.
Yaaah!
KRAK
<It seems the House of the Deadly Hammer has a new champion, Master Zheng Zu!>
Daughter.
Father! I've dreamt of this day! I--
Shang-Chi became the champion of his house three years ago, when he was younger than you are now.
You have only proven yourself adequate.
That's all I ever was to him. Adequate.
Your unavenged grievance is your anger at our father.
Not anger.
Hate!
My love and hate for him knew no bounds! I couldn't tell where one ended and the other began!
Shi-Hua, what he thinks of us doesn't matter anymore!
He's dead!
You may have been brainwashed by our enemies, Brother Hand, but I was not! I've never lost sight of the truth about our father!
He is still with us!
He's--

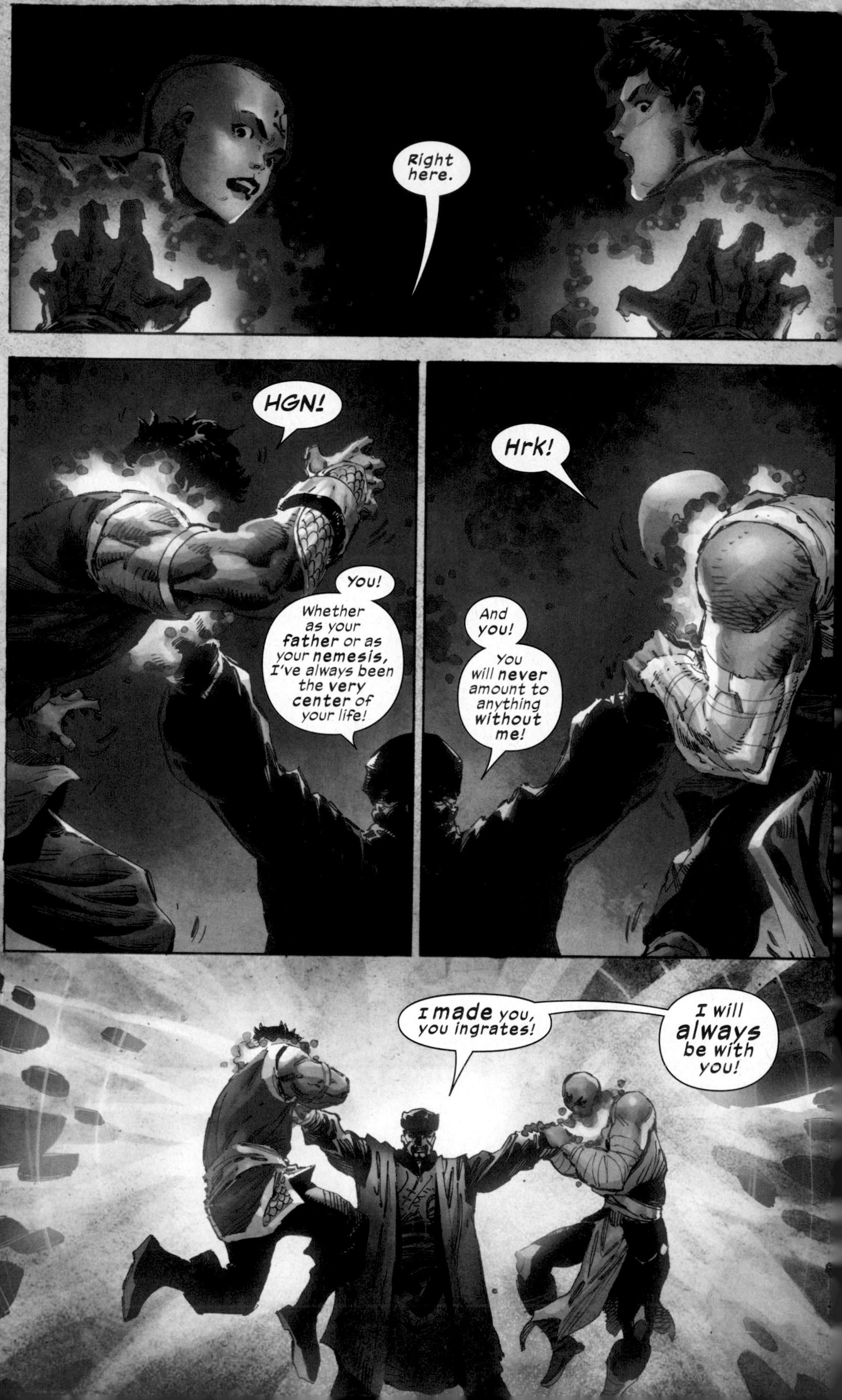

Right here.
HGN!
You!
Whether as your father or as your nemesis, I've always been the very center of your life!
Hrk!
And you!
You will never amount to anything without me!
I made you, you ingrates!
I will always be with you!

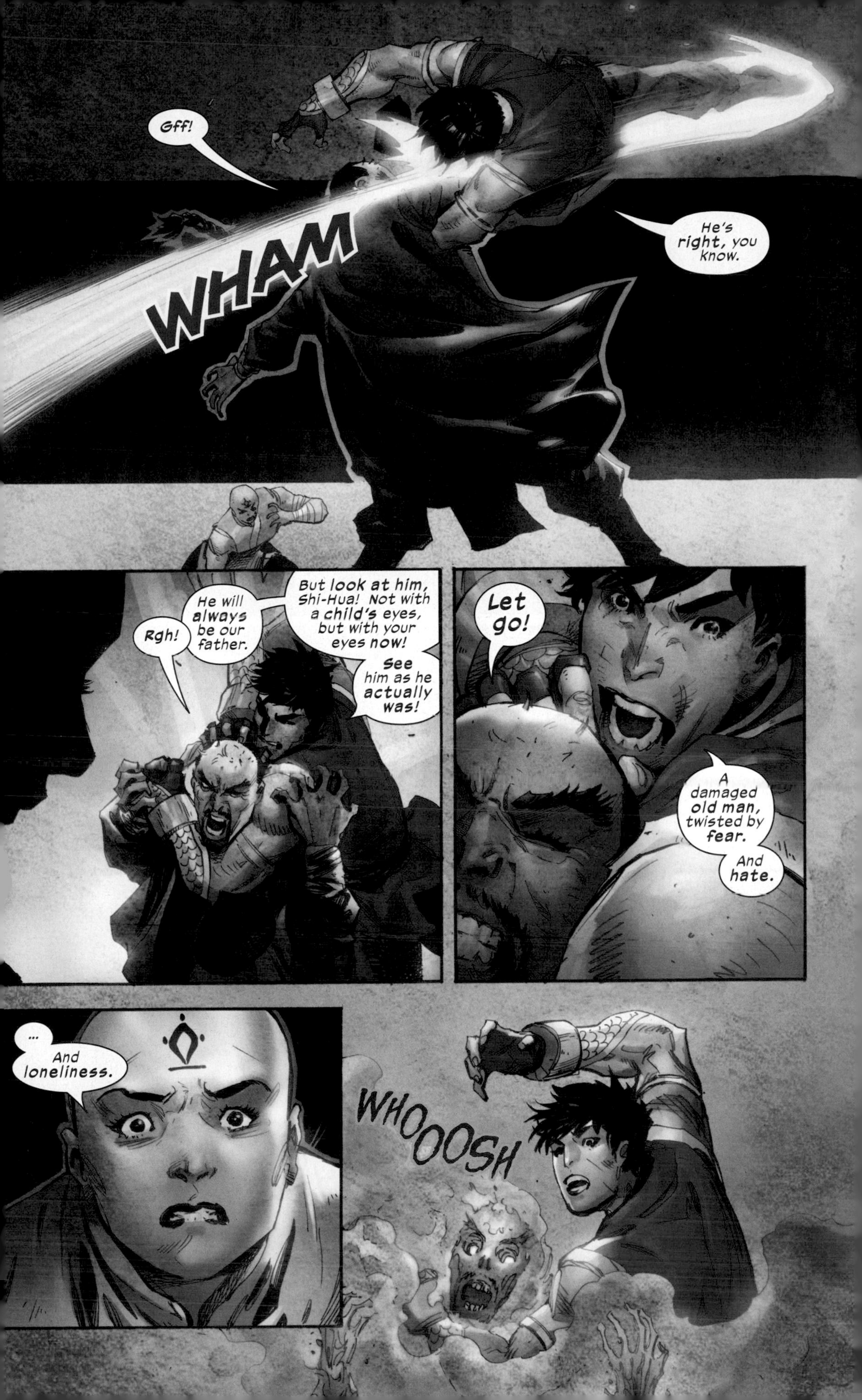
Gff!
WHAM
He's right, you know.
Rgh!
He will always be our father.
But look at him, Shi-Hua! Not with a child's eyes, but with your eyes now!
See him as he actually was!
Let go!
A damaged old man, twisted by fear.
And hate.
... And loneliness.
WHOOOSH

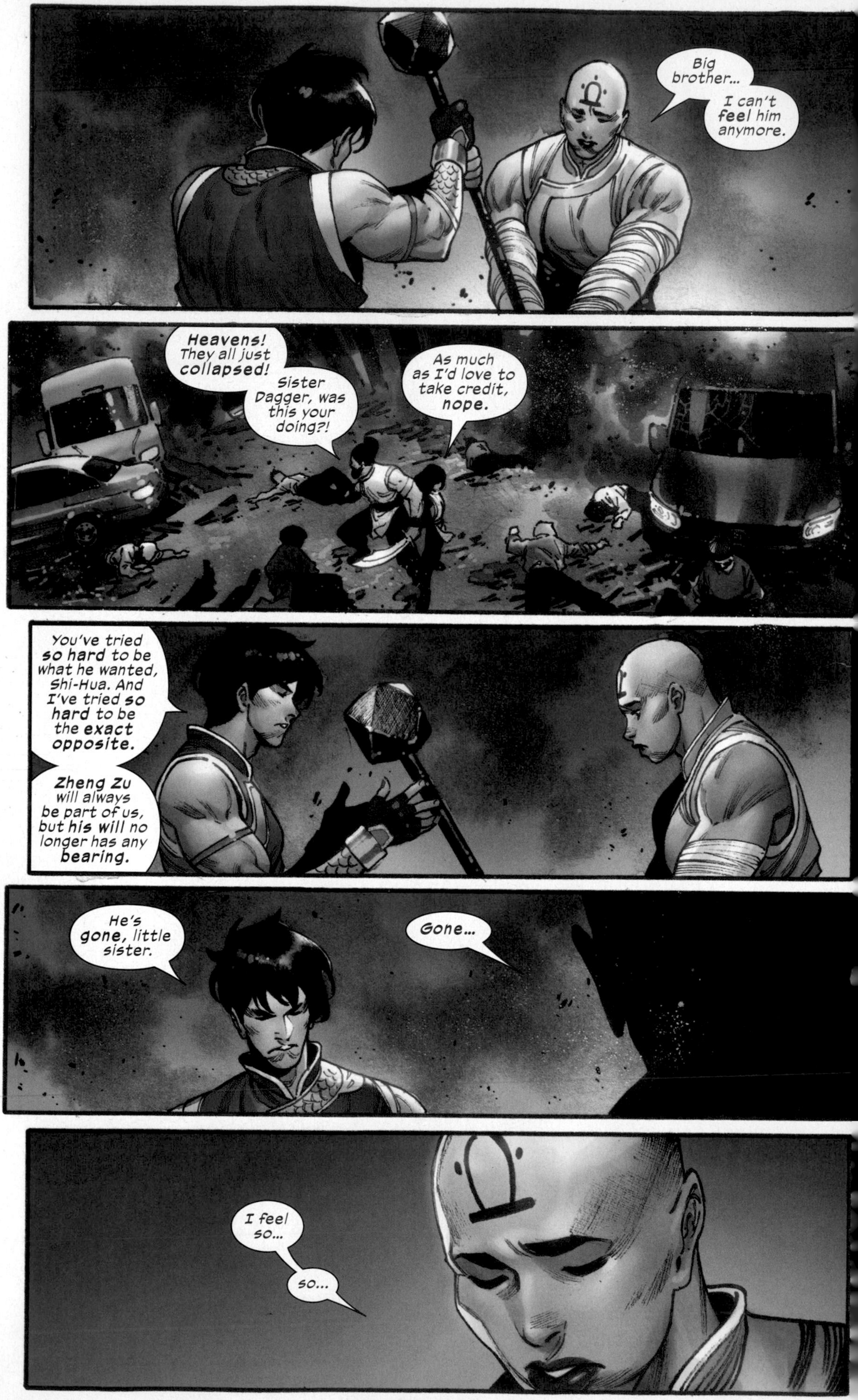
Big brother...
I can't feel him anymore.
Heavens! They all just collapsed!
Sister Dagger, was this your doing?!
As much as I'd love to take credit, nope.
You've tried so hard to be what he wanted, Shi-Hua. And I've tried so hard to be the exact opposite.
Zheng Zu will always be part of us, but his will no longer has any bearing.
He's gone, little sister.
Gone...
I feel so...
so...

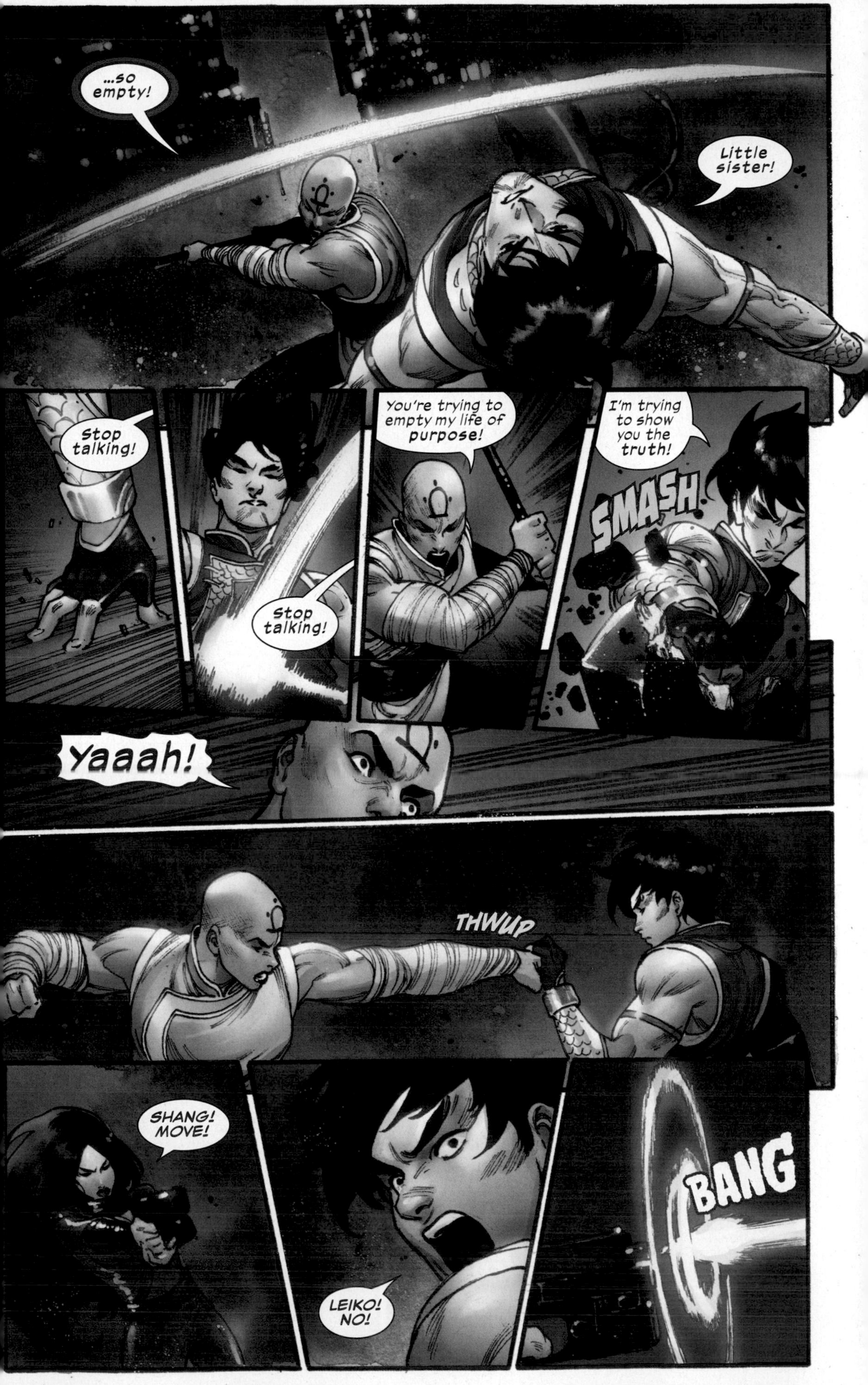

...so empty!
Little sister!
Stop talking!
Stop talking!
You're trying to empty my life of purpose!
I'm trying to show you the truth!
SMASH
Yaaah!
THWUP
SHANG! MOVE!
LEIKO! NO!
BANG

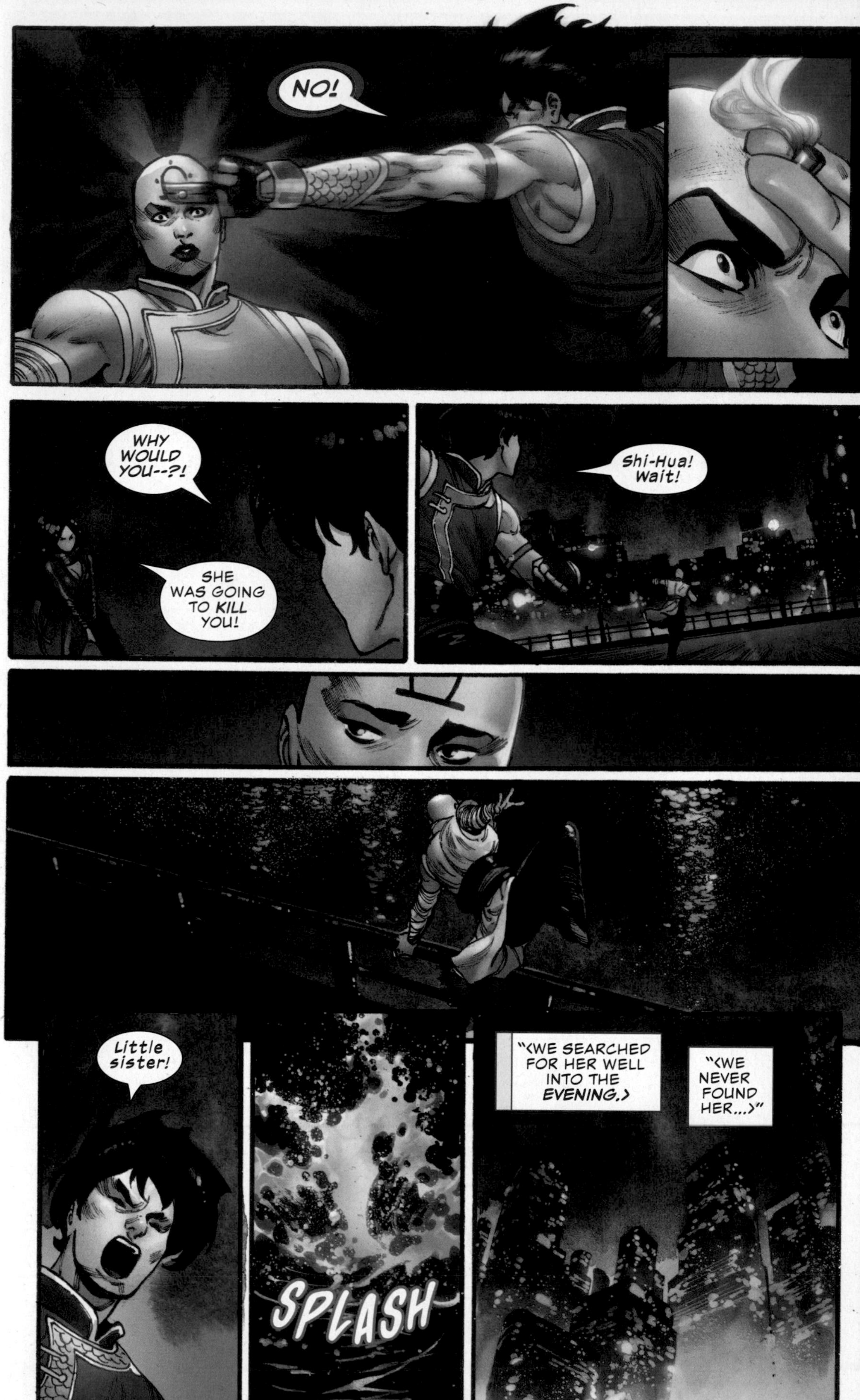
NO!
WHY WOULD YOU--?!
SHE WAS GOING TO KILL YOU!
Shi-Hua! Wait!
Little sister!
SPLASH
"<WE SEARCHED FOR HER WELL INTO THE EVENING.>
"<WE NEVER FOUND HER...>"

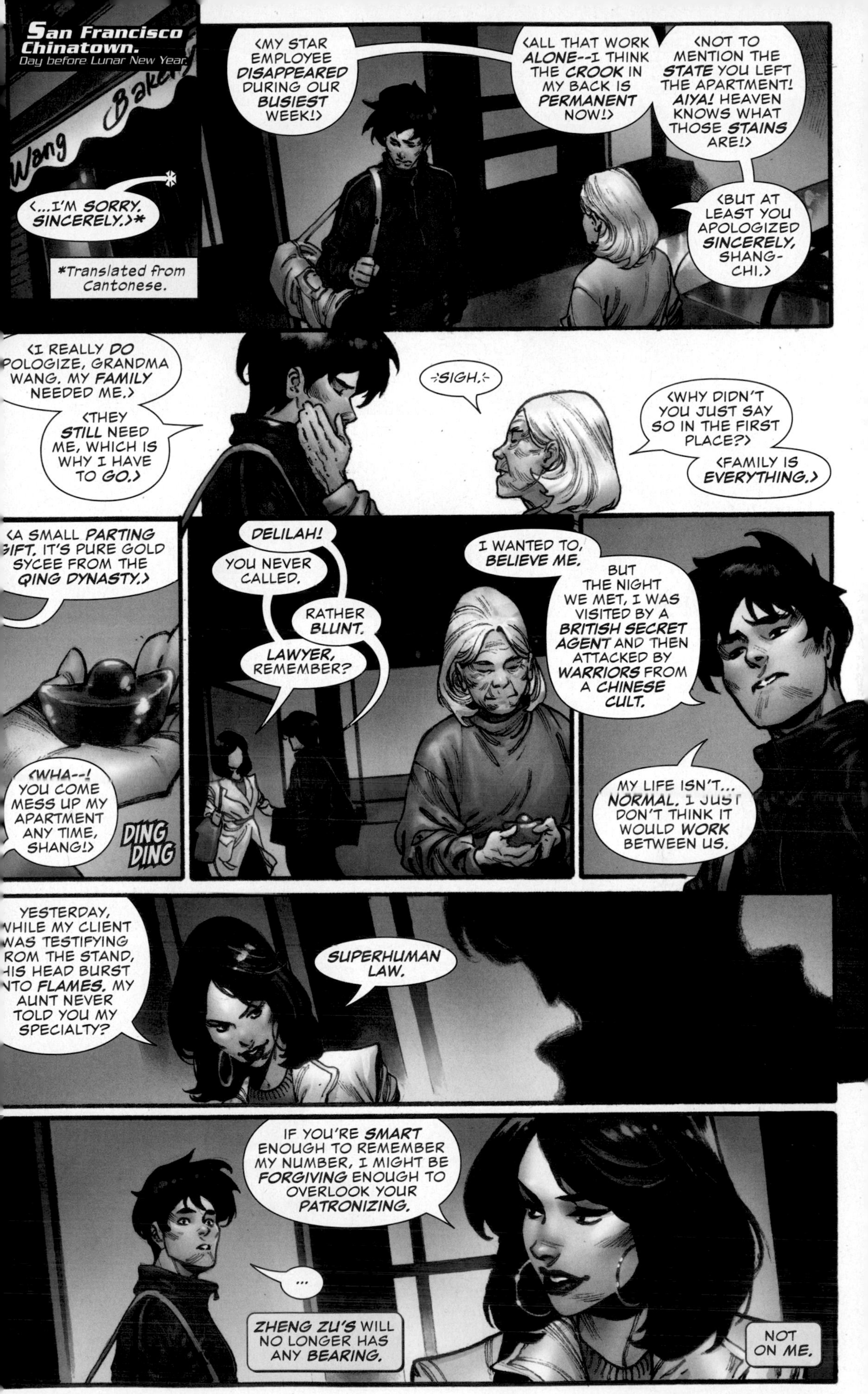

San Francisco Chinatown.
Day before Lunar New Year.
Wang Bakery
<...I'M SORRY. SINCERELY.>*
*Translated from Cantonese.
<MY STAR EMPLOYEE DISAPPEARED DURING OUR BUSIEST WEEK!>
<ALL THAT WORK ALONE--I THINK THE CROOK IN MY BACK IS PERMANENT NOW!>
<NOT TO MENTION THE STATE YOU LEFT THE APARTMENT! AIYA! HEAVEN KNOWS WHAT THOSE STAINS ARE!>
<BUT AT LEAST YOU APOLOGIZED SINCERELY, SHANG-CHI.>
<I REALLY DO POLOGIZE, GRANDMA WANG. MY FAMILY NEEDED ME.>
<THEY STILL NEED ME, WHICH IS WHY I HAVE TO GO.>
SIGH.
<WHY DIDN'T YOU JUST SAY SO IN THE FIRST PLACE?>
<FAMILY IS EVERYTHING.>
<A SMALL PARTING IFT. IT'S PURE GOLD SYCEE FROM THE QING DYNASTY.>
<WHA--! YOU COME MESS UP MY APARTMENT ANY TIME, SHANG!>
DING DING
DELILAH!
YOU NEVER CALLED.
RATHER BLUNT.
LAWYER, REMEMBER?
I WANTED TO, BELIEVE ME.
BUT THE NIGHT WE MET, I WAS VISITED BY A BRITISH SECRET AGENT AND THEN ATTACKED BY WARRIORS FROM A CHINESE CULT.
MY LIFE ISN'T... NORMAL. I JUST DON'T THINK IT WOULD WORK BETWEEN US.
YESTERDAY, WHILE MY CLIENT WAS TESTIFYING ROM THE STAND, HIS HEAD BURST NTO FLAMES. MY AUNT NEVER TOLD YOU MY SPECIALTY?
SUPERHUMAN LAW.
IF YOU'RE SMART ENOUGH TO REMEMBER MY NUMBER, I MIGHT BE FORGIVING ENOUGH TO OVERLOOK YOUR PATRONIZING.
...
ZHENG ZU'S WILL NO LONGER HAS ANY BEARING.
NOT ON ME.

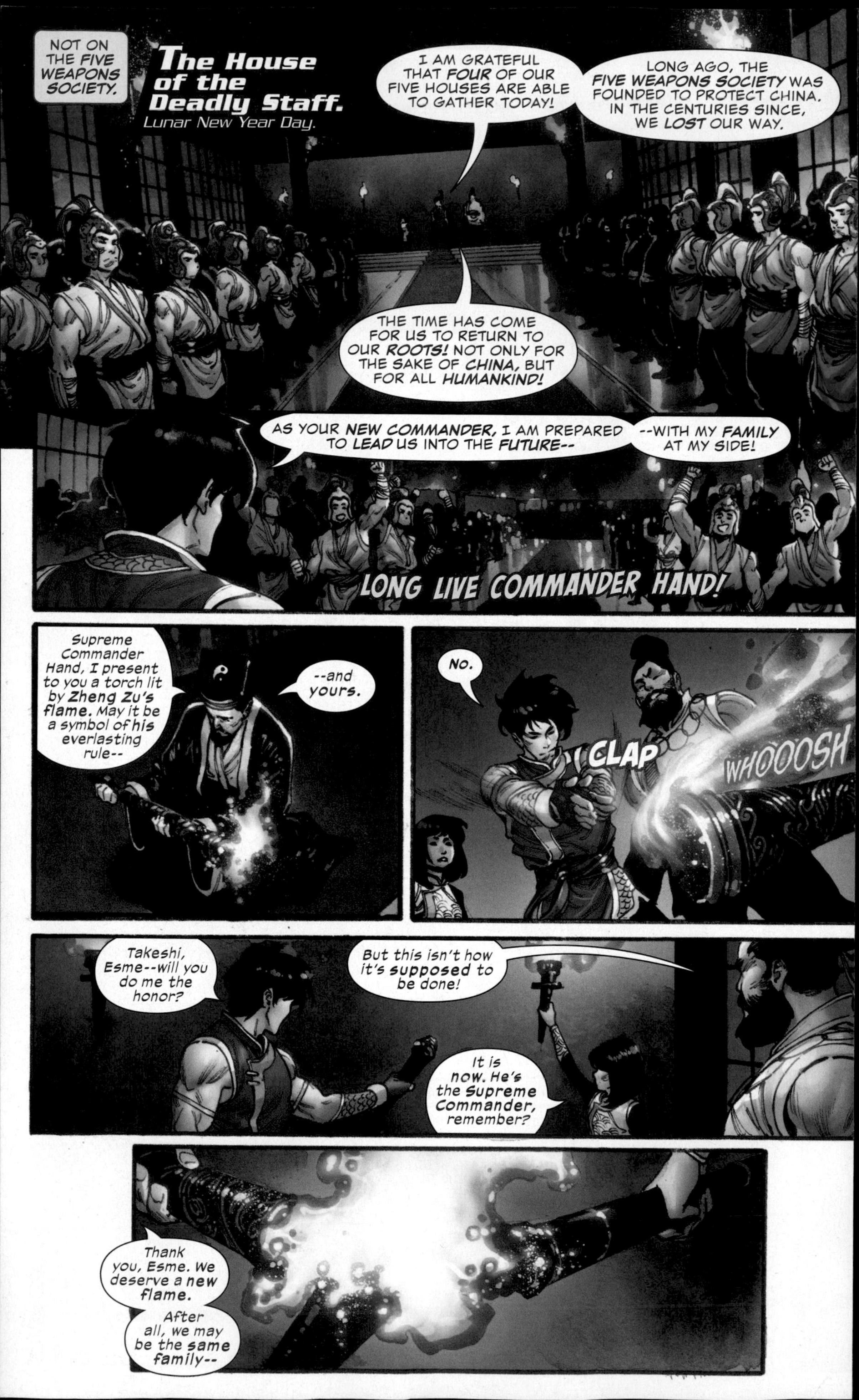
NOT ON THE FIVE WEAPONS SOCIETY.
The House of the Deadly Staff.
Lunar New Year Day.
I AM GRATEFUL THAT FOUR OF OUR FIVE HOUSES ARE ABLE TO GATHER TODAY!
LONG AGO, THE FIVE WEAPONS SOCIETY WAS FOUNDED TO PROTECT CHINA. IN THE CENTURIES SINCE, WE LOST OUR WAY.
THE TIME HAS COME FOR US TO RETURN TO OUR ROOTS! NOT ONLY FOR THE SAKE OF CHINA, BUT FOR ALL HUMANKIND!
AS YOUR NEW COMMANDER, I AM PREPARED TO LEAD US INTO THE FUTURE--
--WITH MY FAMILY AT MY SIDE!
LONG LIVE COMMANDER HAND!
Supreme Commander Hand, I present to you a torch lit by Zheng Zu's flame. May it be a symbol of his everlasting rule--
--and yours.
No.
CLAP
WHOOOSH
Takeshi, Esme--will you do me the honor?
But this isn't how it's supposed to be done!
It is now. He's the Supreme Commander, remember?
Thank you, Esme. We deserve a new flame.
After all, we may be the same family--

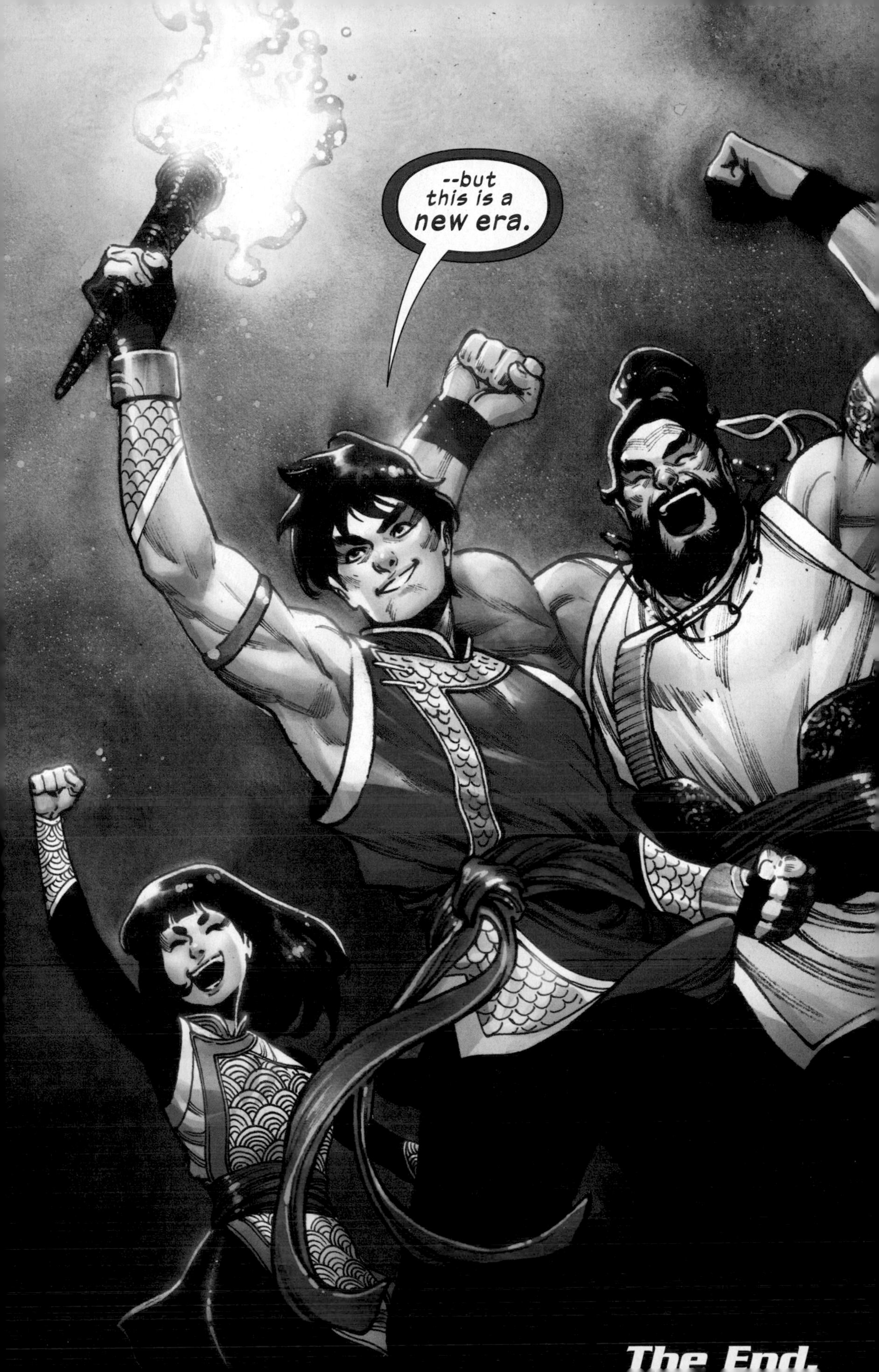
--but this is a new era.
The End.

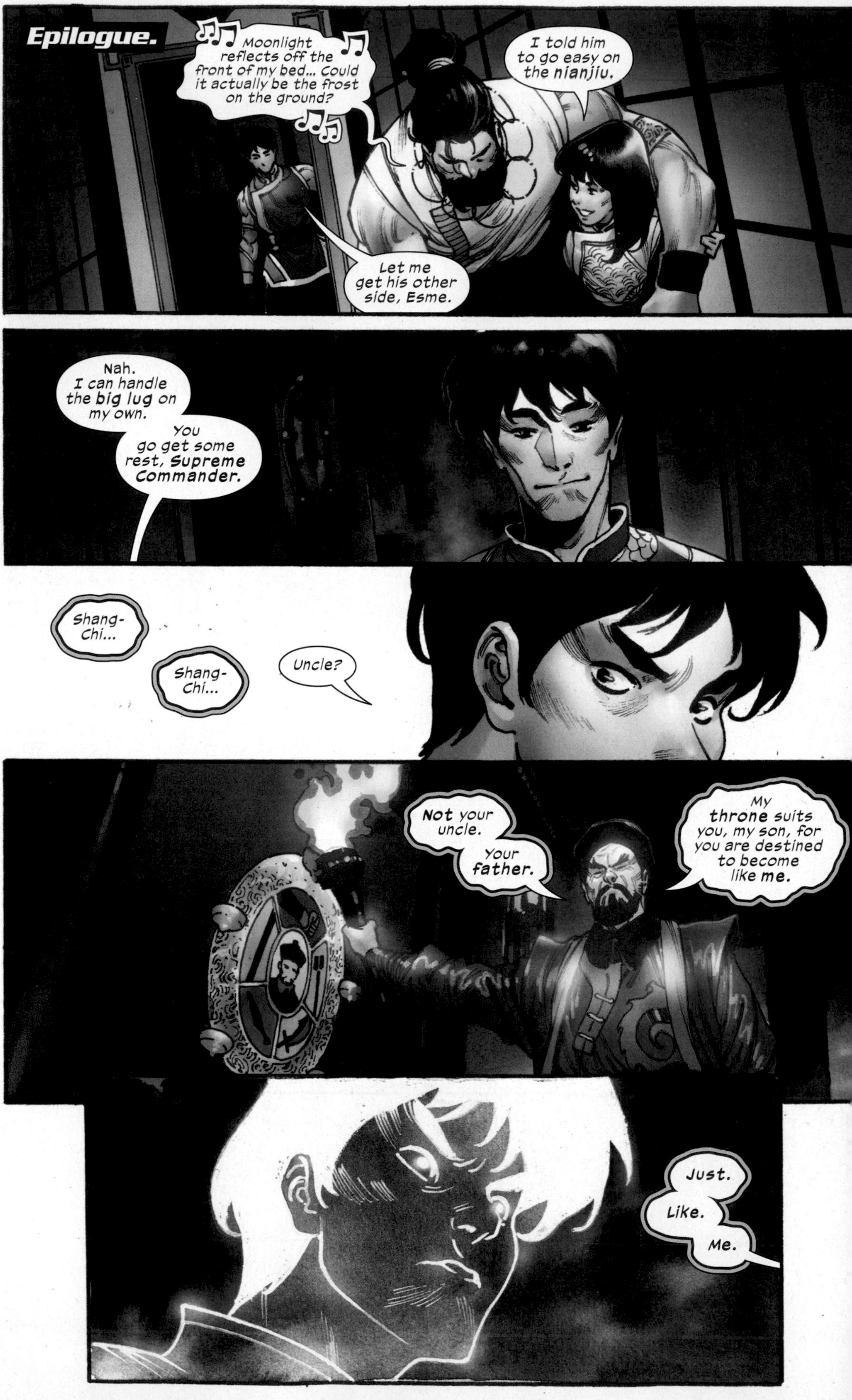

Epilogue.
Moonlight reflects off the front of my bed... Could it actually be the frost on the ground?
I told him to go easy on the nianjiu.
Let me get his other side, Esme.
Nah. I can handle the big lug on my own.
You go get some rest, Supreme Commander.
Shang-Chi...
Shang-Chi...
Uncle?
Not your uncle.
Your father.
My throne suits you, my son, for you are destined to become like me.
Just.
Like.
Me.

CHARACTER GUIDE

TEXT BY **GENE LUEN YANG** · ARTWORK BY **DIKE RUAN**

e Five Weapons Society is made up of five different houses, each dedicated to one weapon. t who are the players in this new part of the Shang-Chi legend? Here is a rundown and ne character designs to help you become acquainted:

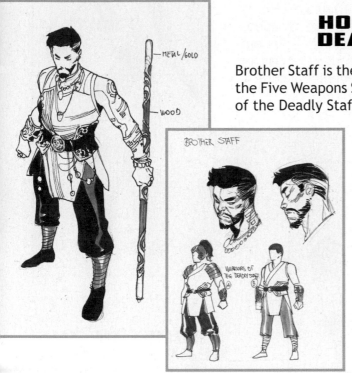

METAL/GOLD
WOOD

BROTHER STAFF
WARRIORS OF THE DEADLY STAFF
A
B

HOUSE OF THE DEADLY STAFF

Brother Staff is the current Supreme Commander of the Five Weapons Society. He comes from the House of the Deadly Staff, located in a forest just outside of London, England. Brother Staff is nothing if not flexible. He's always willing to adapt to the changing times. Under his leadership, the Society focused on economic gain rather than tradition. The ornate bo staff he carries is as much a status symbol as it is a weapon.

HOUSE OF THE DEADLY SABRE

Brother Sabre was raised in the House of the Deadly Sabre near Tokyo, Japan. He centers his life on the Five Weapons Society, the secret organization founded by his and Shang-Chi's father. Though boisterous, he is a true believer. Skilled at all manner of bladed weapons, his favorite is a nine-ring sabre.

BROTHER SABRE

HOUSE OF THE DEADLY DAGGER

Sister Dagger grew up in the House of the Deadly Dagger, a mansion hidden behind a waterfall in France. As one of the most talented martial artists in the world, Sister Dagger is the youngest House Champion in the history of the Five Weapons Society. She trusts Brother Sabre with her life, but no one else. Even when blindfolded, Sister Dagger can throw flying daggers with pinpoint accuracy.

SISTER DAGGER

SISTER HAMMER

HOUSE OF THE DEADLY HAMMER

Sister Hammer is perhaps the most unkno of Shang-Chi's family. She spent most her childhood in the House of the Dea Hammer, located in a Russian desert. Sh strong in body, mind, and will. The tattoo her forehead was meant to be a punishme but she's turned it into a source of pric Her weapon of choice is a long-handled w hammer. Unlike the other House Champio she has kept her distance from the Socie Unhappy with its direction, she can no lon wait patiently to take action.

HOUSE OF THE DEADLY HAND

To date, the House of the Deadly Hand lies in shambles.

The whereabouts of its Champion is currently unknown.

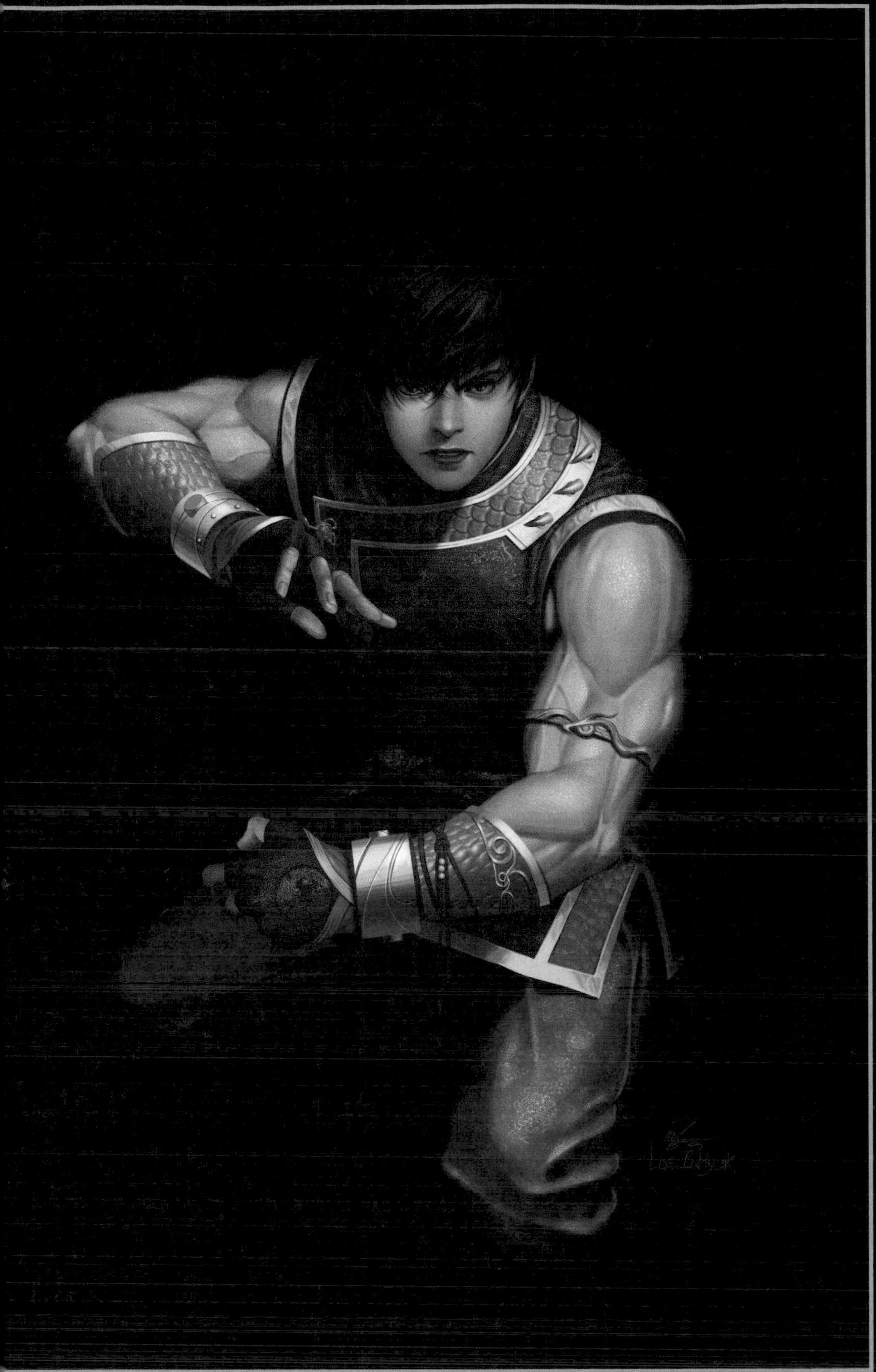

#1 VARIANT BY **InHYUK LEE**

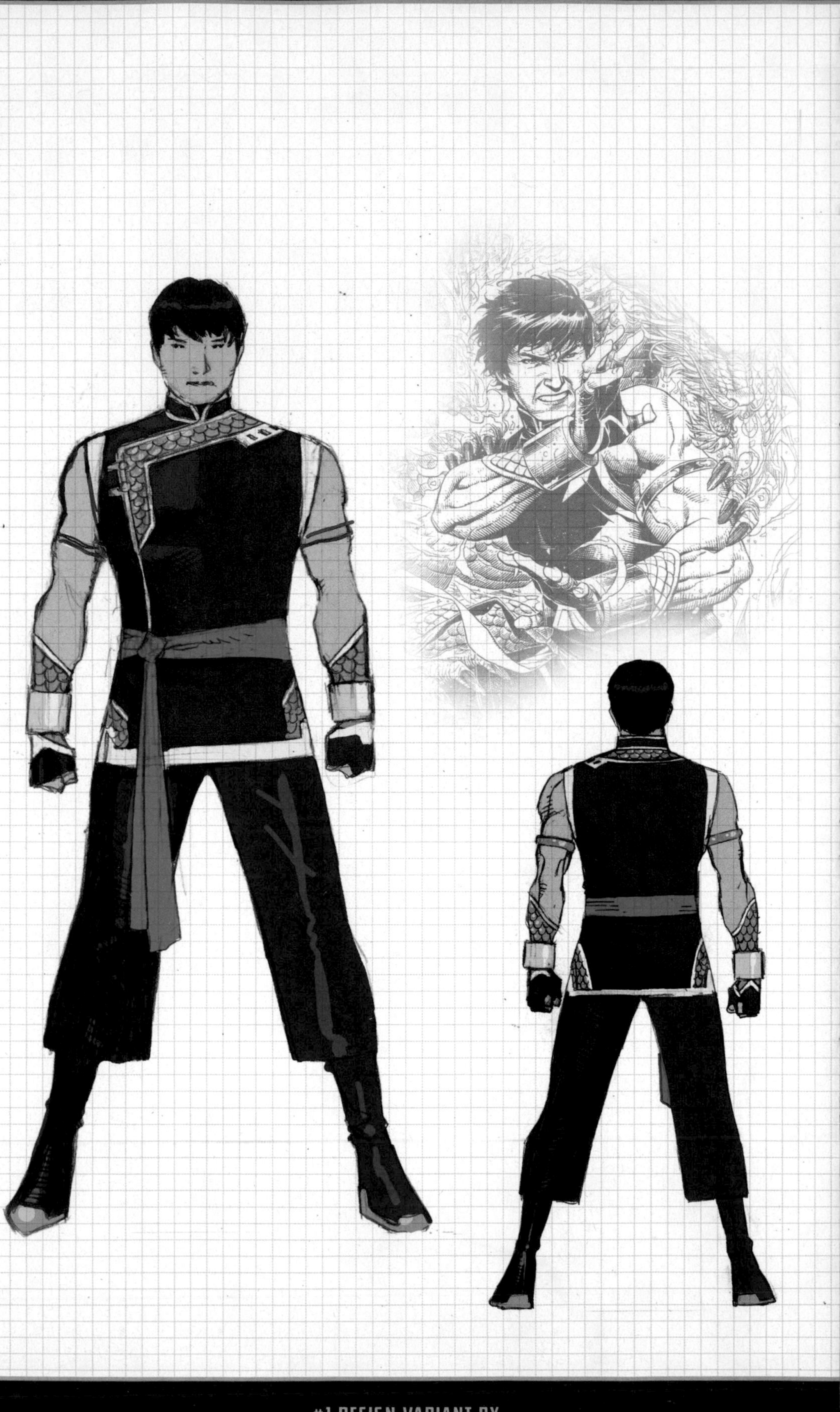

#1 DESIGN VARIANT BY
JIM CHEUNG

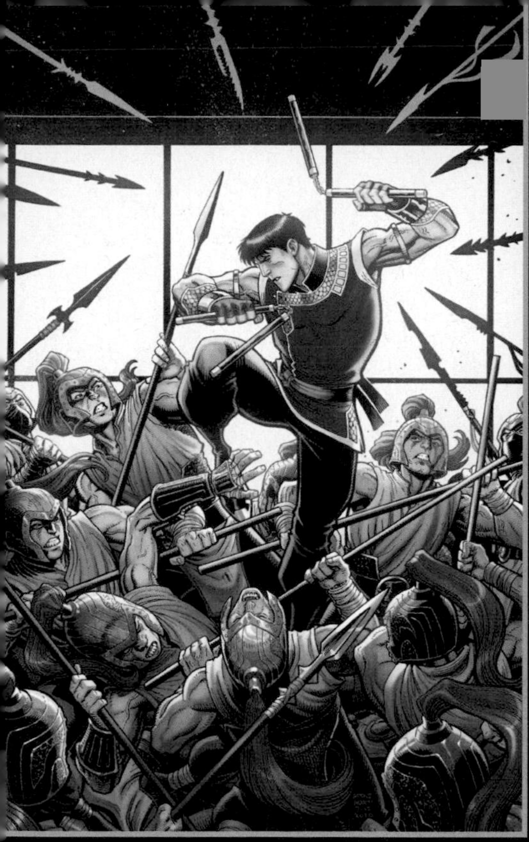

#1 VARIANT BY
ARTHUR ADAMS & SABINE RICH

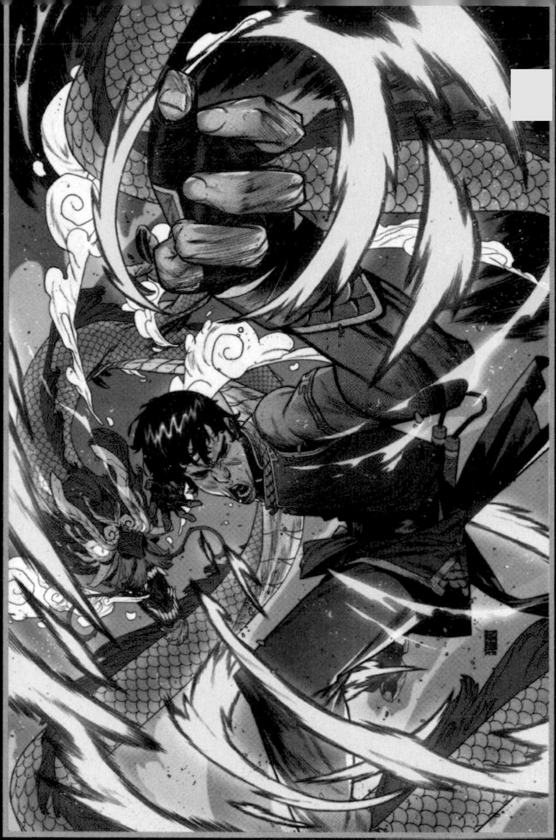

#1 VARIANT BY
KIM JACINTO

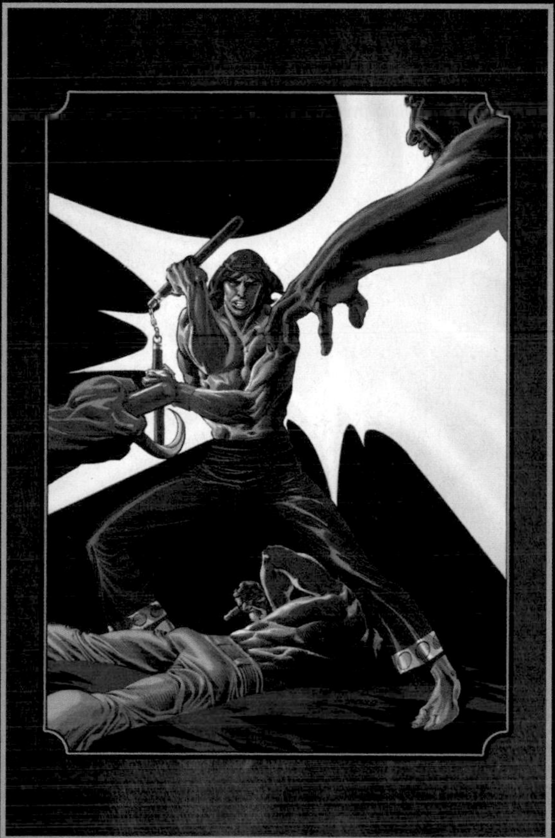

#1 HIDDEN GEM VARIANT BY
RUDY NEBRES & DEAN WHITE

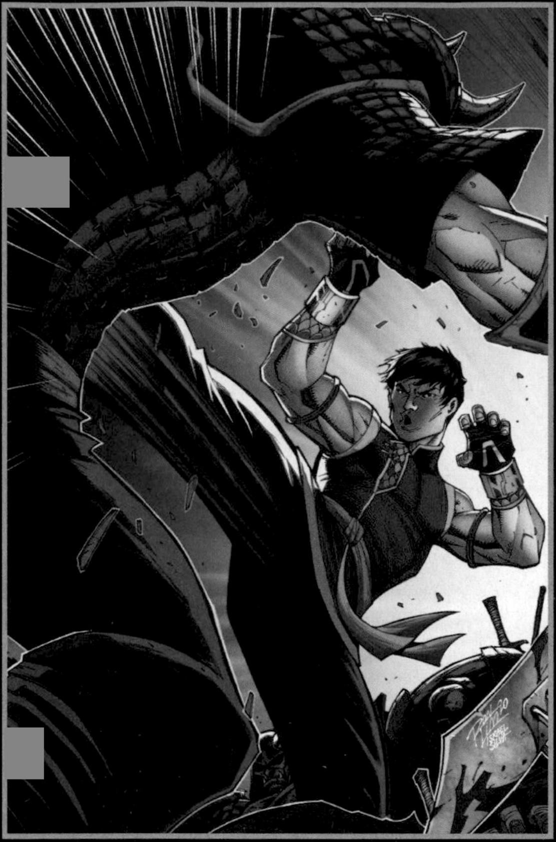

#1 VARIANT BY
RON LIM & ISRAEL SILVA

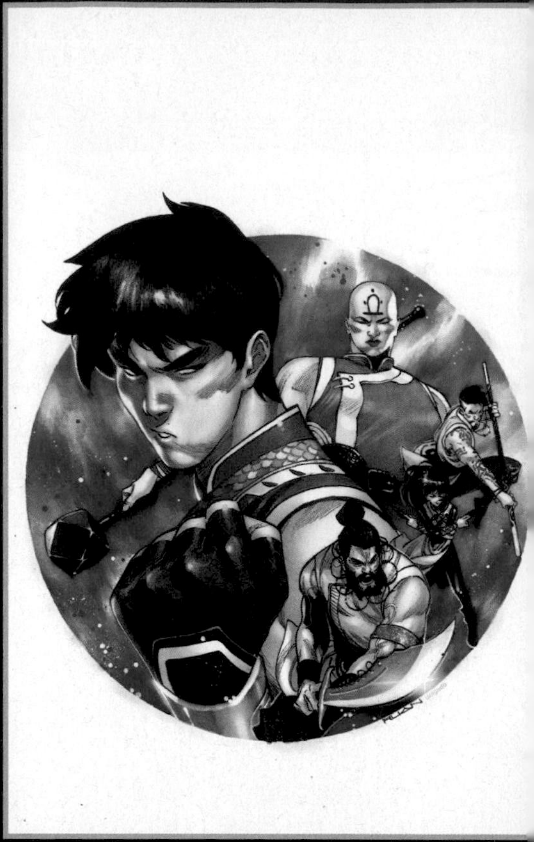

#1 VARIANT BY
DIKE RUAN & EDGAR DELGADO

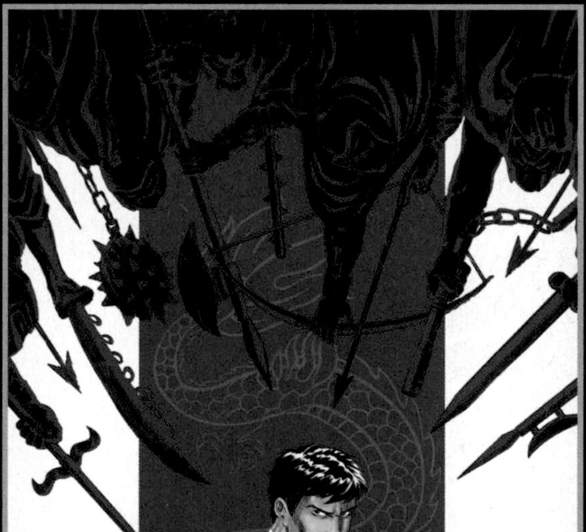

#1 VARIANT BY
BENJAMIN SU

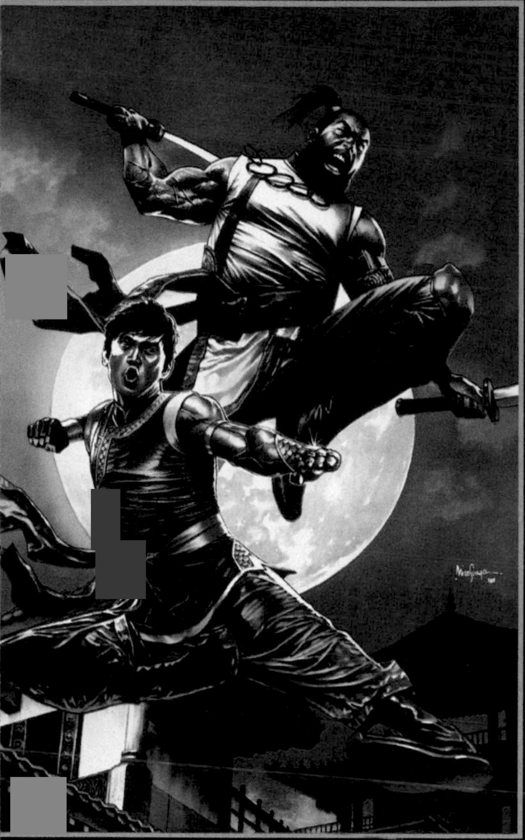

#1 VARIANT BY
ICO SUAYAN & FRANK D'ARMATA

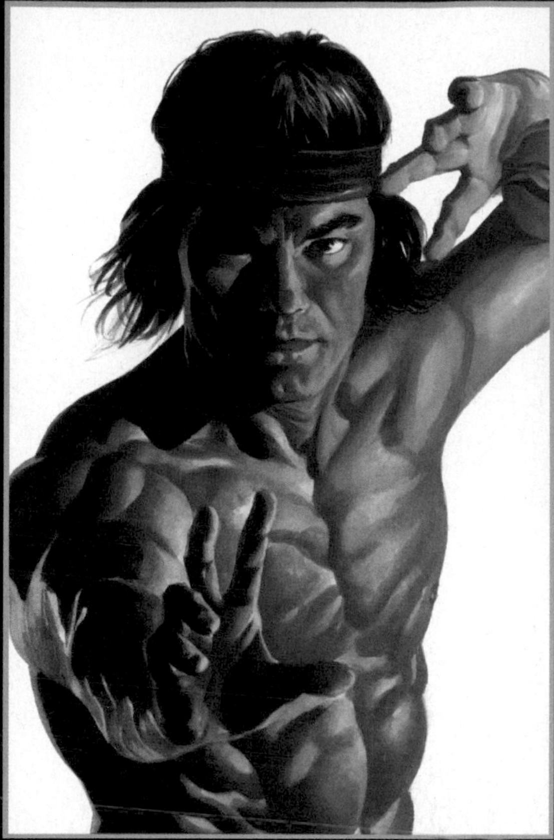

#2 TIMELESS VARIANT BY
ALEX ROSS

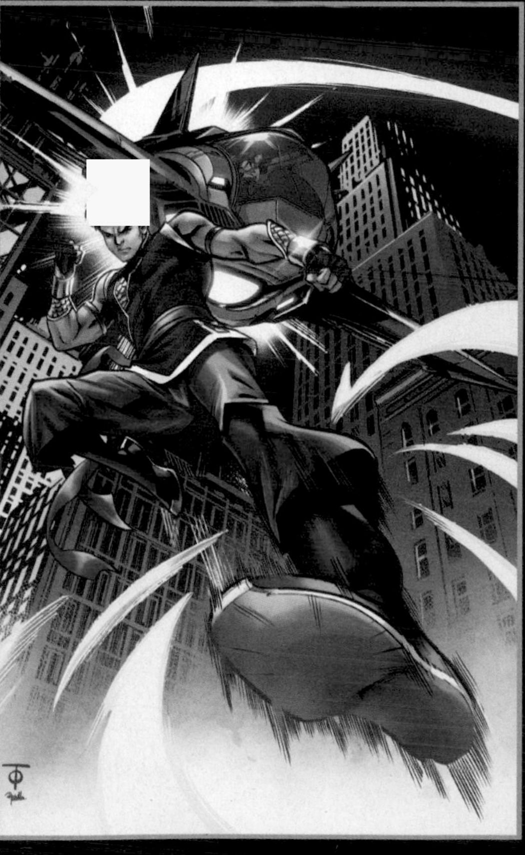

#2 VARIANT BY
ARCUS TO & RACHELLE ROSENBERG

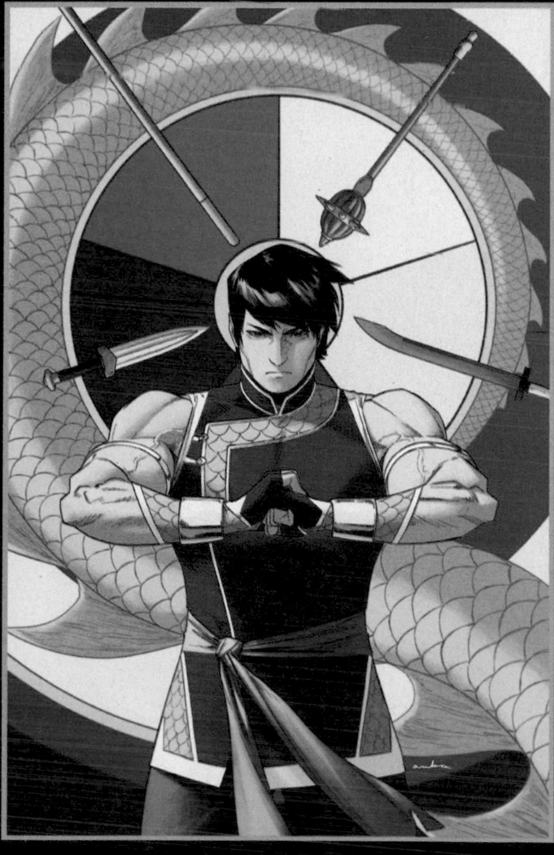

#3 VARIANT BY
KRIS ANKA

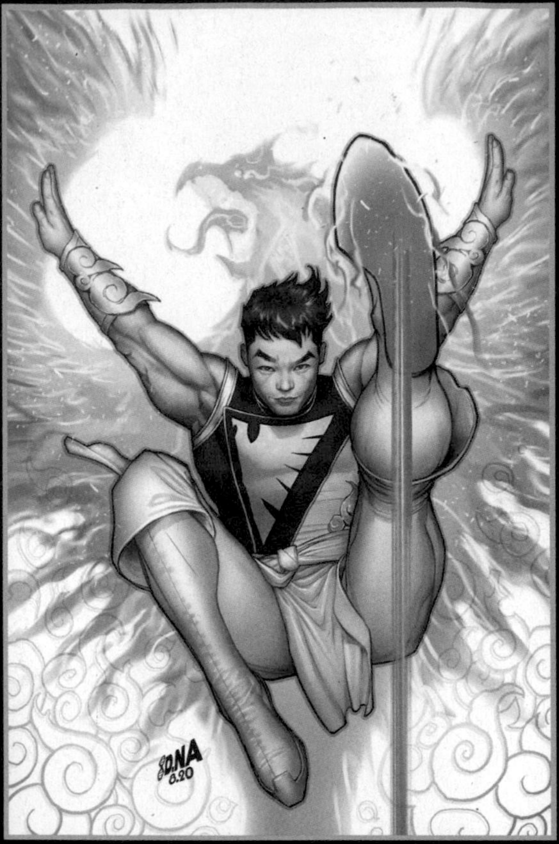
D.NA
6.20

#3 PHOENIX VARIANT BY
DAVID NAKAYAMA

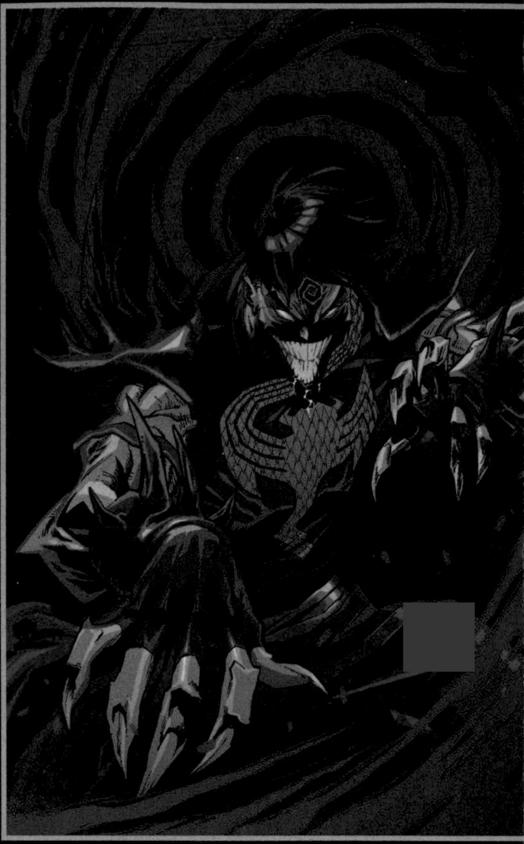

#4 KNULLIFIED VARIANT BY
KHARY RANDOLPH & EMILIO LOPEZ

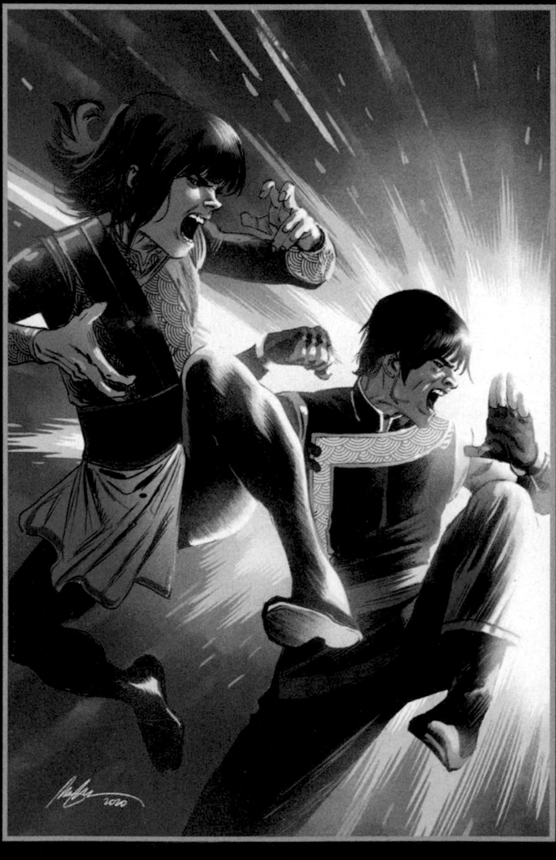

#4 VARIANT BY
RAFAEL ALBUQUERQUE

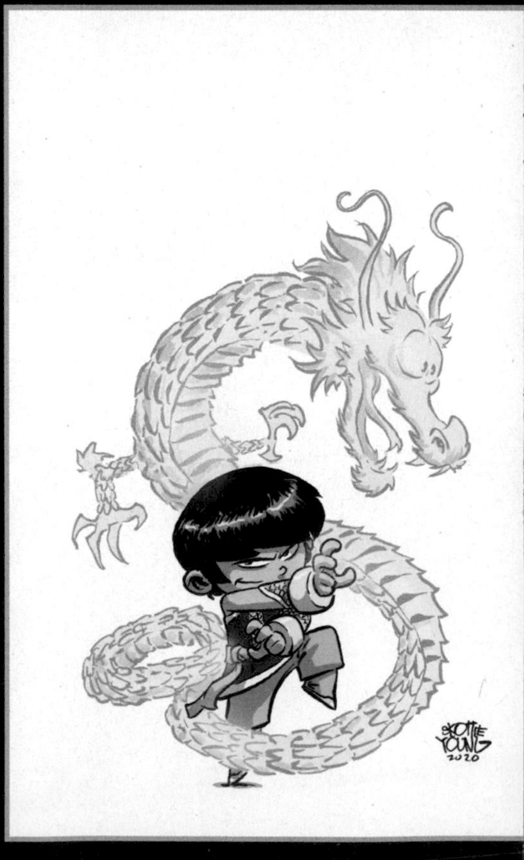
SKOTTIE
YOUNG
2020

#5 VARIANT BY
SKOTTIE YOUNG